L2

NEW HORIZONS IN JOURNALISM

HOWARD RUSK LONG, *General Editor*

ADVISORY BOARD

Irving Dilliard, *Professor of Journalism*
Princeton University

James S. Pope, *Former Executive Editor*
Louisville *Courier-Journal* and *Times*

Donald Tyerman, *Former Editor*
The Economist, London

LORDS AND LABORERS

OF THE PRESS

Men who fashioned

the Modern British Newspaper

By LINTON ANDREWS *and* H. A. TAYLOR

Foreword by HOWARD RUSK LONG

Southern Illinois University Press   *Carbondale and Edwardsville*

Feffer & Simons, Inc.   *London and Amsterdam*

Contents

        Dennis Hamilton, Alastair Dunnett,
        John Edward Sayers, John Giddings

17   Now We Look Ahead   307

     Bibliography   319

     Index   323

Foreword

This book was conceived in the orderly room of a structure intended to serve as a transient residence for troops in World War II, now the uneasy headquarters of a Department of Journalism, for twenty years a vagrant in temporary accommodations.

During his brief tenure as visiting professor of journalism at Southern Illinois University, it was the practice of Sir Linton Andrews to drop in each morning to pick up his mail, and if I were free of obvious vexation, to pause for coffee and conversation. We talked of many things—American young people; his own youth as schoolboy and later press apprentice; the differences and similarities of British and American journalism; the great men he had known in a rich career extending from the reign of Queen Victoria, and, of course, the need for the Americans and the British to know more about each other.

It was a season for the nurturing of projects. Sir Linton was a congenial guest; I was anxious to sign a distinguished author for a new series I was to edit for our university press.

"Americans should read about the great British journalists."

Sir Linton agreed.

"Serious students can run down the standard sources of information about your outstanding people, but materials are woefully lacking for the casual reader and for the undergraduate. A collection of short biographies between the covers of a single volume would help to fill this void."

Sir Linton agreed.

"You could write it, if you would. Since the days of the Diamond Jubilee, you have seen them come and go. . . . Now how is that for a working title, 'I Have Seen Them Come and I Have Seen Them Go.'"

Sir Linton agreed, with silent reservations. I had gained a gentleman's commitment, yes. But neither of us really expected the title to survive.

Within days of his return to England, and to his home in Leeds, Sir Linton was at work on his new assignment . . . perhaps the last he will ever undertake. Research progressed rapidly through the summer of 1967. The first five or six chapters came easily. Then in October there was word of a physical setback, painful, dangerous, and frustrating to a man accustomed to a life regulated by deadlines. Later, work was resumed, but at a slower pace. In March of the next year a letter from Sir Linton confessed that he had undertaken the impossible.

> I have tried to get going again at a professional pace but I am painfully slow.
>
> The best suggestion I can make is that I should hand over half the task of writing the book to H. A. Taylor, C.B.E., author of *The British Press: A Critical Survey* and several biographies, one of Robert Donald, for whom he used to work on the *Daily Chronicle*. Taylor is a well-known Fleet Street personality, and I know from experience he would be an excellent collaborator. He is willing to give all the help he can.
>
> Would you approve of our doing a joint book?

With the work already at hand and subsequent contributions turned out with great effort and considerable discomfort, Sir Linton's portion of the final manuscript would have made an acceptable publication. Yet there were gaps that needed filling. It was most fortunate, therefore, that an old friend of Taylor's competence and professional standing would come forward with the chapters required to round out the undertaking as originally planned.

The chapters by Sir Linton Andrews include W. T. Stead, C. P. Scott, Lord Northcliffe, J. A. Spender, J. L. Garvin, Arthur Mann, Lord Beaverbrook, A. J. Cummings, George Murray, and Lord Thomson of Fleet.

It would have been most unfortunate to have published without the five chapters prepared by Mr. Taylor, including those on Robert Donald, Lord Camrose, R. D. Blumenfeld, W. J. Haley, the combined treatment of Cecil Harmsworth King, Hugh Cudlipp and their associates.

In chapter 16 the two authors shared the labor of coping with the "Viceroys of a Press Empire." It was Taylor who prepared the materials on John Edward Sayers and John Giddings, while Andrews treated with Dennis Hamilton and Alaistair Dunnett. The final chapter, "Looking Ahead," is by Sir Linton Andrews.

Not only did H. A. Taylor save the day with the chapters so essential to a well-rounded treatment of the important leaders of the twentieth century British press, but he also helped to relieve his old friend of many of the housekeeping chores of authorship, such as collecting the illustrations, assembling the manuscript and revising the revisions.

The most obvious omissions from this collection of biographical sketches are sections or even chapters treating with the authors, who in their own right must be counted among the great men of British journalism.

When William Linton Andrews assumed the editorship in 1939 of the *Yorkshire Post,* recognized as the leader among Conservative British provincial newspapers, he was already well in the vanguard of his profession. He was known as the man who at the age of thirty-seven had passed up a promising Fleet Street career to return to the provinces, thereby reversing the progress of the promising journalist who expected to get ahead in his profession. From 1923 when he became editor of the *Leeds Mercury,* his official position always was on the side of management, a conservative management at that.

Yet it was the respect of the rank and file of his profession, gained through his years of association with them in the City and in the country, which, as much as anything, seemed to qualify him to participate as no other man could in many of the most significant journalistic developments of his time.

Hard work, imagination, and an affable disposition combined with an unwillingness to compromise on principle enabled the new editor to make the *Mercury* a much better newspaper. Andrews's own growth brought an influence within the parent company far greater than the dimensions of his own editorial sanctum.

In his autobiography, Linton Andrews is most kind and differential to Arthur Mann, his predecessor as editor of the *York-*

shire Post and his superior while he served as editor of the satellite *Mercury.*

One suspects, however, that some at least of the Mann achievements and triumphs were engineered by the younger editor whose powers were on the ascendency while those of Mann were withering away. In time of crisis certainly it was Andrews who was ready to cope with the emergency. With the beginning of World War II and mobilization of the British press, the *Mercury* was consolidated with the *Yorkshire Post.* Arthur Mann retired because of ill health and Andrews, now editor of the *Post,*. was assigned the task of reorganizing personnel and policy to meet the needs of a people fighting for their lives.

Under Mann's editorship the *Yorkshire Post* was a good newspaper. Under Andrews the *Post* became a great newspaper, foremost among the English provincials and on a par with such respected American newspapers as the St. Louis *Post-Dispatch* and the *Christian Science Monitor* and the Washington *Post.*

Sir Linton retired in 1960, but retained his position on the board of directors another eight years. In January 1968 he was naced Editor Emeritus when he retired from the board. He continues as a consultant and has been accorded the freedom of all meetings of the directors.

The first of many rare honors came in 1954 when Andrews was invested Knight Bachelor for confidential services to Prime Minister Winston Churchill. Sir Linton was awarded honorary doctorates by Leeds University in 1955 and Emerson College (U.S.A.) in 1967; Médaille d'Argent de la Reconnaisance Française, 1947.

From the perspective of the West bank of the Atlantic it would seem, however, that Sir Linton's greatest honors were achieved in his unique accomplishments in the service of his profession as differentiated from his services as an editor.

The record of this impact upon the destiny of British newspapers begins when he became chairman of the editorial committee of the Newspaper Society in a most critical period, 1943–50. This group, organized in the interests of the war effort, survives as the Guild of British Newspaper Editors. Sir Linton was president in 1952 while this organization was playing a definitive role in the establishment of the British Press Council.

The Institute of Journalists, as all associations which had survived the war, in 1945 found themselves in troubled times. This professional society, composed of editorial workers and supervisors, was in need of strong leadership. Sir Linton was elected president in time to preside over the debates relative to amalgamation with the labor-oriented National Union of Journalists. Although nothing came of it at the time, Sir Linton's diplomatic handling of the issue probably had much to do with hastening a later alignment of the two groups.

Most important of all were the contributions of Sir Linton Andrews in the founding and development of the Press Council, that self-regulating body accepted under pressure of Parliament through the agency of the Royal Commission on the Press in 1947. Among proprietors and editors the opposition was considerable, and of the various associations only the National Union of Journalists favored a Press Council.

Sir Linton represented the conscientious element in whose sober judgment it was time for self-imposed restraints. His personal influence, the accrual of decades, helped many of the reluctant to reconcile themselves to acceptance of an authority, however weak, other than their own. As president of the Editors Guild he participated ably in the negotiations that brought the Press Council into being on July 1, 1953.

As representative of the Editors Guild, Sir Linton was one of the first members of the Press Council. He became the first vice-chairman and in 1955 succeeded Colonel the Honorable J. J. Astor (later Lord Astor of Hever) as chairman. Thus Sir Linton not only officiated in the birth of the Press Council, but his was a stablizing influence in the difficult formative years of this body. By the time of his departure not long before retirement from his editorship, the Press Council had progressed from experiment to a trusteeship in public responsibility.

The paths of Henry Archibald Taylor, C.B.E., and Sir Linton Andrews, after crossing many times in their respective journalistic careers, had merged into a high road of friendship by the time circumstances brought them into collaboration upon the present volume. It was a friendship nurtured through a concern for common objectives approached from differing viewpoints.

Thus Taylor was instrumental in defeating the proposed

merger of the National Union of Journalists with the Institute of Journalists, when Andrews, as president of the latter group, favored the move. Taylor devotes a chapter in his book the *British Press: A Critical Survey* (1961) to the Press Council and by no means whitewashes the work of this body under the chairmanship of Sir Linton. In fact it was Taylor's contention that inaction of the Press Council in behalf of the public's rights, when strikes on two different occasions forced lengthy breaks in newspaper publication, represented gross failure of the council to come to grips with its responsibility. Sir Linton in his *Autobiography of a Journalist* (1964) makes it clear that encounters on principle, however painful, caused no rift in the delightful personal friendship of these two professional journalists.

Like most newsmen of his generation, Taylor began his career in the provinces before finding his first post in the City, an assignment for the *Daily Chronicle*. Over the period of many years Taylor contributed to the *Evening Standard* and the *Yorkshire Post* and for a short time was editor of the *Empire Review*. From 1923 to 1964 Taylor was chairman of Newspaper Features Limited. Since 1956, he has been editorial writer of *Country Life*. An impressive list of books are among his writings. Through much of his career, he combined political writing with active services in the cause of the Conservative party including parliamentary candidacies in Doncaster and Northeast Leicester.

Taylor's public services, in fact are many and varied. He was president of the Institute of Journalists in 1938; member of the Lord Chancellor's Committee on the Law of Defamation, 1939–48, and chairman of the Restoration Committee, of St. Brides's Church, Fleet Street, 1951–57. He has been a member of the Court of Bristol University. It was for political and public services that Taylor in 1953 was created Commander (of the Order) of the British Empire.

H. A. Taylor is the author of the following books: *Goodbye to the Battlefields, Smith of Berkenhead, The Strange Case of Bonar Law, Jix: Viscount Brentford,* and *Robert Donald.*

Thus American readers are to receive the benefit of insights from two great British journalists who really have seen them come and seen them go. Sir Linton Andrews and H. A. Taylor have worked shoulder to shoulder with the other great men who made the British newspapers of this century. They have known them as fellow craftsmen, they were associated with them in shaping up the guidelines, vague as they are, governing the conduct of the working press. Each in his way has been critic as well as professional leader.

This is to become a useful book in the United States with a long life expectancy in the hands of students and in the collections of our libraries. The reputation of the authors is sufficient to gain attention in Britain.

Southern Illinois University   Howard Rusk Long
Oct. 12, 1969

Introduction

The making of press history

This book began as a sequel to one of the happiest and most instructive experiences in a long journalistic life. The time had come to lay aside forever my absorbing preoccupations for more than sixty years: reporting, foreign correspondence, subediting, editorial writing, editing. An unexpected offer pierced like a bright ray the sadness I felt on giving up after close on forty years what I thoroughly enjoyed, through all its trials and occasional sunbursts of success, the editing of daily papers, especially the *Leeds Mercury* and the *Yorkshire Post*. The offer was this: Would I care to be a visiting professor in the journalism department of Southern Illinois University? Would I welcome opportunities to combine with this tuition the giving of public lectures? Would I like to bring my impressions of North America up to date? Indeed I would, as I at once assured the president of the university, Dr. Delyte Morris.

My class at the university headquarters, Carbondale, taught me much. I encouraged all the discussion possible, especially on such themes as the British National Council for the Training of Journalists, an organization for which I agitated for many years before it came into being, the British Press Council, of which I was the first deputy chairman and then for five busy years of its development the chairman, and the stinging criticisms of American newspapers by Mr. Cecil Harmsworth King, then head of the gigantic International Publishing Corporation and in some ways the most controversial and most powerful newspaperman in Britain. My students vigorously championed American press training with its insistence on a broad culture. They were distrustful of the proposed press councils on the British model. These, they thought, might jeopardize the exceptionally wide freedom of the press enjoyed in the United States. A movement centered at Washington to gather and pronounce upon ideas from universities for pilot press councils had not yet reached the stage of public documentation. So discussion raised more questions than it answered, more doubts than it settled.

Mr. King's philippic excited the keenest response of all. He did not lack some supporters, even among students in the chauvinistic Middle West. Which country's press ever did lack assailants? Certainly not Britain's. The London papers, especially those of the mass-circulation class, became the target of sharp attack by my students for their alleged shortage of world news and their abundance of scrappy trivialities. At this point I dropped the role of classroom umpire or question-master and joined in the fray. Defending the British press when it deserved defense in lesson after lesson, I said our leading papers might be dwarfed physically by gigantic American journals, but they fitted into the economic and social conditions of Britain that they reported and commented on. They had behind them a gallant history of fighting for press freedom and a record of many brilliant technical improvements.

The more I personalized this history—that is, the more I spoke of creative leaders of the British press, especially those whom I knew well during my almost seventy years of active journalism —the more attentive my class became. Recalling that biography has been described as the best form of history and history as the essence of many biographies, I told of press incidents and press characters I had known. That inspiring teacher and encourager, Dr. Howard Rusk Long, chairman of the journalism department of Southern Illinois University, approved this experiment in personalized history. He thought it might well provide the method for a book. Hence these pages on creative journalists of the modern British press.

Before I reached halfway in the writing of the book I was interrupted by an exhausting illness. My worthy friend, Mr. H. A. Taylor, gallantly came to my help. I owe him the warmest thanks for giving me the benefit of his experience of journalism and authorship. His books about the press include *Robert Donald*

(the editor of the London *Daily Chronicle,* the paper on which
Taylor made his debut in Fleet Street) and *The British Press: a
Critical Survey.* Most of his other books are biographical studies
of British statesmen—Lord Birkenhead, Andrew Bonar Law and
Lord Brentford. At one time he was chairman and editorial director of a leading British syndicate, in which capacity he paid
several visits to the United States; but that commitment did not
curtail his personal journalism or his work for the profession.
Indeed, he was chosen to serve on the Lord Chancellor's Committee on the Law of Defamation. This laborious inquiry into the
anomalies of the law of libel and slander was interrupted by the
Second World War and continued so long that he was the only
member from the newspaper world to survive to sign the ultimate
report. This he did much to publicize and on it legislation was
enacted by Parliament in 1952. He has been most useful in our
many consultations about points that I proposed to make.

Since it should be always a wholesome exercise to define our
terms let me explain what Taylor and I mean by *creative* journalists of the *modern* press. There are always many worthy workers for newspapers: owners and managers of careful, vigilant con-
cerns; editors who serve their own communities faithfully and to
the fairly general satisfaction; subeditors who become brightly
and swiftly efficient in dressing a news story to seize and then hold
attention; reporters who often excel in news-getting because of
their friendly nature, their many contacts, their ingenuity. It is
a most unhappy newspaper that has no staff members who are
excellent craftsmen. But creative journalists are rare.

"The first need and qualification for a journalist in a profession with enormous capabilities," said W. T. Stead to his young
friend, Edmund Garrett, who became editor of the *Cape Times,*
"is enthusiasm. Of course, for journalism a man ought to be fairly
quick in forming his impressions and making up his mind. Some
people take too much winding up. I take my impressions on the
moment. The logical defence is rather an afterthought." Stead
was right so far as he went. But he failed to mention a rare and
precious quality that he himself possessed. Even enthusiasm and
speed, along with craftsmanship, are not enough to endow a newspaperman with creativity. He may tread the worn path eagerly,
but it remains the worn path.

The people we chose for study in this book have broken new ground. They have led the way in the development of the press. They have extended its appeal and power. They have had the fearless pioneer temperament and done something never done before but often done since by imitators. They have opened up new realms of thought and knowledge for their readers and increased their energy of spirit. They have fired new enthusiasms. They have set new trends.

Like any anthology of poetry or prose, our selection of creators or trend-setters of the modern British press is sure to disappoint some hero worshippers. Ought we to have included Sir Winston Churchill? He was proud to call himself a journalist. We of Britain's Institute of Journalists were proud to have him as a fellow member. He stood at one time in the front rank of war correspondents. At another time he excelled in brief newspaper studies of the threatening problems of his day, when he seemed to lay a hand on the reader's shoulder and hold him thinking hard. His memoirs were masterpieces of historical literature. As a vivid, challenging journalist he followed the tradition of such men as that press hero of the Crimean War, Sir William Russell of the *Times*. As an author Churchill steeped himself in Edward Gibbon's splendid eloquence, dry irony, and mastery of a vast historical movement.

But was he a creator of modern journalism in the sense of changing time-honored habits? His impulsive editing of the *British Gazette* during the General Strike in 1926 may have been of value to the government. It did not win plaudits from Fleet Street. But who could suddenly, without detailed planning and long trial runs, create an attractive new daily paper in the midst of a crisis that half paralyzed the country? Now, more than forty years later, we cannot take up the pile of papers of a journalist's breakfast table and say, "Look, we should never have had that eloquent, balanced style of editorial but for Churchill. Look at that analysis of relations between East and West in the *Times*— isn't it just like Winston speaking?" So, not without twinges of regret, we have left Churchill out of our collection and many other great men who contributed much to the journalism of their day but did little to alter its trends.

One more decision must be explained. It is impossible to pin down the start of modern journalism to a date in the calendar. A young person of today looking at a dusty newspaper file of Queen Victoria's middle years would be astonished to find so much small type, long, heavy, unbroken slabs of political speeches, such ponderous, polysyllabic English, no halftone pictures, no light-hearted features, so little of special interest for women, nothing to entertain the children. There were concise halfpenny newspapers before Alfred Harmsworth started the *Daily Mail* in 1896, just as there were great warriors before Agamemnon. But Harmsworth, learning much from American enterprises and innovators, especially Joseph Pulitzer, did more than anyone else to modernize a politically overweighted press. He introduced ideas that still keep their value and vitality. So, in thinking of great men who have helped to spread or to use with exceptional public spirit the rise of the modern press, it seems to us reasonable to start with the closing decades of the nineteenth century.

A book of this kind should avoid a danger pointed out by T. S. G. Hunter in the *Financial Times* of London when reviewing an earlier work on journalism to which I contributed. The critic held that newspapers probably suffer too much from inbreeding and the handing down of techniques from old to young. He said rightly, "The most successful papers of the past decade have been those least conditioned by tradition. Inspired amateurism has marked the breakthrough and is more likely successfully to compete with the electronic journalism of television." This suggestion may apply to some textbooks. It reminds me of a saying by Frank Moore Colby in his book, *Constrained Attitudes:* "Journalists have always been our most old-fashioned class, being too busy with the news of the day to lay aside the mental habits of fifty years before." However, the changes we here record are those that have not only influenced the journalism of our time but will continue to influence it. As Byron said, "The best prophet of the future is the past"—parts of the past, anyway.

Much without doubt is to be learned from journalists of an earlier time, the Defoes and Delanes, but today, when, in a fast-changing society, journalism is called on to be fast-changing too, and in many of its methods revolutionary, it should help us to look closely at the careers of the more recent and the present-day creative leaders. What made them journalists? What qualities made them excel? Whad did or do they see as the proper function of the press? Have they expanded its influence? Have they made it more powerful for ensuring the public good? The more clearly we can answer these questions the better equipped we shall be to face present challenges in the world of communication.

Challenges, especially by other mass media, have started to come so fast and so forcibly, especially since the Second World War, that we can only run into peril if we try to shrug them aside. Let us learn what we can, then, from great men who mastered problems of their own day, opened up new horizons in journalism and wielded by their example an influence on the problems of today and tomorrow.

Linton Andrews

Leeds, England
June 30, 1969

Lords and Laborers of the Press

Courtesy of H. A. Taylor

W. T. STEAD, CHRISTMAS 1907

That Good Man Stead

His defense of young girls was part of the New Journalism

William Thomas Stead (1849–1912), whom Carlyle called "That good man Stead," was one of the fifteen hundred persons drowned when a huge iceberg in the mid-Atlantic tore into the *Titanic* and sank her on the night of April 14, 1912. There cannot be still alive many persons who heard him address a public meeting with all his burning sincerity and who have read the crusading articles in the *Pall Mall Gazette* that made him world-famous. I heard him in my boyhood, when he was campaigning with all his might against the South African War. I read a good deal of his journalism with all the keener interest because as a child I acquired and loved many of his penny *Books for the Bairns, Penny Classics for the People,* and *Penny Poets,* wonderful treasures for a child, and for more than children, and selling in millions.

Stead was often described as the founder of the New Journalism, a title which the newspapermen of today would confer on Lord Northcliffe. His biographer, Frederic Whyte, described him as the bravest and most brilliant of all English journalists and perhaps the most extraordinary man ever seen in Fleet Street. Time may tarnish such superlatives, but that Stead deserves to be honored as one of the grand masters of his craft, though he had a

streak of eccentricity, is incontestable. The newness of his journalism, especially in his *Pall Mall Gazette* days, from 1880 to 1883,
as assistant editor, and then as editor to 1889, sprang mainly from
his own personal initiative, his editorials, his special articles, his
interviews. Some critics even termed it "Government by newspaper." More than any other editor he told prime ministers what
to do. He expressed himself so insistently and so effectively that
London took him most seriously and cabinets had to follow suit.

Stead became editor of a daily paper in exceptional circumstances. He was the son of a Congregational minister and this
qualified him to go to Silcoates School, near Wakefield. Under
parental and school influence he always regarded Congregation-
alists as the heirs of Cromwell, Milton, and the Pilgrim Fathers.
At fourteen he became an apprentice office boy in a merchant's
counting house on Quayside, Newcastle on Tyne. Eager to help
in good works and promote social reforms he soon found the
value of press publicity. This led to his contributing, without
getting any payment for it, to the *Northern Echo,* Darlington.
The editor encouraged him, gave him occasional advice and before long recognized that here was a youth of exceptional journalistic talent. The proprietor of the paper, Hyslop Bell, shared
his view. When his editor left him, Bell offered the editorship of
the *Northern Echo* to Stead, then twenty-two years old. Incredible as it seems the young man had not then seen the inside of
any newspaper office. To get some ideas about editing he arranged
to call on Mr. (afterwards Sir) Wemyss Reid, who as editor of the
Leeds Mercury had charge of what had for a long time the largest
sale of any British provincial daily. Reid, himself the son of a
Congregational minister and himself a junior clerk before he
broke into journalism, warmly admired his young visitor's enthusiasm and self-confidence. Stead explained how he would use
the press as the true and only lever by which thrones and governments could be shaken and the welfare of the masses improved. "I see you think I'm crazy," Stead remarked cheerfully at
one point. "Not crazy perhaps," replied Reid, "but distinctly
eccentric. You will come all right when you've had a little
experience."

In nine years Stead had had enough experience to become
assistant editor of the *Pall Mall Gazette* under John Morley, the

anti-imperialist, philosophic Radical, who became Viscount Morley of Blackburn, secretary of state for India, and biographer of William Ewart Gladstone. When Stead took over from Morley he had full scope to develop his theories of "Government by newspaper." He stirred the creators of political opinion as they had hardly ever been stirred before by Victorian journalism.

The most famous of his peremptory agitations deserves to be told in some detail because of its triumphant outcome and because it gives us a supreme Victorian example of what is now known as the journalism of exposure and sometimes treated as if it were a brand-new development. This campaign imprinted on the public mind the phrase, "The Maiden Tribute of Modern Babylon." Stead's object was to prevent the purchase and violation of child virgins and the international white slave trade. Both these evils had long horrified reformers who knew the facts.

Juvenile prostitution had increased to an appalling degree, but as the law stood it could not cope with the problems presented. The law held that a child of thirteen was competent to consent to her own seduction. It did not let girls under eight bear witness against men who had outraged them on the ground that such victims were too young to understand the nature of an oath. A Select Committee of the House of Lords reported on this problem and Lord Shaftesbury said: "Nothing more cruel, appalling or detestable could be found in the history of crime all over the world." A bill giving effect to the Select Committee's recommendation to prevent the sale of young girls to brothels was strongly opposed by men who regarded it as fanatical or had still worse motives. It was reintroduced in the spring of 1885, but a change of ministry threatened it again with sacrifice.

Mr. Benjamin Scott, chamberlain of the City of London, and Mrs. Josephine Elizabeth Butler, the reformer who fought so nobly against the degradation of women, appealed to Stead as the one man in the country who could save the bill. Stead knew little of the tragedies of the underworld but consulted persons like Mr. (afterwards Sir) Howard Vincent, a former head of the Criminal Investigation Department of Scotland Yard. Howard Vincent (who years later became an encouraging friend of mine at Sheffield) explained to him the business well known to the police of men and women who procured and corrupted young girls. "As soon as the child is over thirteen," he said, "she can be inveigled into a house of ill fame and there violated without any hope of redress, because if she has consented to go into the house she is held to have consented to her own ruin, although she might at that time be and probably was absolutely ignorant of what vice means."

Stead, with a passionate resolve to help, first saw Archbishop Benson, Cardinal Manning, and Bishop Temple and said he proposed to demonstrate in the *Pall Mall Gazette* how he could buy for five pounds a girl just over thirteen, ostensibly for vicious purposes. Later these Church leaders attested the purity of his motive. Stead was helped in his plan by General Booth and his wife, of the Salvation Army. In response to an offer of three pounds (to be increased to five pounds later) a woman handed over her daughter Eliza, just turned thirteen, to a former brothel-keeper now a Salvationist. This helper brought the girl to Stead, who in his pretended character of a vicious man took her to a house of ill fame. Here a midwife certified the girl to be a virgin and she went to bed. Later Stead and a Salvation Army woman officer went together into the girl's room and took her to a nursing home, where a doctor certified that she had not suffered any interference of any kind. This was the chief episode in the articles that Stead now wrote to prove, as he put it later, that British mothers were willing to sell the virginity of their girls for a five-pound note to the procurers of vice.

The first article of the series appeared in the *Pall Mall Gazette* of Monday, July 6, 1885. It ran to about ten thousand words and filled five pages of rather more than tabloid size. But first came an editorial, "We bid you be of good hope." It began: "The Report of our Secret Commission will be read today with a shuddering horror that will thrill throughout the world. After the awful picture of the crimes at present committed under the very aegis of the law has been fully unfolded before the eyes of the public, we need no doubt that the House of Commons will find time to raise the age during which English girls are protected from inexplicable wrong. Terrible as is the exposure, the very horror of it is an inspiration. It speaks not of leaden despair but with a joyful promise of better things to come."

Stead well knew the furious commotion the exposure would

create. He went on to argue against reticence about horrors of evil that cried out for reform. "The Home, the School, the Church are silent," he wrote. "The law is actually accessory to crime. The Press, which reports verbatim the scabrous details of the divorce courts, recoils in pious horror from the duty of shedding a flood of light upon these dark places, which indeed are full of habitations of cruelty." The report of the Secret Commission did not plunge headlong into the sordid details. The "Maiden Tribute" of the title was explained by a reference to Greek mythology about the Minotaur, the monster kept in the Knossian labyrinth and fed with the bodies of youths and maidens whom the Athenians at fixed times had to send to King Minos of Crete as tribute. Also in a long introduction was the admission that to extirpate vice by Act of Parliament was impossible; but it was argued that "because we must leave vice free, that is no reason why we should acquiesce helplessly in the perpetuation of crime."

When the writer came to describe in the first and later issues the steps taken to buy a girl of thirteen there was no lack of detail to cause shuddering horror. The shock in those Victorian times was unprecedented. Such details had never been printed before in a highly reputable newspaper. Headlines of sedate appearance and modest size and, so far as concerned the technical presentment, a staid look did little to lessen the shock.

The Home Secretary asked Stead to stop the articles. Stead said he would do so the moment the Home Secretary promised he would carry the bill through. No such pledge was forthcoming. "I then told him," the crusader wrote later, "I would go on with the publication until the roused indignation of the public compelled the Ministry to do their duty."

The campaign developed on possibly even larger lines than he expected. At any rate, at eight o'clock on Thursday evening nothing had been written for the following day. Stead stayed up all night, the latter part spent with wet towels around his head, dictating to three stenographers. The wonder is that with such stress prevailing during the five days of the series and afterwards, what was written so fast and furiously read so smoothly. There were some unhappy expressions that pained supporters of the campaign. Stead seemed at times to be more reckless than anyone wielding press power has any right to be. But this did not happen often, and nobody now would dream of questioning the purity of his motive.

The demand for the paper exceeded expectation, though in rising from 8,360 to 12,250, sales did not become enormous by modern standards. The paper lost money by the crusade, partly because some advertising was withdrawn, partly because of crusade costs. Yet London seemed eager to know what appalling revelations were made and why. But in what way did they appall? Were people shocked by the crimes revealed? Or by Stead's shattering of conventional reticence? Did he cause sniggering amusement by frank references to virginity and its callous sale? Or did he inspire, as he intended, a determination that Parliament should pass a bill protecting the daughters of the poor, which the House of Lords in three consecutive years had declared to be necessary?

Some of the widely circulated London papers blamed Stead for his methods of exposure since men, women, and children, as one of them put it, could buy copies of a paper containing "the most offensive, highly colored, and disgusting details concerning the ways of a small section of the population." Said the *Weekly Times* (not connected with the *Times*): "The evil will be spread, till there will be scarcely a boy or girl in England whose ignorance will not be displaced by forbidden knowledge, or whose innocence will not be tainted by the disgusting pabulum with which they have been so plentifully supplied. A plague worse than any Egyptian plague has visited the homes of England."

If any children did hasten to buy the *Pall Mall Gazette* in the expectation of reading spicy bits on subjects they were curious about, they would be sadly disappointed. They might learn more from a paper like the *Weekly Times* with its reporting of sex cases in the courts. They would find nothing to giggle over in Stead's highly moral campaign and denunciations of crimes against children. However, Mr. Cavendish Bentinck, M.P., asked the Home Secretary whether the author and publishers of "certain publications relating to objectionable subjects" could be subjected to criminal proceedings. The reply was that the publication of obscene matter could be prosecuted by indictment in the usual way, but is was for the jury to define what was an obscene publication.

In one of the series Stead challenged the government to lay
his disclosures before a judicial investigation. He was sure of his
ground. His articles began to make the impression he intended.
The Criminal Law Amendment Bill had its second reading in
the House of Commons. Calling it the Charter of the girlhood
of the country, Stead rejoiced that it raised the age of consent
from thirteen to sixteen, admitted the evidence of children even
if they were not able to satisfy the judge and jury that they understood the nature of an oath, and increased the pains and penalties
inflicted upon all those who ruined girls, whether by abducting
them abroad or corrupting them at home. Many eminent persons
acknowledged the good that Stead had done. Religious papers
praised the crusade. So did some of the provincial papers.

General Booth summed up accurately: "Multitudes are filled
with horror and while distressed at the dire necessity which
compels publicity cry out with agonising entreaty for the Bill.
Others refuse to look at the black iniquity on a plea that a mistake has been made in the publication. Others try to find comfort in the hope that there is some exaggeration in the facts. Alas,
alas, we who are face to face with the evil are only too well able
to verify them. It is a strong dose certainly, but it is a horrible
disease." Bishop Temple, while agreeing that the *Pall Mall Gazette* exposures had caused the greatest pain to many excellent
people, believed the result of the crusade would be a "general
raising of the moral tone on this subject throughout the country."

Stead's opponents still had a chance to trip him up, though
not to overthrow his work or ruin his reputation. He was tried for
abducting the little girl Eliza, who had not been returned to her
mother but was being cared for by the Salvation Army in Paris.
True, Stead had not had the consent of the girl's father to the
demonstration purchase, but believed he had bought the consent
of the mother. The judge ruled that the consent of the father
was what would have mattered. It had not even been asked for.
The jury had to find Stead guilty, but they said he had been de-
ceived by his agents, recommended him to mercy, and expressed
their appreciation of the services he had rendered to the nation
by securing the passage of a much-needed law for the protection
of young girls. He was sentenced to three months' imprisonment,
and served about two, as a "misdemeanant of the first division."
He could see visitors every day, work at his trade (his newspapers

arrived at 7:15 A.M. and a messenger collected his editorial or other articles at 10:00 A.M.), received mail, fruit and flowers, and thoroughly enjoyed a comparatively restful time. The only person he disliked in prison was the chaplain. All others were sympathetic. No wonder Carlyle, who was happy to meet him, called him "That good man Stead."

Not all Stead's campaigns (or escapades as he sometimes called them) were as successful as the "Maiden Tribute" achievement. He wrote an interview with General Charles George Gordon on the danger in the Soudan where the Egyptian garrisons and all Europeans were in peril from the conquering Mahdi's forces. In a leading article Stead urged that Gordon should be sent to Khartoum "to report upon the best means of effecting the evacuation of the Soudan." Gordon at that time had almost the reputation of a superman with phenomenal personal magnetism owing to success he had achieved in coping with innumerable fanatical rebels in China. But no magical transformation could be wrought in Africa. Gordon was besieged in Khartoum. A relief force arrived too late. The city had been lost and Gordon speared to death. Stead undoubtedly inspired the ill-starred expedition, but why should he be blamed for his faith in a man of Gordon's inspiring record or for the delays in sending the relief force?

His campaign for a stronger navy roused some political opposition, but here, with the help of the future Lord Fisher, a man of Nelsonian foresight, he had a strong case. Many British politicians have often been driven into a neurotic scare by the raising of taxation but accepted without a trace of dismay the lowering of defense efficiency.

One campaign that Stead ran with his usual zeal had a strange end. It is worth recording as an example of how this headstrong campaigner could go astray. On a June morning in 1887 at a boarding house in Whitechapel, London, a young married woman, Miriam Angel, was found dead in bed, obviously strangled after a struggle. Her mouth showed burns, presumably from a phial containing nitric acid found among the bedclothes. Searching the room, police found lying unconscious under the bed Israel Lipski, aged twenty-two, who also lived in the house. His mouth also showed signs of burning. He quickly recovered, having apparently fainted.

The police regarded the case as one of attempted sexual assault by Lipski with resistance met by strangulation and the attempted suicide of the assailant. He presumably had forced some of the poison into the woman's mouth. Tried for murder, he said that while he was going upstairs to his room two men outside Mrs. Angel's door seized him, forced poison into his mouth and must have pushed him unconscious under the bed. The jury did not believe this story and the man was sentenced to death. At that time Britain had no Court of Criminal Appeal.

The Home Secretary, Mr. Henry Matthews, considered the case and consulted the trial judge, Mr. Justice Stephen. Lipski's solicitor, a Mr. Hayward, was duly told that the Home Secretary was unable to advise Queen Victoria to grant a reprieve. The execution was ordered for Monday, August 15. As a last hope Hayward telegraphed to the Queen, "Lipski absolutely innocent. Implore Your Majesty to stay execution," and he asked for Stead's help.

Stead published the telegram exclusively and the following day printed a front-page editorial under the heading "A Legal Murder." He argued that the execution would be convenient for the prosecution since dead men tell no tales. The article said, "We are assured most positively by the prisoner's solicitor that the judge . . . is no longer convinced that the evidence of Lipski's guilt is so strong as it appeared to him at the Old Bailey. The sand in the glass is rapidly running out. Lipski sleeps twice more and then—an innocent man will be called out to be strangled to death in the name of the law and by the will of the Home Secretary."

Questions were raised in the Commons at a Saturday sitting. The Home Secretary announced a week's respite for Lipski, but denied the story attributed to the prisoner's solicitor. How could a solicitor know what the judge was thinking? The *Pall Mall Gazette* explained. Hayward had put down in writing his theory of the crime and shown it to the Solicitor General, Sir Edward Clarke, who urged him to send a copy to, the judge. Hayward protested that it would be contrary to professional etiquette for a solicitor to communicate with a judge. Sir Edward replied, "Never mind that. You'd better do it."

The judge asked Hayward to call on him at the Law Courts,

"a thing never known before." Shortly afterwards the judge requested Hayward to call again and said, "I cannot tell you what I think, but I can tell you this. If I were not *I*, I should heartily wish you success." Hayward told Stead of this interview, but begged him not to print anything about it because publication would ruin him as a solicitor and do Lipski no good. But Stead decided to print, added to his article a mention of Hayward's plea for nonpublication, and said, "We decided to publish and take responsibility for our decision."

Stead's articles had a marked effect, and 109 M.P.s signed a petition asking the Home Secretary to change Lipski's respite to a reprieve. When one of the M.P.s tried to present the petition in the House of Commons the Speaker ruled him out of order, saying the document must go to the Home Secretary. The Leader of the House, Mr. W. H. Smith, protested strongly against an attempt to bring Parliamentary pressure upon the Home Secretary. Then Stead issued a penny pamphlet, "SHALL WE HANG LIPSKI? OR MYSTERIOUS MURDER OF MIRIAM ANGEL, with illustrations and portraits." It described "the race for life" and set out reasons for a reprieve.

Time was indeed running short. On the Sunday before the appointed execution day, Mr. Matthews asked the judge to meet him again at the Home Office at five o'clock. An account of the meeting appeared in *Many Furrows*, by A. G. Gardiner. The source was not mentioned, but I think the silent witness must have been Evelyn Ruggles-Brice, of the Home Office staff. The judge said that after the jury's verdict he had no alternative to passing the death sentence. For four hours this indecisive conference went on. Then an office messenger appeared bearing a missive which almost made the minister jump from his chair. Lipski had confessed his guilt. The document was signed by the condemned man and formally witnessed by the prison rabbi and the governor. Lipski said his sole motive was robbery and he craved the forgiveness of the woman's husband and the two men on whom he had cast suspicion. On the scaffold he said, "I have no more to say. I am guilty."

Did this reduce the silent shame or an abject apology the editor who had said an innocent man was going to be strangled to death in the name of the law and by the will of the Home

Secretary? It did not. Stead was not silent. He headed his front-page editorial, "ALL'S WELL THAT ENDS WELL."

Stead went on surprising people up to the day of his death. He seemed able to get interviews with some of the most important persons on earth. One was with the Tsar Alexander III of Russia. Stead became a close friend of Cecil Rhodes, the English-born imperialist who became the most influential man in Africa. Even at Darlington he had corresponded with monarchs and statesmen. When I saw him he looked a forceful figure with his piercing blue eyes, reddish beard, and proudly erect head. He did not seem to care much about his clothes. But why should he worry about details of appearance when he was acknowledged by so distinguished a critic as James L. Garvin to be Britain's only journalist who was an international figure in his own right?

Stead's unshakable self-confidence inevitably harassed the proprietor of the *Pall Mall Gazette,* Mr. Henry Yates Thompson, many of whose friends detested the New Journalism. Editor and proprietor parted after Stead told Thompson he had arranged to edit a new monthly magazine for Mr. (afterwards Sir) George Newnes, and Thompson replied that he was not "going shares in the editor of the *P.M.G.* with Mr. Newnes of *Tit-Bits.*" The new magazine was the *Review of Reviews.* Here again editor and proprietor were soon in conflict. Newnes said Stead was turning his hair gray. Stead bought him out and confronted almost overwhelming problems alone until he got a manager. The review started with good ideas—a world review, with an illuminating record of the month, a character sketch of the man of the month, interviews, book reviews, cartoons, quotations and information from all over the world. Stead worked in a breathless whirl and not all his projects for the *Review of Reviews* or for new newspapers were properly carried out. Becoming a Spiritualist, he ran *Borderland* for four years.

He wrote fluently and graphically. Visiting Chicago in 1893 he gave a conference address on "If Christ came to Chicago." He did not intend to write a book on Chicago, but became so immersed in the problems of "the great city which has already secured an all but unquestioned primacy among the capitals of the New World" that he felt he must bring his pen into action and record the civic and moral issues that cried out for reform.

The book had its detractors. It also won warm praise as a creditable piece of reporting. It deserves a prominent place in the historical records of Chicago.

Many and fervent were the tributes when it became clear that Stead had perished in the *Titanic*. He was last seen standing alone, without a lifebelt, on the deck. There is evidence that his bedroom steward helped him to put on his lifebelt, but probably Stead gave it to someone else. Such self-denial would have been characteristic.

He was long remembered as a controversial figure, hero-worshipped by many for the good he did, blamed by others for the excitingly, breathlessly novel methods he used.

What of the verdict of history? Such a verdict, despite a popular presumption to the contrary, is rarely unanimous. Few today, reflecting on the changes in journalism in the past hundred years, would think at once of Stead as its greatest transformer. Northcliffe, Kemsley, Beaverbrook, Thomson of Fleet, Cecil King, Hugh Cudlipp, Denis Hamilton—these have done more to change its appearance, improve its techniques and enlarge its number of readers. But Stead made innovations that fashion could never change and set examples that others followed and developed, so that they have become conventions of today. The fear of "Government by newspaper" still recurs. The journalism of exposure has shone torches in many dark and dangerous haunts of crime.

That "good man Stead" could be impulsive to the point of recklessness. He often committed wild indiscretions. A friend congratulated him on his "dashing unscrupulousness." Lord Milner, his assistant editor for a time, said it was fun to work for such "a compound of Don Quixote and Phineas T. Barnum." But, above everything, Stead was a man of action, a man who got things done, not merely a scorer of scoops but also a supreme social reformer. Because of him, newspapers became not only less stodgy but also far more effective in organizing public opinion to oppose wrong.

2

C. P. Scott

*He made a provincial newspaper
a world force*

Charles Prestwich Scott (1846–1932) edited the *Manchester Guardian* for fifty-seven years, from 1872 to 1929. Slowly and not without facing times of dangerous stress he achieved a journalistic feat unparalleled in Britain—he made a provincial newspaper a respected and indeed honored force throughout the civilized world. In the United States and other countries the *Guardian* became as well known as the *Times* of London.

Two classic sayings in journalism are associated with Scott. It was he who said, "Comment is free, but facts are sacred." This was the climax of a passage which every trainee in journalism might well know by heart—"The newspaper is of necessity something of a monopoly, and its first duty is to shun the dangers of monopoly. Its primary office is the gathering of news. At the peril of its soul it must see that the supply is not tainted. Neither in what it gives, nor in what it does not give, nor in the mode of presentation, must the unclouded face of truth suffer wrong."

The other saying is that of Lord Robert Cecil who, at a great dinner at Manchester when the paper was a hundred years old and Scott had been editor for fifty years, said the *Manchester Guardian* had made righteousness readable. This tribute from a leading Conservative, who afterwards became the first Viscount Cecil of Chelwood and was awarded the Nobel Peace Prize for 1937, made an instant and lasting impression.

How did C. P. Scott win this distinction for his paper? What were the lessons he left behind? These are questions for careful research and thought. Scott would not have wished it otherwise. He would not want to be revered as a legend. He hoped to be an example. He still is.

I can claim to have read the *Guardian* longer than most people. The first day I read it with unreserved though juvenile admiration was on May 20, 1898, when it published the news of the death of William Ewart Gladstone, statesman, orator, and scholar. Brought up in a Liberal family, opposed to acquisitive imperialism, I believed while still a young schoolboy that Gladstone was a greater man than any of the laureated heroes of military history. So when the *Manchester Guardian* printed as a supplement a long memoir of the Grand Old Man I read it absorbedly. It struck me as a prodigious achievement for the editor to write all this within a few hours of the great man's death. My father, a frequent contributor to the press, explained that the memoir had been prepared long before, and brought up to date from time to time, as were records of other prominent citizens. Morgues, as he said these stores of biographical matter were termed, existed in all important newspaper offices.

Hearing a secret of the trade did not lessen my admiration of the paper with its many-paged array of tributes to Britain's dead statesman. Thereafter I read it as regularly as I could, especially during the Boer War. At that time I was a schoolboy at Christ's Hospital, London, under masters who were mostly Imperialistic. Indeed some were Jingoes, especially one who used to come dashing into the classroom with the exultant cry, "Soon we shall have another bit of the map of Africa printed red." Most of the boys shared his excitement. I, coming from a *Guardian*-reading home in the north of England, refused to be elated. The greater part of the British press favored the war. The Liberal party split on the issue, but the *Guardian* never wavered, no matter how unpopular its policy was. Police protection was given to Scott's house.

When I became a junior reporter on a Liberal paper at Hull

Courtesy of the *Guardian*

C. P. SCOTT

I quickly realized the influence of the *M.G.,* as we always called it. My evening paper editor, John Forrester, an excellent news-getter but not much of a politician, never dictated an editorial without consulting in the course of the task, as if to refresh his memory, the *M.G.,* the *Yorkshire Post,* a free trade Conservative paper, and the *Westminster Gazette,* a front bench Liberal paper. His doctrines were sometimes a paraphrase of those in the *Guardian,* so used as to reply to some argument in the *Yorkshire Post.* The contrast between his chief intellectual source and the resulting version was rather pathetic, like a dull report of a brilliant speech. But how could a moribund, understaffed little evening paper in those days possess the distinction of a paper like the *Guardian* of C. P. Scott? I quickly learned that to grasp the meaning of the controversies of the day, to find them much more than an exchange of partisan battle-cries, to appreciate the moral and economic inwardness of the issues, eager young people like my-self must study the *Guardian* as well as newspapers that flew the Conservative flag. A time came when cheap and popular papers, like the *Daily Dispatch* of Manchester, and the London papers that printed their Northern editions at Manchester may have threatened the circulation of the *Guardian,* but its reputation for integrity and judicial self-control remained unassailable. A friend of mine working on an evening paper in Manchester wrote to me, "The other papers may scream and sweat, but the *M.G.* has only to beckon with its little finger and in political influence it outdoes the most determined effort of its rivals."

I was still hardly out of my teens when, to my surprise, C. P. Scott asked me to go over to Manchester to see him with a view to a possible appointment on his paper. He wanted a young journalist to help with minor editorials and editorial notes. I knew that he had a team of young writers, whose short editorials on a variety of topics were then a feature of the paper. But I did not know that he liked to get such men both young and cheap. On his reporting staff he had a former *Sheffield Independent* man, Louis Northend, who told him that I was doing editorials and descriptive specials for the *Independent,* a once famous Lib-eral paper. For me the resulting interview was the first I ever had with an editor of national and indeed international reputa-tion. First I was received with almost ambassadorial courtesy by someone who I was afterwards told was probably W. P. Crozier. The name meant nothing to me then, but later Crozier became editor, was very much a scholar journalist on the model of C. P. himself, and was my predecessor as the British Broadcasting Corporation's regular commentator on the news of the North, a freelance sideline that brought much prestige at the time. I was soon taken by Mr. Crozier to C. P.'s room and found him quite welcoming. My friend on the reporting staff must have given me an enthusiastic commendation. Nervous as I was, I warmed to the handsome, bearded, briskly speaking man who commanded so much authority and worldwide influence.

After a few questions on my political faith and my education on the classical side at Christ's Hospital, C. P. approached the, to me, highly important question of pay and mentioned a possible fifty shillings a week, ten shillings less than I was getting at Sheffield. Transparently disappointed, I explained that I must think it over. Then I said perhaps he would like to see some articles I had written for various popular papers, since they showed perhaps a certain versatility. C. P. looked at them and then said most courteously that while he had been glad to see me, he thought that I was not quite the kind of man he wanted. Possibly he thought a man who sold articles to popular papers like the *Daily Mirror* could not possess the moral earnestness needed for the *Guardian,* or did he suspect me of trying to force him to raise his terms? Was I as mercenary as he probably thought? I did much free-lancing, not because I was intensely greedy for money (though I needed it badly to help my father, brothers, and sister), but because I loved writing and wanted to get away from the so dreary routine of reporting in those days, the long slabs of verbatim speeches, the innumerable theft charges, the suicide inquests, the writer's cramp from incessant transcription of shorthand notes without the benefit of a typewriter. Anyway, my failure to join the *Guardian* probably did me no harm. Work under so famous an editor as C. P. would have been an enviable experience, but to join Lord Northcliffe on the *Daily Mail,* as I did before long, was by no means a poor substitute, and much better paid just when I badly needed more money.

In spite of my failure to meet C. P.'s needs, my admiration for him and his journalistic ideals never wavered. When I was able to marry and furnish a home I took warm pride in having his photograph alongside Northcliffe's in my study. The examples of these great men of my world gave me a continuing stimulus to work hard. Northcliffe, great man though he undoubtedly was and in many ways often most generous, had his journalistic detractors. Some of them were not even silent at the time of his death. One evening paper in a Yorkshire town then wrote of him with what seemed to me savage contempt. But C. P. Scott never roused such antipathy. If I, as an outsider who saw him only once, was impressed so deeply by C. P., what an influence he must have had on those who worked for him and came under his constant firm control, his instructive example, his polite reproofs, his encouragements, his moral qualities! He was known to pay modest salaries (as did almost all newspapers in his time) and was once stingingly rebuked for this, to his intense surprise, by a journalistic trade union deputation. But his public spirit shone out so clearly and he made the *Manchester Guardian* so worthy and so distinguished a paper that he became a hero to almost everyone of us in the British newspaper world.

He was not the founder of the *Guardian*. It began as a four-page weekly in 1821 at sevenpence, with John Edward Taylor, a Unitarian minister's son and a Radical, as editor. His son, who bore the same name, took control of the paper in 1861 when it had become a penny daily. He chose as a colleague his cousin C. P. Scott, who had done well at Oxford, and was a serious thinker with opinions like his own. The young man had six months apprenticeship on the *Scotsman,* then edited by Alexander Russel, one of the leading editors of his time. Scott started work at Manchester in 1871 and the next year at the age of twenty-five was given the editorship. He at once devoted himself to his many-sided task so sacrificially that friends thought he might break down, but being a methodical man he soon adapted himself to laborious duties.

Few editors have supervised so thoroughly so many departments of a paper while it was being prepared for the printing press. Above all he took pride in scrupulous political leadership, first-class writing, the best informed contributors, and utterly truthful reporting. W. T. Stead, representing the *Guardian* at The Hague in 1899, mentioned that the word "disgruntled" had been cut out of one of his telegrams. "I do not object to such mutilations," he wrote to Scott, "as I regard them as a sacrifice of force and effectiveness to your theory of the necessity of preventing the English language being reinforced with words which have not received a classic stamp." Stead mentioned that in a telegram he had used the words "hankey-pankey" and "on the sly," and expected they would be cut out. I feel sure they were.

Scott himself said that he started in life with a very strong feeling of devotion to humanity. That feeling never weakened. When he joined the *Guardian* it was not as Radical as it became later. It was cautiously Whiggish, competing with a truly Radical *Manchester Examiner*. But devotion to humanity moved Scott more and more to the Left, especially in the great strikes of the eighteen-eighties and eighteen-nineties. As the paper said during the miners' strike in 1893, "The idea that wages, in other words the living, the comfort, and the civilization of the great mass of men is to be the one elastic and squeezible thing in a business, has got to go." This may be thought a bold utterance at that time in a paper read largely by the employers and well-to-do, but it was in keeping with the humanitarian politics to which Scott and his chief assistants, W. T. Arnold, C. E. Montague and L. T. Hobhouse, were always faithful.

Grave troubles were coming. John Edward Taylor, as senior proprietor, often warmly praised Scott's editing, but in his closing years, anxious about the profits of the paper, he began to develop suspicion that Scott was growing less attentive to his editorial duties. It is true that combined with them were those of a member of Parliament, for he had been elected by the Leigh division of Lancashire in 1895. Taylor did not object to this diversification of Scott's energies for liberalism, but would have preferred his editor to represent a Manchester constituency. Though Scott did not achieve a commanding position in the House and was not a fluent debater, he believed his parliamentary experience improved his editorial qualities. I cannot imagine that the editor of the *Guardian* today would even dream of standing for Parliament. Editing has become a whole-time occupation. Scott, at the time in question, had a brilliant staff, and when in London could exercise careful supervision from his Fleet Street office. Unhappily his wife, who had given him excellent help with his editing, fell ill and Scott, a devoted husband, took her abroad. Nor were these Taylor's only worries. The Northcliffe revolution had transformed British newspaper competition. The *Daily Mail* started in 1896 and soon used special trains and printing facilities in Manchester as well as London to become in a sense the first truly national paper. Meanwhile, as the popular press prospered, the *Guardian's* profit sank in 1905 to twelve hundred pounds.

Taylor died in October of that year and Mrs. Scott in November. Taylor's will, intentionally or not, threatened Scott with calamity. He was given the option of buying the business of the paper, but not the building, for ten thousand pounds, but the executors were not compelled to sell. They thought in fact of administering the paper themselves in the interests of the estate. After the position had seemed hopeless to Scott, the executors decided to sell. The copyright, building and other assets were put at £242,000. Scott had only £48,000, but with this money, sums from relatives, a mortgage on the building, a bank overdraft, small loans and liquid assets in the business, he gained control of the paper his editing had done so much to make famous. He plunged with intense energy into the task of regaining the *Guardian's* prosperity. Now he had to face the increasing opposition created by the Northcliffe revolution. But his vigor seemed to increase, especially in politics. He ceased to be a member of Parliament in 1906, but exercised powerful influence through his editorials, in which he was more fluent and effective than in public speaking. What many readers, myself among them, appreciated most were his articles on votes for women. The ultimate excesses of the suffragettes roused his disapproval, but he remained a convinced feminist who never thought the blunders of militancy should rob women of their moral rights. As one who gave all the help he could to the suffragettes until they resorted to discreditable violence, I think Scott's support for the cause helped to win over the most thoughtful elements in our dissentious society. But it was not until 1918, after women had given invaluable help in winning the First World War, that they were rewarded with the vote. Ireland and foreign policy were other subjects on which Scott wrote with marked effect. His editorials were models of incisive and lucid criticism—the analyses and utterances of a well-stocked and persuasive mind.

The First World War gave Scott increasing opportunities to show his statesmanship. He believed it ought not to have taken place and that Britain ought not to have become a party to it, but once we were in it the whole future of our nation was at stake and there was no choice but to do our utmost to obtain success. As disaster followed disaster in the early stages, he began to believe that with Asquith as prime minister, an impressive public speaker but slow to realize that delays in war are frightful dangers, we could not win. Though he recognized Lloyd George's imperfections, Scott believed that the man had the right spirit, the right energy to hold the well-officered Germans at bay and lead us to victory. Lloyd George, who under Asquith was said by J. L. Garvin to be driven almost desperate by the blindness and nervelessness on every side of him, did not disappoint his champions. Though a hateful gadfly to generals and others whom he thought unequal to their terrific tasks, Lloyd George proved to be a war leader of steely strength. When the conflict, in which we owed so much to the mighty efforts of the United States, came to an end, Scott wrote of Lloyd George, "He has done more than any other man in public life to win the war."

Yes, our side had won the war. Who would win the peace? Scott was soon saying, "Lloyd George doesn't know (it is an intellectual defect) what principle means." To Colonel House, President Woodrow Wilson's friend and adviser and one of the American peace commissioners, Scott wrote: "George, be it never forgotten, is not a statesman; he is a pure opportunist with a good many sound and generous instincts, but an opportunist to the bone." We can see now that if the victors had shown more magnanimity, if after crushing the warmakers of Germany we had made a peace of reconciliation, if there had been more support for the League of Nations, the world would have been spared unspeakable misery. In many respects the ruling spirit was of avarice, vindictiveness, and propaganda-fed hatred. The *Manchester Guardian* pronounced wise and humanitarian principles, but not with strong effect at the Peace Conference.

Scott achieved more success in the next phase of that ancient problem, Ireland. He loathed the policy of lawless violence practiced by the Black and Tans, even though it was a response to many murders. In his editorials he hammered his old friend

Lloyd George as hard as he could. But at length British and Irish leaders, sick of killing and carnage, ashamed of massacre, longing for good will, came to terms in 1921, not perfect terms, not solving all Irish political problems, but highly creditable to Britain and Sinn Fein. Scott's efforts helped considerably to bring about this heartening result. It was a most happy year for Scott, the year of the Irish settlement, the centenary of the *Manchester Guardian* and his fiftieth year of editorship. The King sent congratulations on the jubilee of a courageous and high-minded editor. Resounding tributes were paid to him by the newspaper profession and political leaders. At a great dinner in Manchester he was praised by Lord Derby, Lord Robert Cecil, and Mrs. Fawcett, but the most memorable speech of all was his own, containing this reference to the *Guardian*: "There are papers which will never be sold—which would rather suffer extinction. And it is well that it should be so. The public has its rights. The paper which has grown up in a great community, nourished by its resources, reflecting in a thousand ways its spirit and its interests, in a real sense belongs to it. How else except in the permanence of that association can it fulfill its duty or repay the benefits and the confidence it has received?" Scott was now seventy-five. He worked on doggedly through the fall of the coalition government and efforts to heal and reunite the bruised Liberal party. In 1929 he thought the time had come to hand over the editorship to his youngest son, Edward Taylor, an economist with a rare gift for expository writing. Again Scott received world honors, and in 1930 he was made a freeman of Manchester in the presence of thirty Lancashire and Cheshire mayors.

He died on New Year's Day, 1932, and once again many world leaders paid grateful, glowing tributes to this modest man who gave to a provincial English newspaper a worldwide reputation and influence. Today it is printed in London as well as in Manchester, and has chosen to call itself simply the *Guardian*. Like all good newspapers, it has introduced many innovations, but in its quality and, above all, its devotion to integrity, fair play, and reform it still breathes the spirit of C. P. Scott. When we ponder the duties and ethics of the newspaper press, it is his great sayings—sayings that were his own guides—that inevitably come to mind. He was a determined leader, far ahead of popular feeling. He raised Britain's reputation in the world.

3

Robert Donald

A successful editor who renounced writing

"If it appeared in any other paper, I would not care much. But the *Chronicle* is different."

That remark by David Lloyd George, at the height of his power in World War I, was a significant tribute to the extraordinary influence exercised by the *Daily Chronicle* in the early years of this century.

Robert Donald (1861–1933) was its editor throughout the period in which this Liberal newspaper acquired the reputation that made Lloyd George so fearful of its criticism that he turned aside from his great responsibilities to conspire with rich political friends for the secret acquisition of the paper from a proprietor who, well content with its prosperity, was not disposed to sell. Eventually, the purchasers paid a price then unprecedented in comparable newspaper transactions, to the end that the editor could be confronted with conditions that would ensure his subservience to Lloyd George's will.

Quietly, firmly, and instantly Robert Donald rejected the ultimatum. He resigned. Twelve years later the *Daily Chronicle*, insolvent, disappeared. Not long afterwards, when Donald died, the *Daily Express* said of him: "He gave a vital character to his own newspaper. When he left it, the spark died out of it and nobody in the new generation rekindled it." Here, indeed, was an exceptional editor, one well qualified to rank among journalists who made British press history.

Robert Donald was born in Banffshire in the Scottish Highlands where, as recorded by Ramsay MacDonald, who came from those parts, the land "yields nothing for nothing." Therefore, avowed MacDonald, a Banffshire farm provides "a stimulating nursery" where people know the true values of life and "prepare their sons to go forth to lead a hard life honestly and uprightly and to find work interesting to themselves and of service to others."

Equipped with the best that could be done for him in a rural day-school, plus a zest for reading, Donald found something fascinating even in the newspapers of the 1870's. He became possessed of a desire to enter journalism. So, while he worked at a junior clerk's desk in the office of an Aberdeen lawyer, he taught himself shorthand in preparation for a career more appealing.

Traditionally, Aberdonians have a natural talent for economical administration, of which the *Aberdeen Journal* of his day provided an incisive example. Journalistically minded youths who approached the management were conceded the privilege of "frequenting " the reporters' room for a limited period under the supervision of the chief reporter. In practice, the aspirants performed assigned tasks but received no pay.

At the end of such a trial Donald and another youth were told by the chief reporter that they were not worth engagement, even on the terms of the experiment. Later in life when each of them was editing a daily newspaper (Donald in London and his friend in Birmingham) it afforded them some amusement to hear that the man who dismissed them with so crushing a verdict was still chief reporter of the *Aberdeen Journal*.

Soon after that initial blow to his hopes, Donald took the road to England. Arrived in Edinburgh, an Aberdonian on the staff of the *Evening News* there procured a start for him in the editorial office of that paper, where for the next five years good training made him an excellent reporter.

Though Donald was trained to the style of the period, he was a young man of the same generation as Northcliffe, and he

Courtesy of Madame Saulnier-Blache (née Margot-Donald)

SIR ROBERT DONALD

regarded the press of that period as failing to comprehend the significance of a great, new reading public which universal, elementary education had created during his lifetime. Though he had a Scot's pride in Scotland's capital city, its tradition did not favor enterprising journalism; and he was conscious, too, of London's pre-eminence among the world's news centers.

When he resumed the trail southward he showed good sense by breaking his journey at Northampton, sixty-six miles from London. There, joining the staff of the *Evening Echo*, he added English experience to a training wholly Scottish. He mastered the difference in technique and terminology and thus was able, even while he worked on the *Echo*, to get some free-lance pieces accepted by London newspapers. Also, he made occasional trips to Fleet Street.

The day soon came when he decided to launch himself on Fleet Street without further reconnaissance. Most journalists so situated would almost certainly have begun such an enterprise by writing letters to London editors, soliciting an interview. Donald dispensed with that preliminary gambit, adopting the more direct approach of disengaging himself from his current employment and going in person to seek a London job.

Physical confrontation with the sources of news was part of a reporter's daily round at that time. The telephone had only just emerged from the laboratory; it was not yet a factor in news-gathering. When facts and interpretative information were wanted, the reporter had to get out and about. Whether he elicited what he was seeking could depend on what sort of a person the reporter was. Often, he had to interview individuals temporarily in a state of excitement, grief, or suspicion, and officials who might have an exalted sense of importance.

For such situations, Donald was fortunate in his natural endowments. He possessed those personal characteristics that added up to what the Victorians called "good address," and this asset served him well throughout his career. He was instinctively a friendly man, a good mixer, quick of perception. His sympathy was readily aroused by circumstances that called for compassion. Scottish caution inhibited impulsiveness. Anger was either so alien to his nature or was under such strong control that, in twenty years of association with him (at times in daily contact on a variety of matters) I never knew him to exhibit ill temper; and he could rid himself quickly of a bore or a charlatan without discourtesy. In appearance he was tall, well built, possessing the bearing and distinguished appearance peculiar to Highlanders, even to men of humble origin.

Donald's personality is important in relation to his success as an editor. No one was more strongly convinced that the sustained efficiency of a newspaper depends in large measure upon the loyalty and team spirit of its staff, and that the response forthcoming at times of stress depends upon the sort of leadership to which the staff are accustomed.

Those essentials were always evident in the nightly activities in the *Chronicle* office when he presided there. Not only in the editorial rooms but down in the stereo foundry, and in the basements where giant presses rolled, a visit by the editor was always welcomed. When he appeared, with an unhurried, easy stride, greeting genially anyone who flitted across his path, and dropping an occasional word of encouragement, tension seemed to be dispelled.

Such being his character and temperament, he may have had an awareness even in those early Northampton days, that attendance in person was the best way to a job. Having decided to advance upon Fleet Street, he wrote no letters but bade goodbye to the *Echo* and set out for London where his first call was to collect two guineas due to him for an article.

Before reaching the office of the evening paper concerned, he noticed that a crowd was gathering on a corner near the ancient church of the press, St. Bride's. Investigating, he encountered unexpectedly a reporter named Nankivell whom he had met only once before. Nankivell explained the commotion by saying that supplies of the *Pall Mall Gazette* were just reaching news-sellers, and the whole population of London was agog to read the next installment of the "Maiden Tribute of Modern Babylon," a factual serial by the *Pall Mall's* editor, W. T. Stead. (See "That Good Man Stead," chapter 1.) Nankivell added that he himself was now on the staff of that paper. When Donald disclosed that he was seeking a job in London. Nankivell suggested that an inquiry at his own office might be worth while; and they made off together.

Thrusting through a crowd of newsboys waiting for supplies and into the *Pall Mall*'s building, they discovered that the editor was not available; but meeting the manager, they learned that his staff was overburdened with mail orders for back numbers containing the "Tribute," and that he could do with an additional man to address postal wrappers.

Neither the work nor the pay attracted Donald, but he reasoned that here, at least, was an opportunity to get a footing in the office of a London daily newspaper, and a newspaper that obviously was making the running. Two days later, Donald's intimation that he was a shorthand writer, resulted in immediate promotion (and increased pay) to help with managerial correspondence. At the end of a week, in an exploratory visit to the editorial department, he made known his journalistic qualifications and thus, during his second week in the employment of the *Pall Mall Gazette,* he was a reporter again, assigned in the mornings to stockholders' meetings in the City, and, in the evenings, to the press gallery of the House of Commons, an experience he found most agreeable.

One day, in the interval between these two assignments, he was asked to go to the editor's room, to take by dictation the next installment of the "Tribute." In three weeks, the unemployed reporter had become the aide of Britain's most controversial editor.

From contemporary assessments of Stead an amusing anthology could be compiled. Lord Milner, statesman and fastidious writer, saw him as "a compound of Don Quixote and Barnum." Prime Minister Asquith considered his methods "as novel and as sensational as those of General Booth" (founder of the Salvation Army). R. D. Blumenfeld discerned in Stead "a Caesarian chronicler, a stern moralist, a visionary and a journalistic buccaneer; but as great a journalist as we have ever known."

Donald shared Stead's own view of himself—a crusader who had discerned in journalism a new means of crusading. Though never tempted to adopt Stead's eccentricities, the young man was much influenced by his editor's principles, and so cherished his friendship that after Stead's death he took the initiative in promoting a project that resulted in a public memorial to Stead in the form of a plaque set in the wall of the Thames Embankment

where the river comes nearest to Fleet Street. At the unveiling of
the memorial in 1913, he made a speech.

Only an urge to vary his experience caused Donald to leave
the *Pall Mall Gazette.* He wished to add to his journalistic qualifications some knowledge of the work of a foreign correspondent.
Stead recognized the desirability of his taking that step at that
stage in his career, and though Donald went to France as a free
lance, he received authority to describe himself as the Paris correspondent of the *Pall Mall Gazette,* a helpful tag though it carried
no salary.

There is no evidence that he scored any sensational success
with his stories from Paris, but he learned much about the foreign
correspondent's functions, and he acquired a good knowledge of
the language. But there was a priceless bonus to come. In the
course of his contacts he met the young Parisienne who, a few
years later, became his wife in a marriage that proved ideal.

Moreover, the Paris experiment encouraged Donald to extend his experience similarly by visiting the United States. There,
he concentrated his attention on American institutions, and
studied the system of local government. Also, his interest was
actively engaged by the structure of public companies, commercial corporations, and of great trusts then in the making.

But by far the most important result of this first visit was the
conviction it established of the universal importance of Anglo-
American relationship in the new century soon to dawn. Throughout his career Donald never modified that estimate. Always he
supported movements seeking to foster cooperation between the
two nations. Early in the new century he associated himself with
the project to acquire Sulgrave Manor in Northamptonshire,
ancestral home of George Washington's family, to commemorate,
in 1914, one hundred years of Anglo-American peace. The property was then vested in trustees, and since that day the Stars and
Stripes flying over the house have greeted the tourists, students,
and the sightseers to whom the house is open daily.

Donald appears to have left New York abruptly on hearing
from home of a move to establish a new evening newspaper to
serve London, a venture with which the name of T. P. O'Connor
was associated as prospective editor. Donald knew O'Connor only
by repute, as a rising Irish journalist who, after service on the

Daily Telegraph and in the London bureau of the New York *Herald*, had entered Parliament as a Liberal.

So swiftly did Donald move that, when he confronted "T. P.," the editor of the unborn newspaper had engaged only one man for the staff. O'Connor was impressed particularly by Donald's knowledge of local government at a time when the administration of London was on the eve of a revolutionary reform. Donald was to promote that cause with zest and much success in the *Star,* as the new newspaper was named.

O'Connor was an exceptional "talent spotter." Of the small staff which he engaged initially, eight became editors of leading newspapers or periodicals. The most famous of the recruits, however, was not destined for editorship, one George Bernard Shaw, who, engaged as editorial writer, appointed himself to the additional role of music critic.

An excellent *esprit de corps* developed in the office of the *Star.* Having chosen good journalists, O'Connor showed confidence in them. He did not "handcuff" his men (as Donald put it) in what they wrote for a newspaper dedicated to a crusade for social reform. In personal relationships with his staff, the editor was avuncular. Late in life, "T. P." claimed with some pride that never, in his most flamboyant mood, did he compose such a eulogy as one he wrote of Donald. It was contained in a letter sent when he was "consulted by a French gentleman about the young man who was paying suit to his daughter."

After some four years on the *Star,* Donald left to devote his knowledge of London's local government to a new weekly newspaper planned, under his editorship, to foster public interest in a thoroughly modern pattern of administration lately decreed by Parliament for the metropolis. At first, the new paper went well, but as the reforms took effect, public interest declined.

All the same, the paper did not perish. It evolved into a periodical of the magazine type, catering for the governing bodies and technical staffs of cities and towns, and meeting the advertising needs of manufacturers of the equipment needed for public works and services. Today, the periodical launched as *London* now prospers as the *Municipal Journal.*

One of the public spirited men who backed *London* financially, Frank Lloyd, was the chief proprietor of the *Daily Chron-*

icle and its Sunday associate, *Lloyd's Weekly News*. He knew
Donald's worth. So also did the then editor of the *Chronicle*,
H. W. Massingham, for he was one of Donald's colleagues on the
Star. Thus Donald became news editor of the *Chronicle* and
seems to have been satisfied with that role until he was lured from
it four years later by the attractive terms of an offer from a company owning a group of hotels situated in the West End of
London, at fashionable seaside resorts and at Monte Carlo and
Cannes. Before the title was invented Donald became a press and
public relations officer. He seems to have been successful in the
job, and the leisure it afforded enabled him to contribute on his
favorite subjects to newspapers, magazines and reviews. Alfred
Harmsworth (Lord Northcliffe) commissioned him to write a
series of articles on the industrial trusts of Britain and the United
States, an experience of his work that caused Northcliffe, later, to
describe Donald as "a first-class reporter, as accurate as a stop
watch."

It was natural, therefore, that as his contract with the hotel
company neared its end, Donald sought a way back to his original
course. Frank Lloyd, minded to make a change in the editorship
of the *Daily Chronicle*, offered the job to Donald.

The *Chronicle*, then fifty-two years old, began life humbly
as the *Clerkenwell News*, a local sheet living on the news and
advertisements of the watchmaking industry of which that quarter
of London was the national center. In the course of its first twenty
years the paper evolved into a daily issue so profitable that thirty
thousand pounds was paid by Edward Lloyd, father of Frank
Lloyd, when he acquired it as an associate for his successful
Sunday paper, *Lloyd's Weekly News*.

Building on the Clerkenwell readership and the revenue
from specialized advertising, Edward Lloyd enlarged the scope of
the *News* and renamed it the *Daily Chronicle*. Thus it became a
general newspaper, Liberal in politics; price one penny. Such it
was when Frank Lloyd succeeded his father as proprietor.

Having served as its news editor under Massingham for four
years, Donald was familiar with its ways. Though on good terms
with Massingham as a former *Star* colleague, Donald was not
happy about some of the *Chronicle's* practices. Indicative of its
editor's habits was the legend that early each evening a dummy

was prepared of the next day's issue incorporating the news already in hand, and what was known to be coming; and thereafter, any story that arrived unexpectedly had a poor chance of appearance next day. A reporter who pressed such an offering, saying it was absolutely exclusive, was likely to be told that he had given a good reason why it could wait for another day.

When, however, Donald came into the editorship, the *Chronicle*'s chief handicap was a legacy from the South African War (1899–1902). As a Liberal newspaper with a radical tradition, it had leaned toward the pacifist position fundamental to radical philosophy; and concerning the South African War, the Liberal party (already suffering the disadvantage of being out of office) was perilously divided about the justification for Britain's waging war on the Boer republic.

Consequently, Liberal newspapers were in a dilemma in their efforts to serve a party thus at war within itself. Those that sought a middle course, as the *Daily Chronicle* did, pleased neither faction and lost readers.

A highly regarded editor of the *Daily News* was ejected from his post overnight when a radical group, led by Lloyd George, acquired the paper. The group could not afford to buy the *Daily Chronicle,* which they would have preferred. All the same, Massingham, harassed by the Liberal party's internal conflict, resigned his editorship of the *Chronicle,* and it was from Massingham's successor that Donald took over in 1903. By that time, the war was ended, but the fortunes of the *Chronicle* were at a low ebb and newspapers dedicated to Liberalism were generally out of favor.

The new editor came to his task with a determination to break with the traditions and habits of the 1880's whose influence still lingered among the "quality" papers with which the *Chronicle* was classed. The editors of such journals cultivated a cloistered remoteness. An extreme example cited by Donald was Mr. Mudford of the *Morning Standard,* at whose home a "great statesman" called one evening, only to be turned away by the butler with a message that "the editor of the *Standard* is at dinner." Even Mudford's successor was said to be as inaccessible to his staff as the Dalai Lama.

Most of the numerous daily papers of the period were pre-

eminently political organs. Their editors were chosen for the in-
flexibility of their political opinions and their ability to expound
their views on any question of the hour in terms of their political
beliefs. They sat, chairbound for hours, writing editorials, long,
cogent, scholarly, and strictly impersonal, in which the editorial
"We" was associated with the kind of high authority implicit in
the pronouncements of monarchs and popes, while, in the news
columns, said Donald, they assigned an inordinate amount of
space to politics and foreign affairs.

Donald was resolved never to be a "writing editor." Journalists were to be found to whom editorial writing, under the
direction of the editor, could be delegated, leaving the editor free
for the supervision of all the other contents of the paper and for
daily contact with the staff.

Again, in Donald's view, the editor of a daily newspaper
should cultivate the acquaintance of people predominant in all
those aspects of life that the news columns of a modern newspaper should reflect. He had been deeply impressed by the examples of Delane of the *Times* and of W. T. Stead. Delane wrote
little but moved freely in high places. Stead, though he was capable of filling quite a high percentage of the space in his relatively small paper, seemed to go everywhere, and especially where
he was not wanted.

Two of Donald's earliest achievements as editor were to
persuade the proprietor to reduce the price of the *Chronicle* to a
halfpenny (thus putting it in the same price range as the soaring
Daily Mail) and to secure the services of E. A. Perris who, as news
editor of one of the general news agencies, had demonstrated
in the output of that organization, the best conception of what,
for the millions, constitutes news.

This was to prove an ideal combination. Perris, once described as "the newsman rampant," had an eager temperament
and an uncanny instinct for news. As a news editor the only
desirable quality he lacked was an extrasensory perception of
where news was about to break.

The defect that usually accompanies such qualities is a liability for zeal to outrun discretion. There, Donald's Scottish
caution could, and did, provide the corrective to Perris's drive.
Thus, while the news columns of the *Chronicle* always exhibited

liveliness and enterprise, they never frothed into the sensation-
alism that provokes lawsuits. Under Donald's editorship, the
paper seems never to have been sued for libel or incurred a summons for contempt of court.

The selection of Perris was an example of the advantage enjoyed by an editor like Donald, whose career had lain solely on
the journalistic side of the press. Donald knew, generally, where
to find the qualities he required in his staff, if they were not already within the office as a consequence of his readiness to consider young aspirants of promise and ambition. Moreover such
was his personality and his sense of good leadership of his team
that he could get men who were antipathetic to work harmoni-
ously under his direction. His strong resolve was not to become a
"writing editor" but to have time to devote to all that was essential to a grasp on every aspect of the paper's life.

Such was his success, and such the command over his work
that after a few years in office, Frank Lloyd and his two co-direc-
tors, invited Donald to accept, additionally, the responsibilities of
editorship of their Sunday newspaper, *Lloyd's Weekly News.* Also,
they appointed him managing director of the company, United
Newspapers Ltd., with complete editorial control subject only to
the maintenance of a Liberal policy. His contract of service gave
him, as managing director, "control and direction of the business" with power to engage and dismiss employees, to enter into
contracts and "generally to do all things connected with the staff
and the undertakings which in his judgment will be conducive to
its success." It is doubtful whether, at that time or since, any
journalist, save Northcliffe (who had become a wealthy man and
a proprietor) had a position of comparable authority over national newspapers.

In one respect, the incidence of Donald's editorship had been
fortunate. About a year after his appointment, the political tide
in Britain began to turn, slowly but perceptibly. As the war re-
ceded into history, neglected social problems claimed increasingly
the conscience of the nation. A desire for a change of government grew. It was a mood helpful to Donald's modernization of
the *Chronicle.*

His resolve to create a paper whose reputation would be
based chiefly upon its efficiency as a medium of news and of popu-

lar features did not imply neglect of the paper's political mission, nor did it weaken his resistance to the temptation to write editorials, despite his assiduous cultivation of contacts with Liberal leaders.

His attitude toward the relative importance of news, features, and political opinion was made plain to me when, as I was leaving his room after he had engaged me for his staff, he had an afterthought. "By the way," he exclaimed, "what are your politics?" Detecting some hesitation due to my not having attained voting qualification, he added, "Don't tell me if you'd rather not. We're a Liberal paper of course, but most of the staff seem to be either Socialists or Tories; and, anyhow, your duties won't be much concerned with politics."

Time and again the soundness of this attitude has been proved. If a newspaper is produced with political propaganda as its primary purpose, and party politics are poured into its columns to the detriment of its new content, it will fail as a saleable product. As nothing loses money so quickly as a losing newspaper, its political patrons will soon be frightened into closure, and their propaganda effort will have been wholly unavailing.

Donald's political value lay in his contacts with leading politicians and the guidance he gave to his editorial writers each day. One of them has said he valued it "for the penetrating, though kindly, shrewdness with which he appraised personalities in the field of politics," and "for his unquenchable public spirit."

That shrewd appraisal of personalities was the outcome of his practice of breaking away from the office as frequently as he could for the purpose of making contact with leaders in all spheres of public life; not only with politicians but notably with scientists and businessmen. Receptions to welcome distinguished foreign visitors always claimed his attention. He accepted readily invitations to evening functions, public or private, that enabled him to keep his friendships in repair and make new acquaintances; but generally, he was back in the office before midnight to cast a keen eye over page proofs of the principal editions of the paper before they went to press.

For recreation, he resorted to golf at Walton Heath, fifteen miles from London. Accessibility from Westminister as well as its setting on the breezy Epsom Downs made it a favorite playground for politicians. The wealthy proprietor of the *News of the World*, Lord Riddell, who had a financial interest in the course, conceived the idea of buying up desirable villas close to the course and offering leases of them to selected members of his circle who were almost exclusively Liberals. Among those who thus became his tenants were David Lloyd George and Robert Donald, whose villas were so situated as to make them (and their families) near neighbors.

This colonization of the perimeter of the golf course, did not develop until after the general election of 1906 had put the Liberals in office with the largest majority any party had enjoyed hitherto. For that electoral battle, the first in his editorship of the *Chronicle*, Donald prepared with such success that, after the event, he caused an illustrated brochure to be published describing the part the paper had played.

Strange as it may appear today, sixty-four years later, the booklet claims proudly that the *Daily Chronicle* had proved the value of the automobile as a news-gatherer, adding that "the time certainly will come when no well-equipped newspaper will be without a private garage with cars ready to depart for any place at a moment's notice." With pictures taken inside and outside the office, the booklet reflects such enterprising efforts as the personal service by which each of the two thousand readers, who had availed themselves of it, received the result of the poll in any particular constituency, by a telegram dispatched immediately the news appeared on the tapes in the office.

Telephones, specially installed, enabled the results as they came into the office, to be transmitted to certain theaters to be thrown onto screens at intervals in the performance. In the open, at various populous centers, *Chronicle* screens displayed results, interspersed by comedy films to hold the crowds between announcements. In the center of London, on a site lately cleared for redevelopment, opposite the Waldorf Hotel, three thousand people faced the screen, while on that same Fleet Street corner where Donald encountered Nankivell twenty-one years earlier, the front of a large building, now the *Chronicle*'s advertisement department, electrically operated devices passed the latest election news to another large audience.

Within the editorial offices, an adding machine, computing

the aggregate vote hour by hour, on a national basis, and tended
by a woman operator represented the last word in modernity.

No doubt many minds cooperated in organizing such testi-
mony that the *Chronicle* was in step with what science was providing; but Donald himself initiated the operation. It expressed
an interest born in his youth in Scotland and always active. An
example of his observation of technological progress provided a
news story for the whole of the daily press when, in his presidential address to the Institute of Journalists in 1913, he touched
upon the future of wireless communication.

He predicted, "People may become too lazy to read, and
news will be laid on to house or office, just as gas and water are
now. The occupiers will listen to an account of the news of the
day, read to them by much improved phonographs, while sitting
in the garden."

Even the assembled journalists (who might be supposed to
have a little more vision than the rest of the community) were
reported as greeting this forecast with loud laughter; and next
day the cartoonists and versifiers exploited the idea enthusiastically. The *Manchester Guardian,* which tended to respect every
crank as a prophet unjustly stoned, showed caution about this
prediction, "Amusing Picture of What may Happen." Lord Riddell, in an after-dinner speech, toyed entertainingly with the idea
and expressed the hope that he would never have to attend a
banquet of "Liquid Speech Distributors." All the same, he lived
to preside over the board of a company that printed all the broadcast programs in the best-selling *Radio Times.* Today, that passage from Donald's speech seems to have an established place in
the history of British broadcasting.

Notwithstanding the amusement created by this fragment of
Donald's presidential address in 1913, his prestige among newspapermen was high, and the year 1914 marked an all-time peak
in the progress of the *Daily Chronicle.* In the summer months the
whole of the staff was moved from offices that had become con-
gested as a consequence of its prosperity, to a new building on an
adjoining site. A large part of the plant, however, was not moved.
What happened was the installation in the new building of a new
plant for almost every mechanical process.

Had life proceeded normally, there would, no doubt, have

been a suitable ceremony to mark the greatest year in the paper's history; but by the time the move was completed, World War I had begun. Ironically, the plant designed for the production of larger papers had, before long, to produce papers that had shrunk, by stages (as imported newsprint was restricted by wartime regulations), from twelve pages for a halfpenny to four pages for one penny.

Editorially, the contents were transformed by the war. Peacetime problems were consigned to cold storage, and scope for enterprising news-gathering was restricted by the insensitive hand of censorship. The familiar political alignment in the dialectical warfare at Westminster changed incredibly with the coalescence of parties, which paradoxically made the former pacifist, Lloyd George, political head of the War Department, and later prime minister with a mandate to win the war and to take whatever powers he needed to fulfill his mission.

Up to a point more than halfway through the war's duration, Donald's relationship with Lloyd George was close and friendly. When with good reason, in 1917, the prime minister was dissatisfied with the official arrangements for disseminating information in neutral countries, he appointed Donald to act as a one-man committee of inquiry. On Donald's recommendation the whole structure of the propaganda department was changed. But deeming a place in such a government agency incompatible with his independence as the editor of a newspaper, he withdrew from the new organization once it was set on its course.

When Donald had considered it necessary in the national interest to criticize Asquith during his premiership, the *Daily Chronicle* voiced that criticism. Though Asquith had a certain intellectual disdain of "popular" newspapers, even those of Liberal complexion, it did not deter him when, being about to exercise his retiring privilege of recommending a few persons for honors, he sounded Donald on his willingness to accept a knighthood. Donald, mindful of his editorial status, declined.

Until the last year of the war, Donald was in close touch with Asquith's successor, Lloyd George, and when the prime minister was heavily engaged, breakfast at Downing Street would be made the opportunity for consultation. Indeed, their relationship was well symbolized by their neighborly location at Walton

Heath. Evidence that such close companionship was waning appeared one morning when the prime minister, exercising his privilege of entering the Donald home without formality, walked into the garden with a copy of the *Daily Chronicle* in his hand. Donald being absent, the visitor proceeded to express himself forcefully to Mrs. Donald about something in the paper. Undoubtedly, he was very angry—he had been criticized.

Mrs. Donald, recalling Lloyd George's addiction to biblical quotation, reminded him of the text, "Whom the Lord loveth, he correcteth." But the aggrieved neighbor was not to be tranquilized. "Tell Robert I will not have it," he commanded. But that Mrs. Donald refused to do, saying that she did not interfere in her husband's professional affairs.

About that time, Major General Sir Frederick Maurice, director of operations at the War Office, addressed a letter to the *Times* challenging the accuracy of a parliamentary statement by the prime minister about the strength of the British forces on the western front. Well aware that unauthorized communication with the press by a serving soldier was a grave disciplinary offense, but feeling that his duty as a citizen in such a situation overrode his duty as an officer, Maurice wrote simultaneously a letter to the proper quarter resigning his appointment. That, he knew, would end instantly his long military career.

On reading Maurice's letter in the *Times,* Donald would have been devoid of journalistic instinct had he not considered the possibility of securing the services of the ex-director of Military Operations as military correspondent of the *Daily Chronicle.* Accordingly, although he had only a slight acquaintance with Maurice, he set out at once to track him down. That was not easy. The general, foreseeing that reporters would be deployed to interview him, had taken evasive action overnight. But Donald located him and succeeded in his mission. All that remained was to publicize the appointment as soon as the prime minister's reaction to Maurice's letter had created the right moment for an announcement.

In retrospect, Lloyd George has been described as a pacifist crusader who, during the First World War, became a military tactician, but even in that changed role there survived sufficient of the pacifist radical to inhibit any respect for British generals, as a class or individually. What he expected of the generals was victory without bloodshed, and what he saw himself getting was bloodshed without victory.

In 1918, a year that began with serious British reverses on the western front, that antipathy became too evident to be disguised. But so incalculable are the fortunes of war that in midsummer the calamities of March produced an opportunity which the long-term prediction of the British commander in chief had alone anticipated. Thus there followed a series of British operations that achieved victories so exceptional as to evoke public congratulations form allied countries and from British organizations so varied as to include even the stolid Trades Union Congress.

The British War Cabinet, however, maintained a silence so disciplined as to be noticeable, especially by the commanders in the field. The new military correspondent of the *Chronicle* on a visit to France such as military correspondents were permitted to make from time to time, reported in one of his regular articles, the resentment he encountered in the army. Soon thereafter Lloyd George inflamed the soreness that already existed by praising the Allied generalissimo, Marshal Foch, but studiously omitting any reference to the British commander in chief.

On the day following that calculated affront, the *Daily Chronicle* published an editorial headed, "Well Done, Haig!" and ending, "It is a small mind that petulantly refuses to acknowledge the services of a great soldier." Within a month of the appearance of that article, the *Daily Chronicle* and its Sunday associate had been acquired, at the instigation of Lloyd George, by a group of rich supporters under whom Robert Donald refused to serve.

When the history of that transaction had been sorted out, it was seen that soon after General Maurice began to write for the *Daily Chronicle,* a secret approach was made to the paper's chief proprietor. Frank Lloyd rebuffed the prime minister's emissaries. Later the visitors returned with a firm offer, which Lloyd again rejected, adding an intimation that he had decided not to sell the papers for at least two or three years, a statement loyally consistent with what he had told Donald much earlier at a time when the editor had hopes of acquiring the properties in association with business friends and with the participation of the staff.

From what Lloyd himself told Donald it became clear that on the day that the "Small Mind" editorial appeared, the prime minister swept aside his emissaries and intervened personally. In a talk with the proprietor, the prime minister complained of criticism by the *Chronicle*, saying "We cannot trust Donald." What followed was an offer such as the proprietor could not bring himself to refuse, although as he wrote to Donald afterwards, "Throughout the twenty years, there has never arisen a shadow of a shade between us, and I shall carry to the grave the memory of your loyal support and friendship." Evidently, he had entertained a hope that Donald would continue under the new proprietors, but Donald, knowing that the price of continuance was the forfeiture of his editorial independence, tendered his resignation within an hour of the announcement of the sale.

So began the tragedy of the *Daily Chronicle*. Four years later, Lloyd George's coalition government burst asunder from internal dissension, and he lost office at the relatively early age of fifty-nine. He was never to regain power though he remained a member of Parliament for twenty-two more years, and made several strenuous efforts to return to Downing Street.

The immediate reaction to Donald's withdrawal from the *Chronicle* was impressive. Within the next few days he received about 150 letters, telegrams, and cables, many of which not only expressed high regard but also profound indignation at the prime minister's arrogant interference with freedom of opinion. Moreover, newspapers, whose editors ignored the dictatorial attitude that Lloyd George assumed increasingly as victory in the war became assured, used plain language about the *Chronicle* transaction.

Overseas journals that commented put emphasis on the character of the editor. The New York *Times* described Donald's retirement "a loss to journalism and to public life . . . . Holding strong and steady beliefs, he was the creature of no man and no party. . . . No British editor in recent times had so wide a range of respect from leaders in the various fields of thought and action."

Fleet Street men lost no time in demonstrating how well Donald was regarded by those who knew him best. Presiding at a luncheon in his honor and surveying the company H. A. Gwynne, editor of the *Morning Post* declared, "In all my expe-

rience both as to the numbers and character of those present, I
have never seen it equalled—indeed it surpasses anything I have
ever seen . . . Mr. Donald and I [continued the chairman] have
never seen eye to eye on any great question of politics, but I have
never yet met a man in journalism for whom I have had greater
respect."

The veteran T. P. O'Connor avowed, "There is no reason
except conviction why Mr. Donald should not still be editor of
the *Daily Chronicle*. Not the smallest." And "T. P.," who knew
better than most journalists what was going on behind the scenes
in Fleet Street and Downing Street, added that the new proprietors would have been "only too glad to retain him, but he, being
a man of honest conviction all through his life . . . was ready to
sacrifice what, after all, is one of the greatest prizes of this world
—the editorship of a great and widely read newspaper. I therefore join most warmly and willingly, not merely because of the
long friendship I have had with him and his family, but I join
to do honour to a man who has vindicated the independence
and integrity of the great and powerful profession to which he
belongs."

J. A. Spender, characteristically, put the essential point of all
the tributes, "We can only express our hope that, in like circumstances, we may be able to follow his example."

Donald, deeply moved, acknowledged these tributes of his
fellow editors and journalists as the highest honor that he could
receive at their hands.

Some seven years later, another Fleet Street luncheon was
organized to celebrate the appointment of Donald, on the King's
birthday, to be a Knight Grand Cross of the Order of the British
Empire. This distinction was accorded by the King on the recommendation of the government of that day in acknowledgment of
Donald's service as chairman of an official committee set up to
advise on how effect might best be given to the aspiration for a
chain of wireless stations linking all the units of the Empire.
The subject had been bedeviled by controversy and procrastination for four years, and the cynics were quite prepared to see this
new committee conform to the old definition that "Government
commissions are appointed to take evidence—and time," a tag
with which Donald was as well acquainted as he was with the

subject to be discussed. In the sequel, the Donald Committee presented its report exactly fourteen days after its first sitting, thereby astonishing both the press and Parliament. Further, the policy the committee recommended proved feasible and acceptable.

That was not the only official body to which Donald was appointed after his retirement from editorship. Previously he had served on a Royal Commission to examine the system of local government for Greater London—a less fruitful experience. Also, he was appointed to the board that was to plan and launch the projected British Empire Exhibition that came to fruition in 1923. Donald provided the liveliest chapter in the story of its planning.

Much of his time in the 1920's was devoted to work of this kind. As chairman of the Empire (now Commonwealth) Press Union, he engaged himself more closely in its affairs and made a notable appearance at its first postwar conference, which took place in Canada, chiefly in Toronto, whose University accorded him (and three other representatives) the honorary degree of LL.D. For Donald, whose only formal education had been receceived at a parish school in rural Scotland, this academic honor afforded a sense of pleasure that he made no effort to conceal.

The postwar aspect of Donald's career however, lies outside the story of his editorship. On his departure from the *Daily Chronicle*, he came to the conclusion that, as the tale of his years was nearing sixty, he could not expect again any term of energetic editorship long enough to achieve the kind of results that would satisfy his standards. Accordingly, he took various directorships of newspaper undertakings, but never again did he have an office in a newspaper building. For a few years he maintained a detached, personal headquarters until failing health caused him to relinquish his directorships, one by one.

There was to be yet one more echo of the dramatic events of 1918. It was rendered inevitable by the closure of the *Daily Chronicle* in 1930. The news of it revived the story of his renunciation of its editorship; but when interviewed, Donald was chiefly concerned with what the collapse of the paper meant for the staff, one of whom had called its last phase "as foul a page as the history of Fleet Street can produce."

Looking over the paper's decline, Donald saw the first blow to its prestige in its becoming the organ of Lloyd George, which meant that its independence of opinion was sacrificed and its political news had to be "shaped" to suit his policy. Lately, he said, the *Chronicle* seemed to be striving to imitate the techniques of other papers instead of being itself and developing its own characteristics.

His comments showed that despite indifferent health and a reduction of commitments, his interest in what newspapers were doing was as lively as ever. Indeed, when he suffered the seizure that was soon to end his life, he was engaged in the morning routine he most enjoyed, even in his retirement—his scrutiny of the new day's papers, copies of which lay around his chair.

A memorial service at St. Bride's Church, Fleet Street, brought another manifestation of the affection in which he was held in his profession. In the large congregation there were, too, several well-known politicians of all parties, headed by the prime minister, Mr. Ramsay MacDonald, but it was predominately a journalistic tribute. There was hardly need of an address to recall Sir Robert's character and service. Those present would have endorsed the published tribute of Mr. E. A. Perris who worked with him for many years and succeeded him in the editorial chair, and who was no sentimentalist:

> He was a just man, a considerate man, and a born leader. I never knew him weaken in his principle or fail those who worked for him and loved him. He retained his courage in troublous times and has left behind tender memories and splendid examples.

Assuredly, a man who deserves to rank with the best of those to whom this book is devoted.

4

Viscount Northcliffe

*Learning much from American journalists,
he revolutionized British newspapers*

Alfred Harmsworth (1865–1922), who revolutionized the British
press of his time, is better remembered as Northcliffe, the name
he chose when King George V made him a viscount. One author
gave him a more significant title—the Napoleon of Fleet Street.
So far as it meant a careerist of dynamic, restless quality, a supreme strategist and tactician in the battles of the newspaper
business, the phrase did not exaggerate. For years Northcliffe,
though a target for many contemptuous attacks, stood forth as
the most original and most successful leader of his craft.

His *Daily Mail*, far more pithy, far more enterprising, far
more readable, far closer to the life of the ordinary man and
woman than any of its forerunners, introduced a new journalistic
epoch. Many of his pioneer experiments in newspaper and magazine development won abounding success. He lifted circulations
to heights never known before. He did much to build up the advertising industry. He realized what was then a discovery, that
large numbers of women could be induced to read newspapers.
He hailed and hastened, though many were at first sceptical, the
development of the motorcar, the airplane and radio. He paid his
staffs and contributors better than anyone else had done. He

studied the American press of his time, especially the newspapers
of Joseph Pulitzer, James Gordon Bennett, Sr., and William
Randolph Hearst, and learned much from their dash and boldness. Not all their methods were suited to old-fashioned British
newspaper readers, but Northcliffe adapted to his use what he
considered authentic improvements. He saved the *Times* from the
danger of extinction. His innovations were copied by rivals who
at first mocked his efforts. Not least of his achievements, he improved the social standing of the British journalist.

His prowess in giving the public newspapers and magazines
that met an increasingly literate nation's needs did not satisfy all
his ambitions. It whetted them. He had political intentions that
sharpened as his influence increased. Yet some critics thought of
him as a genius without a purpose, the wielder of immense influence at the mercy of a capricious mind. Intensely patriotic, believing in the value of civilization of the British Empire, a
sworn friend of the United States, a master of propaganda, he
wanted David Lloyd George, wartime prime minister of Britain,
to cooperate with his driving power.

Though they worked together for a time two such strong
personalities were almost bound to break away from each other.
Lloyd George was at his best a brilliant politician. Northcliffe
was a brilliant journalist, but he lacked some of the necessary
qualities for politics. He represented power without responsibility. He had been amazingly successful in his main career. He was
so fierce a critic of politicians that the men in office thought he
would be an impossible colleague if he did not always get his
own way.

Did he want Cabinet office, as was often said? "I am not a
politician, nor am I interested in such people," he wrote to a
professor who denounced his views on Kitchener as "written for
the gutter from the gutter." As the power behind his newspapers,
including the *Times*, he had a genuine desire for independence.
But he was not always consistent in his thinking and his actions.
In some conceivable circumstances he might have thought it his
duty to take over tasks which he condemned others for fumbling,
to the dire danger of the country. It was on this assumption, right
or wrong, that controversy went on simmering.

When Northcliffe died, worn out by overwork, the place he

Courtesy of the *Daily Mail*

ALFRED HARMSWORTH, Viscount Northcliffe

would hold in British history remained in doubt. To millions, especially those who had fought in the First World War and were grateful to him for his powerful agitation against inadequate shells, his premature death seemed a national loss. Who now would strive with such mighty resolution against the myopic politicians whose blunders cost hundreds of thousands of lives? So asked ordinary men who, without the phrasemaking power of the Aga Khan, felt much as he did when he described Northcliffe as "one of the greatest cosmic and world forces for good."

There were those who, while admitting Northcliffe's phenomenally forceful qualities, deplored his lack of ordered consistency. H. G. Wells wrote, "His skull held together, in a delusive unity, a score of flying fragments of purpose." Lloyd George said, "An alliance with Northcliffe is something like going for a walk with a grasshopper." C. P. Scott wrote, "The tragedy of his life seems to me to lie in the fact that though he knew how to create the instruments not only of profit but of power he had not the least idea what to do with his power when he got it. Only in Ireland does he seem ever to have counted for anything that was not commonplace and flashy."

These were verdicts on a man struggling with a multitude of self-accumulated responsibilities and without the training or the temperament to reduce them to manageable proportions. The immense success that crowned his ceaseless efforts as a journalist shone for all to see. As a politician he did many services to his country and the Empire. At his best he achieved quick master strokes of judgment when experienced Cabinet ministers wavered. It ought never to be disputed that he was a great force in helping Britain and her allies to grasp victory in the First World War.

A swift survey of his life may be held to reveal an almost unparalleled success story. It also reveals intense and indeed sacrificial effort in national crises. The journalist in him is seen to triumph almost more often than is good for any man. The patriot—he was a patriot of steely determination—is seen to fight agonizing battles that shortened his life.

As a schoolboy Alfred Charles William Harmsworth, like a multitude of others, showed no desire for careful study of any subject that made no direct appeal to him. For example, he had no aptitude for arithmetic. But he had some promising qualities.

He had a zest for reading. Dickens gave him pure pleasure, and he read other novelists of classical stature. He asked his headmaster to start a school magazine. Meeting with the reply, "I'm too busy," he said, "Let me do it, sir. It shall give you no trouble." So the *Henley House School Magazine* appeared with the credit line, "Edited by Alfred C. Harmsworth." The editor was then fifteen. He loved to haunt the printer's where the tiny four-page magazine reached the final stage of production.

A friend of the family had founded the *Hampstead and Highgate Express*. Alfred when on holiday was allowed to do small reporting tasks for the paper. "Tasks" is probably the wrong word. We may be fairly sure that the future press magnate thoroughly enjoyed getting his report on paper and then seeing it in the impressive formality of print. His father, a barrister but not a highly successful one, especially in his later years, did not encourage his intention to be a journalist, but the boy's heart was set on it. This enthusiasm was one great advantage.

Then there were his good looks. Almost all who have written of Northcliffe's youthful days speak of his handsome and indeed captivating appearance. *Northcliffe,* by Reginald Pound and Geoffrey Harmsworth, the best and most authoritative of all the biographical books his life inspired, and there have been many, leaves no doubt on this point. The book mentions that the young Alfred—his father was also named Alfred—impressed Edward Abinger, of the Middle Temple, who saw the two dining in Hall, as "having the face and figure of a Greek god." In later years, when I worked for him on the *Daily Mail*, the weight of responsibility, especially in wartime, was to take away the air of diffidence which was one of the attractions of his youthfulness. He could still charm almost anyone he wished to charm by his appreciative listening and other attractions.

An observer's description, a "clear-cut, senatorial face," was apt; with it went a Napoleonic forelock of light, fair hair, shining eyes, a healthy, pink complexion, a strong jaw and a figure not much too massive during most of his life for a man of five feet ten inches. He was said to believe in choosing as reporters only good-looking men who dressed well, on the theory that such men would impress and please people and so get information most easily and possess a useful self-confidence. He may have professed this, looking back on his own experience, but I cannot believe that so good a judge of character and talent would ever limit himself to these considerations. His appearance helped him, but it needed much more than that to bring a Northcliffe to the summits of power.

Success came to him early, but not before he had endured the instructive disappointments and successes of a free-lance correspondent's life. He was editing an ill-fated paper named *Youth*, part of the *Illustrated London News* organization, for two pounds a week, when word came that the proprietors had sold it. Young Harmsworth had hardly anything to live on, but he fell back on free-lancing and later said proudly that though hampered by ill health he kept the wolf from the door. *Tit-Bits*, a highly successful popular weekly, began to take his work. He wrote on such subjects as "Some Curious Butterflies," "Q.C.'s and How They Are Made," and "Organ Grinders and Their Earnings." When offered by Iliffe and Sons, of Coventry, the editorship of *Bicycling News* at £2.10 a week, he was glad to accept the steady pay, especially as he had been ill with congestion of the lungs after a drenching on a long cycling run. He soon put up the sales.

By this time he had begun to dream of starting a magazine that would appeal to the same numerous class as *Tit-Bits* did, but would be a more professional job. The young aspirant had proved that he could write lucid, catchy prose. He had a fertile mind for ideas that would attract the public he had in mind. He knew how to choose and arrange type. His harassing problem was how to raise the necessary capital, at least one thousand pounds, and this when his father, with eleven children, was getting no briefs at all. But having saved all he could, young Alfred was helped by friends who believed in his ability.

In June 1888, not long after he married, there came out *Answers to Correspondents* (a name soon shortened to *Answers*), which professed to be interesting, extraordinary, amusing and on every subject under the sun. It consisted of snippety information for which readers were supposed to have asked. This was a good time to start such a paper. Britain's Elementary Education Act of 1870 had produced ability to read in a larger number of young people than ever before, and the market for simple, pastime reading was increasing every year. *Answers* soon made a great leap

ahead. Alfred and his brother Harold (later to be Viscount
Rothermere, with a masterly grip on the financial side of journalism to supplement, indeed to complement, Alfred's editorial
brilliance) were asked for help by a man in rags on the Thames
Embankment. They talked to him about his life. He asked about
theirs. What did they do for a living? Apparently one of them
said they ran or thought of running prize competitions. The man
remarked hopelessly, "There's only one prize I want—a pound a
week for life." The drawing power of such a prize flashed into
Alfred's mind. Within a week he announced "The Most Gigantic
Competition The World Has ever Seen" and "A Pound A Week
for Life!"

This unprecedented reward would go to the reader with the
nearest guess to the amount of gold coinage in the Bank of
England at the close of business on a certain day. Guesses were
to be submitted on postcards. Each postcard must give the names
and addresses of five witnesses, not related to or living in the
same house as the sender. The results included 718,218 postcards
and a sale of 205,000 copies of the magazine announcing the
winner. When *Answers* proposed to repeat its contest with a
prize of two pounds a week for life the Treasury forebade it as
a guessing competition. Why the first competition was tolerated
and the second vetoed is hard to understand, but so is much in
British legislation to regulate gaming. Did the question asked of
competitors not call for skill in judging the trends of trade, problems of finance and any other factors influencing the money
market? The careful calculator would surely stand a better chance
of winning the big prize than a Jubilee Plunger, to mention one
of the most reckless gamblers in British history.

Alfred did not let himself be unduly depressed by the ban-
ning of a tried and justified project. Cecil, his brother (later to be
Lord Harmsworth), said, "Alfred is the life and soul of the business. He is brimful of ideas." And, unlike many people brimful
of ideas, he carried them into effect. Early productions were
Comic Cuts and *Chips,* halfpenny papers mainly for boys. They
did much to kill the old penny dreadfuls. They were not high-
brow or middlebrow but certainly not of low moral tone. The
holding up to ridicule of the lazy characters, Weary Willie and
Tired Tim, vastly amused a generation imbued with the spirit

of Samuel Smiles's "Self-Help," and the conviction that industrious personal effort and thrift led the way to personal independence. Northcliffe's insistence from the outset on clean
journalism was to have a widespread effect when he dominated
the newspaper field. The Harnsworth magazines went ahead at
a great pace and proliferated *Sunday Companion, Home Chat,*
and *Marvel* with magazines like *Forget-Me-Not.* Harold was quick
to advise knifing (as he called it) those which were not quickly
profitable. The profits came flowing in, and the larger they were
the greater became Alfred's ambitions. The prospect of becoming a millionaire spurred him on.

He became an evening paper proprietor in 1894, six years
after he had started *Answers* and two years since it had reached
a sale of a million copies a week. The *Evening News,* one of nine
evening papers then on sale in London, was in a bad way and
could be had cheaply. The Harmsworths paid twenty-five thousand pounds for it, lock, stock and barrel. A little doubtful at
first, Harold especially so, they soon found this a wonderful
bargain, mainly because of the editorial changes Alfred made.
About this time, Reginald Pound and Geoffrey Harmsworth tell
us, somebody said of him, "He has a mental searchlight which
reveals to him glimpses of the future." He made a short story a
daily feature of the paper, as it still is, started a women's daily
feature, pared down the old-fashioned, stodgy, political reports
and editorials, printed investigatory series of articles on such
subjects as "Anarchy" when foreign revolutionaries in London
were active, simplified the news and had it illustrated with
plenty of maps. The paper was soon paying its way and in time
became a gold mine that never failed, the most prosperous evening paper in the country.

Standing as a Conservative candidate at Portsmouth in the
General Election of 1895, Alfred Harmsworth, though buying a
local evening paper and transforming its homely provincial character in order to help his campaign, met with defeat. He decided
that that kind of contest was not for him. He had not the sure,
ringing voice for a platform speaker in those pre-microphone
days. Neither had he much talent for the compromises and persuasions of the committee room or for the patient research which
should be a foundation of policy-forming. What he excelled in

were the smart, deadline-heeding, headline-feeding, autocratic
judgments of the editor's room. Portsmouth hurt his self-esteem,
so accustomed to public success, but gave him a useful lesson.

He turned back to those campaigns in which his mental
searchlight would help him to score his most effective feats. He
planned the *Daily Mail*. There were many secret trial runs before
the paper came out on May 4, 1896. Its success as a penny paper
for one halfpenny and as the busy man's daily journal (these
were how it described itself) was immediate. It went all over the
country. Being a Hull schoolboy unable to afford a daily halfpenny but deeply interested in journalism, I used to walk a long
way to town to a news agent's where the main news page and
the women's page were displayed on the window. I decided that
was the paper for which I would work if I possibly could.
Twenty-three years later, on the strength of a world scoop I
secured, Lord Northcliffe welcomed me to the staff.

By then he was the undisputed but not the unchallenged
Napoleon of the press, head of the *Daily Mail*, the *Evening News*,
the *Times*, and other newspapers and many magazines. He and
Harold were making their own newsprint in Newfoundland.
They wanted so much of it. Their magazines, with the imprint
of the Amalgamated Press, flourished prodigiously. So did the
Daily Mail and *Evening News*.

He made one distressing miscalculation in 1903. He thought
women should know what women wanted. He believed they
would welcome a paper produced for them by an all-women editorial staff. But though curiosity created a great demand (276,000
copies) for the first issue of the *Daily Mirror*, after that the sale
quickly sank to 24,800 copies. This was the worst blow that
Northcliffe had ever known. He had snatched defeat from the
jaws of victory. Harold wanted to knife the paper. But his obstinate brother held on and sought a less ignominious way out of
disaster. He found it. The halftone block had been invented, but
did not give good results on a fast rotary press. An improvident
journalist, Arkas Sapt, devised methods of improvement and the
penny *Daily Mirror* for women changed into the *Daily Illustrated
Mirror*, a halfpenny tabloid for men and women. It became in
time a reputable success and today the *Daily Mirror*, run by the
International Publishing Corporation, has the largest sale of any

British daily paper. Northcliffe, remembering its dismal start, never had the kindly feeling for it that he had for the *Daily Mail*.

In 1908 Northcliffe won a coveted prize, control of the *Times*. This once most flourishing newspaper, victor in many encounters, had still a great and honored name in Britain and the world. But it had fallen on evil days. Its most grievous misfortunes began with its innocent, if somewhat careless, use of what turned out to be a forged letter to incriminate the Irish leader, Charles Stewart Parnell. The paper's reputation sank and its resources suffered calamitously. Under the valiant managership of Moberly Bell it struggled on, but it became necessary to sell the concern. After negotiations cloaked in a tricky secrecy that Northcliffe took a delight in, he gained control when C. Arthur Pearson, a less able newspaper magnate, thought the prize was virtually his. Northcliffe now had before him one of the most difficult and exasperating struggles of his controversial life. The *Times* had a loyal and scholarly staff, but their ideas were not his. He began to complain of the "mephitic atmosphere of Printing House Square," where the paper had been printed since 1785, and to declare that "Abandon scope all ye who enter here" should be written over "the portals of that mid-Victorian barrack." He accused the subeditors of a "morbid taste for ancient news." When trying to improve the *Times*, he complained that he was always " 'up against' some vested interest, some unreasonable prejudice, or some meaningless habit." (I imagine he put "up against" in quotation marks to show that be considered the expression an Americanism.)

Such taunts became more and more bitter and offensive. Northcliffe began to accuse the editor, Geoffrey Dawson, of disobedience. This Yorkshireman stood out as an able man in his old-fashioned way, a pillar of the Establishment and a friend of many political thinkers who despised the popular press and its ways. Northcliffe thought the editor's place was at his desk and not at the dinner tables of Mayfair. Dawson, unwilling to stand continuous, nagging distrust, resigned but was destined to return to his post after the Chief's death. Meanwhile Wickham Steed, whom Northcliffe regarded as the best special correspondent in Europe, took over the editorship. Northcliffe was undoubtedly a very sick man with exasperating and exasperated nerves in his closing years, during which I was on his *Daily Mail* staff. He could be rough with us, but his cruel sarcasm and explosive wrath found in men of the *Times,* but not Wickham Steed, his worst-suffering victims. Even those who hated the methods of an irritable perfectionist—methods that at times amounted almost to mental torture—had to admit that Northcliffe saved the *Times* from the danger of death. I cannot think that Charles Arthur Pearson or any other contemporary could have made so many and such drastic, wise and lasting improvements as Northcliffe did.

The biggest and most tragic struggle of all in those years when Northcliffe was the acknowledged Napoleon of Fleet Street was one in which he had a conspicuous influence and one that had an immense influence on him. What we termed the Great War, and now term World War I, made an unforeseeable turning-point in British, and indeed, world history. Britain had been shocked by the reverses it had to endure before it won the South African War. When war with Germany broke out in 1914, it was known in military circles as the Real Thing. Many citizens thought it would produce decisive victories in a few months— victories which our forces, trained for a war on the European continent, had been so slow to gain against unorthodox adversaries on the veldt and the kopjes.

Once again inadequate preparedness blasted British hopes. From the first, Northcliffe felt a sense of mission, a need to command. He astonished the *Daily Mail* editorial conference on August 5, 1914, the day after Britain had entered the war at midnight, by declaring that "not a soldier of ours shall leave these shores." He thought Britain would be doing enough with the Royal Navy and would need her troops to defend the country against invasion. The editor, Thomas Marlowe, strongly opposed this doctrine. Northcliffe gave way.

It was very rarely that he did give way. As the fighting went on he objected to the secrecy of the authorities, who, he said, "suppress everything except optimistic twaddle." Britain's failure to achieve her objects at Gallipoli and Neuve Chapelle led Northcliffe to expose the "scandal of the shells." We were pathetically and disastrously short of the right munitions, especially high explosive, to breach enemy lines. Northcliffe had supported the appointment of the famous Lord Kitchener as secretary of war, but now blamed him for ineptitude and muddle. He wrote a *Daily Mail* editorial condemning him and said on the single contents bill for all editions, "Kitchener's Tragic Blunder." This excited a storm of anger in the country. Both the *Daily Mail* and the *Times* were burnt at the London Stock Exchange. But the men in the front line (I was one of the men in the trenches) felt that Northcliffe was the soldier's friend. Cruel experience of battle frustration, slaughter, and wounds convinced us that he was right. Northcliffe had a contemptuous feeling for Mr. Asquith as a war leader and for a time worked well with his successor in the prime ministership, the much more energetic and imaginative David Lloyd George. The master of the *Times* was ready to do all he could to help in winning the war.

As head of the British War Mission in the United States, he accepted the task of coping with endless harassing problems, hostile influences, even the jealousy of fellow Britons and the limitations of his power after being long accustomed to absolute authority. Believing that the United States was where the war would be decided, he worked there with remarkable success, especially in financial dealings to pay for vast supplies we desperately needed. He waged a campaign of propaganda. He made speeches, which because of a weak voice he never enjoyed doing, in many cities. On his return to Britain he and Lloyd George became the central figures in a political storm of the utmost virulence. Northcliffe wrote to the prime minister on November 15, 1917, that he had "given anxious consideration to your repeated invitation that I should take charge of the new Air Ministry." He declined "that great honour and responsibility" because "I feel that in the present circumstances I can do better work if I retain my independence and am not gagged by a loyalty that I do not feel towards the whole of your Administration." The circumstances referred to were the alleged dallying with such urgent questions as that of the unity of war control, the eradication of sedition, the mobilization of the whole man-and-woman power of the country, and the introduction of compulsory food rations.

This letter of Northcliffe's appeared in the *Times* before Lloyd George had received it. In his war memoirs Lloyd George describes it as a lamentable breach of confidence and "one of those lapses into blundering brutality to which his passion for the startling gesture sometimes led him." Lord Cowdray, who had been a sound and successful chairman of the Air Board and who expected to be minister in the new regime, was bitterly offended at being passed over and promptly resigned. The press which Cowdray controlled, says Lloyd George, "became a vehicle of his implacable resentment and hostility, which helped to widen and deepen that schism in the Liberal party that has led to its crumbling and collapse." Lloyd George did not admit in the memoirs that he had repeatedly invited Northcliffe to become Air Minister, but said he had sounded him about it at luncheon in Downing Street without making a definite offer. The storm abated somewhat.

Northcliffe's brother Harold became Air Minister, Northcliffe accepted a viscountcy and presently he agreed to be Director of Propaganda in Enemy Countries—director not minister, since he had no intention of sharing responsibility for government policy and depriving his newspapers of their independent point of view. A German army order called him the Minister for the Destruction of German Confidence, a hostile tribute to his work. He insisted that propaganda must be truthful to be effective. The outcome showed how right he was. Bestriding the war-torn and stricken world like a Colossus, Northcliffe inevitably made enemies of people who suffered from his scourging criticisms or distrusted his motives. He had the strongest possible views on what kind of peace should be imposed. It was said that he angered Lloyd George by demanding to be a British plenipotentiary at the Peace Conference, but there is no written evidence of such a demand and he was much too ill at the time to undertake such an overstraining task. He and Lloyd George had reached the point of being unable to stand each other. Lloyd George in the House of Commons indicated by tapping his forehead that he believed his former associate had become a mental case.

When the thunder of the guns on the battlefields had died away at last, it was not long before Northcliffe's mental searchlight brought us one of the most exciting victories of peace— the first nonstop airplane flight across the Atlantic. He had long foreseen and encouraged the development of the airplane after the triumph of the brothers Orville and Wilbur Wright when in North Carolina, on December 17, 1903, their first airplane made the world's first powered, sustained, and controlled flights. The *Daily Mail* offered a gold trophy and a prize of one thousand pounds for a flight across the English Channel. It was won by the Frenchman, Louis Blériot, in 1909. A prize of ten thousand pounds for a flight from London to Manchester (the two cities in which the *Daily Mail* was printed) went to another Frenchman, Louis Paulhan, in 1910. Three years later Northcliffe offered an award of ten thousand pounds for the first direct Atlantic flight. The prize was won on the night of June 14–15, 1919, by two British airmen, John Alcock and Arthur Whitten-Brown, in a Vickers Vimy Rolls-Royce twin-engined biplane. ("The most important part of an aeroplane is the engine. Always give the name of the engine," Northcliffe instructed his staffs.) This triumph of aviation gave the warworn British people enormous excitement and elation.

By this time I had done with the army and was subediting the great splash story for the *Daily Mail*. What good fortune took me to Carmelite House?

As a Territorial in the Black Watch I had taken part in the three-day battle of Neuve Chapelle and with a comrade, Private J. B. Nicholson, who was killed soon afterwards, I had written of our experiences in action. There were then no officially accredited war correspondents, but my colonel welcomed our sending letters to the Dundee papers since it encouraged recruiting, at that time voluntary. Lord Northcliffe saw our account of the battle, quoted it in the *Daily Mail,* and assured me of a place on one of his staffs, if I survived the war. So, after contributing as often as possible from the trenches and battlefields to his papers, I went to the *Daily Mail* as soon as I was demobilized. Northcliffe was then abroad, but his influence permeated the office in a way I had never imagined possible. I had known discipline as a soldier, but never such control from the top as prevailed in Carmelite House.

On my first night as a subeditor I was told a dozen times, "That heading won't do. The Chief would never stand for that." We always called him the Chief, to his face or to each other; it was his own wish. He was like an unseen presence in the room. Not a paragraph was given out for subediting, not a headline passed, not the position of an item in the paper decided, without consideration of the question, "Would the Chief approve?" He seemed then to be an all-seeing, eccentric, ferociously critical mentor, who reveled in finding fault. His daily communiqués often confirmed this impression. When I was told to report to him, a senior colleague, Douglas Crawford, inspected me as if I were a private with orders to appear before a general. In those days wearing a colored handkerchief in the breast pocket was a fashion among young men. When my colleague saw I was sporting one, a Christmas present from my wife, he looked at it with consternation. "The Chief would never stand for that," he said with a frown. "Hide it at once." Then we went into the great one's handsome room, and Crawford formally presented me.

I found the Chief better looking, more impressive, more gently spoken, more friendly than I expected. He talked about my regiment, the Black Watch, and asked what school I went to. When I answered, "The nearest to Fleet Street, Chief—Christ's Hospital, Newgate Street," he replied, "One of the best public schools we have. I've had excellent boys from there." He mentioned a few of them, but I recognized only one name, H. C. Marillier. I reminded him that Thomas Barnes, under whom the *Times* became admiringly known as "The Thunderer," was also an old Bluecoat boy. Then he asked me how I would improve the *Daily Mail*. I mentioned two of my pet projects—better training for journalists, especially those dealing with foreign news, and a daily personal commentary, "It seems to me," for those who preferred a lively columnist to the impersonal editorial writer. The Chief dismissed them both, but not discourteously.

He said he could always get proficient subeditors to handle foreign news. I felt doubtful of this, having the day before seen how a cable from Florence had been savaged. The subeditor, unacquainted with the Italian name of the city, Firenze, had datelined part of the message as from Paris. Halfway through the cable came the word para, obviously short for paragraph, since here a new item began. The subeditor, perhaps thinking of Pará, a state in Brazil, duly datelined the message from Pará. I did not mention this, lest the subeditor should suffer. Nor did I press my columnist suggestion, knowing that the Chief himself sometimes wrote the *Daily Mail* editorial and regarded it as a powerful political weapon, as indeed it was. My suggestion was adopted in part later, but it was entrusted to another hand than mine, Richard Curle's.

The Chief interest in minute details of journalism appeared, on the face of it, phenomenal, but many of his unnerving discoveries of error were made for him by paid readers of the paper and those he called his spies. His communiqués were not all devastating complaints. He could praise most generously. Work for which no one on a provincial paper would ever get a thank you might be rewarded with a bonus. A man once pleased him by speaking clearly on the telephone. He was given a reward of one hundred pounds. For some time after that, everyone on the paper cultivated a telephone voice of elocutionary audibility. The Chief's moods brightened or darkened the whole office. If he frowned almost everyone was on edge. Lightning and thunder seemed to be about. If he smiled he radiated sunshine. At times he was unjust but not nearly as much as his victims thought. He was intensely sensitive to criticisms of the paper. If somebody made a public blunder in it, he felt it as a personal affront, almost an act of treachery and certainly a revelation of the offender's unfitness to remain on the staff for another day. He expected everyone to read his mind and see the news as he did. But his mind was liable to change unpredictably.

Once, when I was acting as chief subeditor, he condemned the chief news page of that day as overweighted with political news, lacking in surprise, and indifferent to the human desire for something fresh. So the next night I looked round for some news story that would make a million readers exclaim, "My goodness! Did you ever hear the like of this? Listen!" There was a cable from New York or Chicago that a gangster's pet canary had died and he had put it in a coffin of gold and given it a funeral of sumptuous splendor, watched by a vast crowd. It seemed to me the surprise item of the night, about something that did not happen once in fifty years, and it shed light on the sentimental extravagance of a notorious person. I made it a top, not a bold one, in the main news page. The night editor approved. But next morning the Chief blazed with wrath at the prominence given to what he seemed to regard as a silly triviality. Perhaps some American friend had complained to him that we did not give enough of the important news of his country but always had room for its crazy eccentricities.

In the main the Chief's communiqués were stimulating and had an almost Churchillian sparkle. Anyone who studied them would learn a great deal from and about the mind that brought about the Northcliffe revolution. Though the Chief sometimes incensed me, I owe a great deal to his friendly encouragement and occasionally angry criticisms. In my many years of editing later in Leeds, I never had a challenging problem on my hands without asking myself, "What would the Chief have done?" It helped me to take a bold and resolute line.

Northcliffe was a hard, exacting employer, but generous too. All who worked for him for any length of time knew that watchful at the head of all his staffs was a superb master of his craft, whom they were fortunate to serve. When the illness that doomed him, then known as malignant endocarditis, became known, the affection expressed for him among his many staffs would have astonished him could he have known of it. His death caused a sense of public loss, rarely felt on such a scale. At a service in Westminster Abbey every seat was filled. Then enormous mourning crowds watched the coffin being taken to North Finchley for burial beside his mother, a woman of strong and trusty character, for whom throughout life he felt unceasing devotion.

Now that a generation has passed since his career closed, soon after the war he helped to win, we can assess his merits and demerits far more fairly than his contemporaries could amid clashes of war and of political strife. Because his newspapers and some rivals provided substantial dividends it was said the Northcliffe revolution put money before public policy. It was argued that because of the lead he gave, newspaper ownership had passed to a large extent from the hands of individual proprietors, who could treat their papers as a personal trust. They had gone into the hands of companies and syndicates who made public issues of shares and had to earn interest on them. This, it was said, made for rampant commercialism. But commercialism does not necessarily conflict with the public good. A successful newspaper can be exceedingly public-spirited. It can be bold and fearless. Northcliffe *was* bold and fearless. If he had truckled to this interest or thought mainly of dividends, he would never have become the power in the world that he undoubtedly was.

It was said that while he could make newspapers and magazines abundantly successful in a commercial sense he achieved with them no reforms of lasting value, only demonstrations of his publicity-stirring power. Well, he urged the immense responsibilities of the British Empire and opposed Little Englanders. Britain would have fared badly in two world wars without the help of her many friends in the Empire. They recognized that her dominant spirit was far from being the jingoism denounced by old-fashioned Radicals. How readily Canada and Australia and other lands of the Empire came to our help!

When to do so was not as popular as it is today, he championed the "little man" against ministerial and bureaucratic tyranny. In encouraging the development of the motorcar, the airplane and radio, he gave invaluable help to British industry and fostered in his countrymen a better and much-needed appreciation of science. He warned of the bellicose ambitions of Germany. When the First World War put Britain's stamina to the test with besetting perils and showed up our military and political weaknesses, he did more than any other public man to get the right munitions for the troops, to prevent fatalistic lethargy and faintheartedness among leading politicians, and to keep the much-tried nation in good heart. His wartime services gave a powerful impetus toward final victory.

If in the politics of war he was at times too hot-tempered and dictatorial, too ready to dismiss an opponent's arguments as worthless, to be quelled with a slashing phrase or even suppressed in his papers as mere propaganda, for he believed not only in the power of the press but also in the power of suppress—if he had these faults, and I think he had—we may consider something that Cesare Lombroso wrote in *"The Man of Genius"*: "Good sense travels on the well-worn paths; genius, never." Northcliffe's genius lay in the spirit of discovery. It often put him in advance of others, no less patriotic than himself. He could not tolerate their slowness. Many of those around him in the First World War think Britain would have been conquered in that ghastly encounter but for his efforts. They even said he won the war. It seems to me fruitless to try to calculate what exact credit was due to and in the various Services, to and in the various Allies, and to the various leaders in civil life.

As a journalist, Northcliffe's prescience and gadfly tactics made thousands of newspaper people tenfold more efficient than before. Those qualities, in the stern emergencies of war, were also effective with politicians and others who were obstructing with their complacency the methods and measures needed to wrest victory. We should be grateful for his confessedly rough ways, what he termed his flogging of jellyfish into action. We should be no less grateful for his many-sided enlivenment of the press. He did more than anyone else in modern history to increase its attractions. He had eccentricities and occasional lapses of judgment, especially toward the sadly afflicted close of his life, but he made the press more powerful for ensuring the public good.

Courtesy of Thomson Newspapers, Ltd.
Photograph by W. Field

J. A. SPENDER

5

J. A. Spender

The persuasive writing editor of a
long-vanished kind of journalism

Ought we to include J. A. Spender among the great editors who left a legacy of meritorious example? He undoubtedly stood out as a great writing editor, a great journalistic statesman. Lord Francis-Williams in his anatomy of newspapers, under the title of *Dangerous Estate,* included Spender with the "almost legendary possessors of political influence at its journalistic greatness." Wilson Harris, who wrote a warmly sympathetic and engrossing life of Spender, described him as the "very mould and pattern of the highest type of journalist, alike in competence and in character." Contemporaries also hailed him as the chief Liberal editor and the most scholarly newspaperman of his day, an unofficial Cabinet minister and the adviser of the advisers of the Crown.

But the *Westminster Gazette,* to which he devoted almost thirty years of his life, twenty-six of them as editor, belonged to a type of London evening paper no longer in existence. When I first knew Fleet Street four out of London's nine evening papers were issued from political motives, were exceedingly well written, were content with a rather meager news service, had tiny circulations by the standards of today, and rarely if ever made a profit. They were subsidized by rich men as a matter of party loyalty.

The *Westminster Gazette,* during most of its life as an evening paper before it became an unsuccessful morning paper, sold fewer than twenty thousand copies a day. In the South African War it rose to twenty-five thousand and then fell back until the First World War, when it reached twenty-seven thousand. These are pitiably small figures by the scale of today's circulations. They could not draw much advertising. So the paper always lost money, from ten thousand pounds to fourteen thousand pounds a year, until rising costs in the First World War forced up the deficit to at least twenty thousand pounds a year. But what influence the *Westminster Gazette* had in its evening paper days! Its readers were men of culture and political power in the West End, the Houses of Parliament, and Whitehall. The *Westminster Gazette* also went to probably all provincial newspaper offices that supported and were supported by the then powerful Liberal party or wished to bandy arguments with it. Not all country editors were well equipped for national polemics. Some held their positions as veterans with ample local knowledge. If they had to write editorials, and this was then their traditional duty, they found the *Westminster Gazette* usually provided Liberal editors with a well-researched subject and faithful guidance. This they more or less faithfully followed. Not to read Spender's editorials was, for them, to be sadly out of touch with Westminster.

Now that the paper Spender made so influential has gone, along with its well-written rivals, the *Pall Mall Gazette, St. James's Gazette,* and the *Globe,* what can we learn today from J. A. Spender? A great deal, I think. The techniques of journalism change, but not its principles and its basic needs. We cannot trace Spender's career without realizing the power of integrity, the value of a disciplined aptitude for grasping the essentials of a political problem, and the persuasiveness of honest, factual, and lucid statement. It will rarely happen that an editor can enjoy anything like the confidential relations between Spender and his Liberal Cabinet friends. Still, almost every editor is in friendly touch with some opinion formers, in Parliament or perhaps only in his own community. The principles Spender followed in his almost uniquely privileged position are well worth study as a matter of journalistic ethics.

His long life can be quickly outlined. He was born at Bath,

a city much favored for its medicinal waters, in 1862, the eldest son of John Kent Spender, a physician to the Mineral Water Hospital. The doctor's wife wrote twenty-one novels and many essays to pay for the education of their eight children. Her *Parted Lives,* published in 1883, won from a *Spectator* critic the comment that it ranked as the best novel of the year after George Eliot's *Middlemarch.* Not only did she pay the school bills, but she also built up a fund for holidays and for her husband's retirement. She invested much of her savings in the *Western Morning News* and had no cause to regret it.

Her son Alfred (he was always known by his second Christian name), a boy with bright red hair and many freckles, went to the Bath Classical and Mathematical Preparatory School for the Sons of Gentlemen, and then had the good fortune to come under the influence of an excellent headmaster of Bath College, T. W. Dunn. Young Spender learned not only the classics but also the art of living, integrity, loyalty, and unselfishness, of all of which Dunn was an unceasing advocate. All I know against this teacher is that he said out of long experience he had never known a musical boy who was not morally infirm.

In 1881 Spender won a classical exhibition at Balliol College, Oxford, the pre-eminent college in the university. The Master was then Benjamin Jowett, a great moral teacher who has been described as the greatest trainer of able young men that England has produced. He is the Jowett of whom Henry Charles Beeching wrote in the Masque of Balliol:

> *First come I; my name is Jowett,*
> *There's no knowledge but I know it.*
> *I am Master of this college:*
> *What I don't know isn't knowledge.*

Spender found the Master a curious and rather chilling character. Invited to dessert he found the interview most formidable. Writing home, he said:

> The Master sat at the top of the table and appeared to go to sleep, but eyed one keenly all the time. There was one other man there besides myself—an Armenian (for at Balliol we have all nations and languages), who at first waxed talkative in broken English. The Master's answers were monosyllabic, "really," "indeed,"

etc., and the Armenian was frozen into silence. My reception was not much warmer. I told him, at his own request, that there were four debating societies in Balliol. That, he said, was entirely absurd. He asked me what was the next Bill to come on in Parliament; I said I thought the "County franchise." That he also said was absurd (however, I shall probably prove right, unless obstruction prevents). After that, both the Armenian and I subsided, and after talking to one another a little across the table pulled out our watches simultaneously, and the Master said we might go. He invites a man on purpose to stare at him, and to inspire him with awe, and is invariably silent himself, and contradictory. He makes good use of these occasions, for he seems to know all about everybody in College.

Herbert Henry Asquith, destined to be prime minister at the outset of the First World War and to be later the Earl of Oxford and Asquith, had added luster to Balliol's record. So had Alfred Milner, afterwards Viscount Milner, a brilliant colonial administrator in the great days of the British Empire. The tradition set by such eminent men was well upheld in Spender's time.

His contemporaries included George Nathaniel Curzon, who after being Viceroy of India, foreign secretary, a distinguished orator, and acclaimed in a popular rhyme as a "most superior person," became the first Marquess Curzon of Kedleston. Another was Cosmo Gordon Lang, who rose to be Archbishop of Canterbury. He stood firmly for the standards of the Church of England in the controversy that led to the abdication of King Edward VIII. When, earlier, in 1918, he was Archbishop of York, and the First World War still raged, he paid a successful visit to the United States to emphasize the spiritual issues of the conflict. Benjamin Jowett, who loved his students to be spectacular successes, must have been proud of Curzon and Lang. Perhaps he was not always proud of Edward Grey, who was sent down for idleness in 1884, but who in time became a much respected foreign secretary, served as ambassador at Washington, was appointed chancellor of Oxford University, and is known to history as Viscount Grey of Fallodon.

Spender gained a great deal then and later from the brilliant intellectual society at Balliol, for personal contacts mean a great deal to an editor. He himself contributed the influence of a well-liked, athletic, and highly intelligent young man, whose zeal for playing Rugby football and swimming matched his zeal for playing the violin, painting in water colors and debating politics. He was expected to get a first in *literae humaniores*, but an attack apparently of pleurisy handicapped him in the examination. His failure to get a first, though embittering, may have been a blessing in disguise. It led, though by a roundabout route, to a splendid distinction in journalism. He left Balliol with a sense of failure and no hope of a career in Oxford's academic world. Coming of a literary family, he thought of journalism, but Jowett said sharply, "Journalism is not a profession, not a profession, Mr. Spender." Perhaps it is not a learned profession in the old-fashioned sense often applied to medicine, law and theology, but, as H. A. Taylor has well maintained, it should be recognized as a profession within an industry. Jowett said also that journalism was an impossible profession which delivered you over to foolish partisanship and was fatal to good manners and honest effort—an assertion that Spender's career, like C. P. Scott's and the careers of many lesser men, was sternly to disprove.

Spender thought teaching would be his fate, and registered with an agency that might find him a modest post. Then an uncle came to his aid with an offer of two pounds a week as a private secretary. The uncle, William Saunders, who had married Dr. Spender's sister Caroline, hoped to be elected M.P. for East Hull, and later was. Politically Uncle William was a Radical and a devoted follower of Henry George, the American who, mainly by his book, *Progress and Poverty,* created a considerable vogue for the Single Tax movement. Saunders not only supported the new social creed but also showed a pioneering spirit in the newspaper world. He founded the *Western Morning News,* which still flourishes, at Plymouth, the *Eastern Morning News,* no longer in existence, at Hull, the Central Press (a London news agency) and the Central News. He is sometimes described as the inventor of news agencies.

Before Alfred accepted the offer of the private secretaryship he was invited by Uncle William to join him on a tour through Wiltshire with Joseph Chamberlain, then a Liberal leader, though he was to die a Conservative, and Jesse Collings, champion of a Radical scheme for small holdings summarized in the phrase, "Three acres and a cow." They studied rural conditions. Presumably uncle and nephew made a good impression on each other as the party drove in a carriage and pair through a beautiful county. Soon we find the young man installed in the *Eastern Morning News* office and helping to organize his uncle's nursing of the East Hull constituency. The newspaper staff were paid meager salaries but were provided everyday with tea and a midnight sandwich supper. Spender shared in these perquisites. As he paid only ten shillings for bed and breakfast at his lodging, went without luncheon, and could get a good dinner for one shilling and twopence, he fared reasonably well on his salary of two pounds a week. Soon, though he lacked shorthand, he began to write reports of his uncle's speeches and editorials about them. The editor went for a holiday and the young man took over the editorial chair for the time being. But when the holidaymaker returned, Uncle William complained of a number of shortcomings in the young deputy and gave him ten pounds in lieu of notice. Perhaps Spender had not shown enough enthusiasm for the Single Tax movement, which had put such a spell on his employer.

Off he went to London. He stayed at Toynbee Hall, Whitechapel, the first English university settlement. He did some freelancing and for three happy months worked for three hours a day on the *Echo*, a paper at one time owned by Andrew Carnegie. His duties were to do any pieces of writing that were needed. They earned him six guineas a week—not bad for those days. He saved enough to go off to Switzerland with his mother. On his return to England he spent six weeks in hospital with malignant scarlet fever. When he recovered he had two offers. He could go again to the *Echo* or to the editorship on probation of the *Eastern Morning News*, with a salary rising to five pounds a week. Spender was then twenty-three. He chose, I think, wisely. He preferred the editor's chair, with managerial duties as well, and so had a fine opportunity for all-around self-training in running a paper. This training, he wrote later, was of immense use to him in afterdays for "it gave me an outlook which put learning and all that in its place." The paper, read largely by Conservative business men, was losing money when he took it over, partly because of Saunders's devotion to Henry George's unconventional

ideas. But in many respects it met the news needs of a great city.
Hull bore the name of Britain's Third Port, yielding pride of
place only to London and Liverpool, and had important deep-sea
fishing interests. The paper provided fuller shipping news than
its county rivals, the *Yorkshire Post* and the *Leeds Mercury,* and
was the recognized medium for the Hull property market advertising. The London papers did not saturate the provinces in those
days as they did when some of them started to print North
Country editions at Manchester and all of them derived great
benefit from special newspaper trains. London papers in Spender's Hull days did not reach the town till its business men had
spent hours at work and digested the news and scorned the views
of the local morning paper. In accordance with the custom of
the time, the *Eastern Morning News* printed the speeches of
statesmen verbatim, using the Press Association's telegraphed
service that came from the town's chief post office in handwriting
often difficult to read on flimsy paper. As the sections of a speech
flowed in, some were late and some wrongly numbered, making
it an exasperating business to get a clear sequence. Before the end
of a speech arrived, you might have to write an editorial on it,
and there was an inevitable fear that amid the hurry and confusion of the double task you might miss some point of cardinal
importance. I remember such trials well from days long after
Spender left Hull.

Though, like other editors of the time, he accepted the importance of praising or dispraising the speeches of statesmen—
how predictable was the line of those rushed editorials in most
papers!—he could be a strong, crusading editor. One campaign
he waged was long remembered as I, who started my newspaper
career on the *Eastern Morning News,* can testify. The town had
appalling slum areas. Spender demanded that these disease-breed-
ing districts should be cleaned up. Citizens who lived in more
wholesome quarters were slow to support a costly scheme, but
Spender hammered away and got the support of the Archbishop
of York and other leaders. His most powerful ally of all was
an epidemic of typhus. This finally drove the authorities into
action for the good of the whole community.

Among those at Hull who were gratefully to remember the
bright-haired, poetic-looking young editor (that was how Spender

impressed visitors) was the then youthful and shy J. L. Garvin, who had been sending excellent letters to the paper. Spender gave this unpaid contributor ready encouragement, and later they were warm friends. I mention their first meeting in a chapter on Garvin. Spender's Hull editorship ended unfortunately, or was this another blessing in disguise? At Toynbee Hall he had met a beautiful girl doing social work, Mary (May) Rawlinson, daughter of William George Rawlinson, a London silk merchant and art collector. Another warm admirer of Miss Rawlinson was Robert Louis Stevenson. Spender became engaged to the girl and thought, perhaps because of that, it would be helpful if he went to London for a time to be closer to the source of political developments. Uncle William did not think the editor of a Hull paper should leave his desk in that way. Spender disagreed, and in March 1891 lost his job. No doubt William Saunders was a difficult employer, but on this question I think he deserved some sympathy. The editor of an important provincial morning paper in England, as my experience has shown, needs to be bilocal. His contacts with leaders in his own provincial community and with leaders at Westminster have a high and indispensable value, but neither set should be sacrificed for the other. When, later, a distinguished Yorkshire editor proposed to make his home in London and have a deputy to take charge in Yorkshire, his chairman sternly vetoed the scheme.

Deprived of the chance of being an absentee editor, Spender resorted to free-lancing in London and wrote his first book, *The State and Pensions in Old Age,* 1892, a work that brought him high compliments from John Morley, the journalist, author, and statesman who became Viscount Morley of Blackburn and wrote the official life of W. E. Gladstone. Free-lancing produced too uncertain an income to marry on, but articles the young author had written for the *Pall Mall Gazette,* then a small-circulation Liberal paper, and the *Echo,* rather more popular and Radical, proved the way to marriage. For E. T. Cook, editor of the *Pall Mall Gazette,* short of an assistant editor in an emergency in 1892, thought at once of his contributor who had edited a paper at Hull and appointed him to fill the vacancy. Thereupon Spender married Miss Rawlinson. Among the wedding presents was a house, 29 Cheyne Walk, from her father. Again the uncertainties of journalism struck at the young husband's security. He had not been married for three months when the Liberal proprietor of the *Pall Mall Gazette* sold it for fifty thousand pounds to Conservatives, members of the Astor family, connected with a German emigrant to the United States who amassed an enormous fortune mainly in the fur trade. The *Pall Mall* staff showed the sincerity of their political faith by resigning. Help came speedily. Mr. (later Sir) George Newnes founded the *Westminster Gazette* on the lines of the Liberal *Pall Mall*. He took on the staff who had resigned. Being rich on the profits of *Tit-Bits,* the *Strand Magazine,* and other popular productions, he cheerfully faced the prospect of losing money on the *Westminster*. In 1908 other Liberals, including Lord Cowdray, joined him in ownership. Cowdray, known as Weetman Pearson before he gained his peerage, was an engineer and contractor of world renown. His company made the tunnel under the East River, New York. It was also engaged on the Tehwantepec Railway, Mexico.

Newnes chose green paper for the new Liberal organ. This, he thought, would be easy on the eyes. Later admirers often spoke of the *Westminster* as the Seagreen Incorruptible, Carlyle's phrase for Robespierre in his *History of the French Revolution.* Perhaps the green paper was a little more restful to look at than the pink of the *Globe*, but both seemed to me attractive.

Cook edited the new paper, which appeared in January 1893, and wrote most of the editorials. Spender reviewed many books, wrote art criticism, and did a series of articles exposing the financial complexities of the notorious Jabez Balfour.

Then Cook in 1895 was chosen to edit the *Daily News*, the paper whose first editor was Charles Dickens. In 1896 Spender, an obvious choice though a surprising number of men "of high position in the intellectual world," as Newnes put it, applied for the post, began at the age of thirty-three the editorship of the *Westminster Gazette*. He was destined to preside over the paper until the unhappy evening in 1921 when it appeared in its familiar green for the last time and tried to establish itself under another editor as a national morning paper. Among the congratulations Spender received on his appointment, one from his old headmaster, T. W. Dunn, spoke of him as "a much-loved pupil who now commands the ear of the world." That was a grand phrase, perhaps too grand. Could an evening paper, selling few more than fifteen thousand copies a day in the British Isles, where the population stood at around forty million, be said to command the ear of the world? Like the *Times* it was read by the people who inspired the thinking of the people; it was read in foreign chancelleries; its more significant utterances were quoted in the chief newspapers of many nations. It could be said to have the ear of the world in the sense in which a Gladstone or Disraeli, addressing an adequately reported meeting of perhaps three hundred persons, had the ear of the world. It was a time when great world questions, threats of war and outbreaks of war were pressing upon us, when in our anthems of Empire, we prayed that God would set our bounds wider and wider yet. The Victorian era, which had seen such an astonishing transformation of Britain's commercial and naval power in the world, was drawing to a close when Spender took charge of the *Westminster*. War in South Africa threatened. It began before the good Queen died. It was not the quick, enriching, glorious triumph the imperialists expected. In 1904, three years after Queen Victoria died, a Russian fleet from the Baltic, going out to the East to battle with the Japanese Admiral Togo, came across trawlers from Hull fishing the Dogger Bank in the North Sea. The Russians fired on them with deadly effect, believing them to be enemy destroyers. Infuriated citizens crowded into Whitefriargate, then the newspaper street of Hull, where Spender had been a youthful editor, and marched up and down furiously demanding that the British navy should blow the Russian ships to bits or that the admirals and captains responsible for the slaughter should be seized from their ships and hanged for piracy. I shall never forget my first experience of being, as a reporter, in the midst of a maddened mob baying for vengeance. Happily the Czar and his government speedily offered an ample apology and compensation. War fever at Hull died down. The survivors of the attack on the trawl-hampered ships, helpless like sheep before their slaughter, agreed to give evidence at an inquiry in Paris on condition they were given English food, including Yorkshire pudding. The Russian ships met their doom near Tsushima. Balkan wars threatened European war. Strife with the Kaiser's Germany drew closer. Home Rule for Ireland never ceased to stir dangerous disputes.

Amid all these alarms and perils Spender exercised an increasing influence for moderation. He was no bellicose Thunderer, but strove for settlement of international jealousies by conciliatory methods. Britain badly needed social reforms, for behind all the glitter of Imperial power lay a sordid maldistribution of wealth. Spender played a sturdy part in the campaigns for old-age pensions (in those days we usually spoke of them as old-age pensions for the poor), health insurance, unemployment insurance, and labor exchanges. He did not think Joseph Chamberlain's plan for Tariff Reform would help a country that had prospered so much, if unevenly, under Free Trade. He argued the case with exceptional lucidity. When Chamberlain announced his plan, a great many people, including large numbers of the Conservative party to which he belonged, were shocked. Economists were sharply divided. Though there were the usual partisan sneers and smears, the long-continued discussion became a far more educative process than political issues in Britain usually produce. It was more like a nation's training in economics than an electioneering wrangle. The *Westminster Gazette*, with its editorials by Spender, notes of the day by Charles Geake, and cartoons by F. C. G., offered something like an excellent textbook. Geake excelled in the deadly parallel and other pithy revelations of opponents' inconsistencies. Francis Carruthers Gould's rough draftsmanship made effective points with plenty of fun.

Spender and Geake were not content to score heavily off exaggerations and slips, but met squarely the main points of Chamberlain and his supporters. Spender was greatly helped by his intimate friendship with Liberal leaders, notably Lord Rosebery, Campbell-Bannerman, Asquith, Haldane, and Morley. He acted scrupulously in keeping private conversations private. He probably contributed as much as any minister or shadow minister to the common stock of wisdom on current issues. Not that other members of the party's governing circle always liked this form of cooperation. A time was to come when Lord Loreburn, the Lord Chancellor, objected furiously when he found Reginald McKenna, First Lord of the Admiralty, talking with Spender on staff talks with France. Loreburn angrily wanted to know why a mere journalist knew secrets which he, Lord Chancellor, did not know. There had been no wrongful disclosures; Spender must have known of the staff talks for years. The wonder is that Loreburn seemed to know so little about them when every intelligent editor knew that Britain and France were bound to collaborate in view of threatening German actions. Spender, the soul of discretion, could never be accused of disclosing secrets given to him in confidence.

What was then called the Great War, and is now called World War I, ended what Spender regarded as the best years of his journalistic life. He had tried hard to improve Anglo-German relations, but contended for a strong navy. When the assassination on Serbian soil of the Austrian Archduke Franz Ferdinand brought a highly contagious war very close to numerous treaty-bound allies, he strongly supported Edward Grey's efforts as foreign secretary to stave it off. On the evening of August 3, 1914, Spender went to see Grey at the Foreign Office. Peace was doomed. Britain had to face her direst peril. Grey looked out across St. James's Park. He said, "The lamps are going out all over Europe, and we shall not see them lit again in our lifetime." The next night Spender talked with Winston Churchill, then First Lord of the Admiralty. "At midnight," said Churchill, "we shall be at war. Think of it if you can—the fleet absolutely ready, with instructions for every ship, and the word going out from that tower at midnight."

When war came Spender made what he later confessed was a mistake. He denounced attempts "to drive us into the reckless project of embarking our Expeditionary Force in continental warfare." But what had Haldane and his Liberal colleagues planned the British Expeditionary Force for? Even Haldane now seemed to waver. Lord Northcliffe tried to stop the expedition, but was overruled by Thomas Marlowe, the courageous editor of the *Daily Mail*. Protests that we ought to defeat the German navy before sending our troops across the Channel caused a delay of several days when time was all-important. Lord Beaverbrook afterwards wrote: "It is not pleasant to reflect that the issue of the Mons retreat and the Marne, where a few divisions either way would have turned the scale, hung for some days on a hair, and that the timidity of journalistic, military and Ministerial minds nearly exercised a fatal influence on the whole future of their race and the world."

However, Spender made few mistakes in his judgments of war policy. An outstanding service that he rendered was to urge and plan a remedy for the serious shortcomings which revealed themselves in the Expeditionary Force medical arrangements. In this he had the help of his wife, who had founded a hospital at Tankerton, Essex, and done much other social work. He was also greatly helped by Mr. Myron Herrick, the American ambassador to France. The Spenders went over to Paris and found "a shortage of everything, doctors, nurses, ambulances, hospital equipment." There were no hospital trains for bringing the wounded from the Front and no base hospitals, the planners having thought the men on the casualty list could all be shipped straight to England. Spender wrote out the reforms he thought necessary and on returning to London discussed them with Grey and Haldane, who no doubt realized that unless something effective was done at once the *Westminster* would expose the truth and agitate the public. They agreed on the reforms and persuaded Kitchener to act quickly.

The ill-starred Dardanelles campaign brought the unofficial Cabinet minister again into action on behalf of the wounded. Sir Alfred Keogh, Director-General of Army Medical Services, when Spender approached him was in despair over his Gallipoli complaints file and the many departmental delays before the file could reach a decisive authority. Spender offered a short cut. "Look the other way," he said, "and I'll purloin the file and take it straight across to Balfour." The harassed official agreed. The trusted journalist took the file to the First Lord of the Admiralty, and reform was achieved. Nowadays, when the British press is so often assailed with honestly meant but unjustified criticism, I wish more could be said about the reforms we owe to public-spirited editors. We have no need to go as far back as the Crimean War and the cruel inefficiencies exposed by William Howard Russell, correspondent of the *Times*, to realize how good journalists can cut Gordian knots with the quick efficiency of an Alexander the Great.

Spender tried hard to keep the Liberal party a powerful unified force. Its fissiparous tendency for a long time seemed capable of being checked, though the party at the time of the South African War split into Little Englanders and pro-Boers on the one hand with Liberal imperialists on the other. The Great War forced a more fateful split. Asquith, an eloquent Free Trade leader, made a strong prime minister in peacetime, though sometimes accused of intellectual aloofness. He was less effective in wartime. His best qualities were not those of a Winston Churchill. He did not work as smoothly with his Service chiefs as Churchill did with his. (Here I am tempted to interpose a personal reminiscence.) Though not a man with an easy warmth of manner, Asquith used to give me a most friendly greeting at his meetings in Fife. This was because of my editorials in the *Dundee Advertiser* on a bitter Kirk dispute. A divine at a meeting said the proprietors of the paper, unable to get a Scotsman to do their dirty work, had imported a damned Yorkshireman to slander a sacred cause. Asquith would always greet me as a damned Yorkshireman. He was amused by the implication that a Yorkshireman was a particularly odious form of Englishman, since he himself was a Yorkshireman and perhaps foresaw that he would be condemned as I was.

Lord Beaverbrook summed up Asquith in these words: "Within his own limited sphere, the management of Parliament in quiet times, he was perfection, and he was a failure because outside those limitations, and yet within his own range of time, lay a world of battle, murder and sudden death—and that time called for men of a different range of genius. And more than most politicians of our period Asquith looked often to the past, always to the present, and seldom to the future."

The *Westminster Gazette* supported Asquith with all its strength. It could not overcome the widespread belief that, though of sterling moral worth, Asquith was not the man to lead the nation to victory. So Lloyd George replaced him at 10 Downing Street and became the acclaimed pilot of the storm. The *Westminster* continued to lose money. Lord Cowdray, who, by the time the war ended, had put so much money in the paper as to become the chief proprietor, did not like to be running a commercially unprofitable concern, however far-reaching its influence had been and could still be, and however little its losses of rather more than twenty thousand pounds a year meant to so successful a man. He asked his editor how it could be made to pay. Spender said it couldn't. Northcliffe had once argued that he could make it pay in six months. Perhaps he could have done this by denying it a separate office, housing it modestly with his *Evening News* and letting it share that prodigiously successful paper's distribution system. On another occasion Northcliffe offered Spender one hundred thousand pounds to help a paper he admired. Spender declined, I think wisely, lest the relationship between the two men should become that of master and servant. I doubt whether Northcliffe, an impatient perfectionist, could have resisted impulses to improve the paper's rather scanty news service.

Cowdray, faced with his editor's discouragement, turned to other advisers. They recommended him to turn the Seagreen Incorruptible into a morning paper. The change took place in October 1921. It began as a disaster; it remained a disaster; it was lucky to last six years. Cowdray wanted the old editor to remain, but Spender did not like the thought of night work and probably believed that a paper of opinion such as he was accustomed to preside over would never succeed against the two Liberal veterans, the *Daily News* and the *Daily Chronicle*. I was among those invited to consider joining the paper, presumably because of my experience on the *Daily Mail*, then enjoying the highest sales of any British morning paper. It would have needed exhausting, nonstop effort to make the new *Westminster* attractive. Nor did it stir any do-or-die ambition when the managing director told me he was not going to pay any fancy London salaries—he would stick to sound provincial lines. Lord Northcliffe said in his booklet, *Newspapers and Their Millionaires*, "When I look at his [Lord Cowdray's] wasteful *Westminster Gazette*, its ignorance, provincialism, extravagance, mismanagement and muddle written all over it, and no Alfred Spender, I cannot in any way connect Cowdray with it. . . . For the life of me I cannot understand why, having got one of the few men who knew how to edit a daily political newspaper, Mr. Alfred Spender, they did not grapple him to their hearts with hooks of steel." In the Shakespearean phrase "hooks of steel" is perhaps a misprint for "hoops of steel," but the meaning is crystal clear.

When the morning *Westminster* was in the early stages of its puny life, Spender was at the Washington Naval Conference. He would not have gone if he had thought it his duty to guide the infant steps of the newcomer in the morning paper field. He probably meant to be as helpful as possible to the new controllers. His mind must have been quickly made up. He resigned the editorship in February 1922, but continued to write special articles for the paper. Even with constant contributions from the greatest Liberal editor in London, the new *Westminster* never recovered from a bad start and in 1928 it was absorbed by the *Daily News*, for which Spender agreed to write regularly. At first he was happy to have this new platform, but after a few years the *News Chronicle*, as it had become, liked his opinions, especially those critical of Lloyd George, less and less. Some of his articles were thrown into the wastepaper basket. His contract with the *News Chronicle* was terminated by mutual consent in 1935, and he arranged to write regularly for the provincial group of morning papers owned by the Westminster Press, a Pearson family concern. This worked out smoothly and happily; he kept up the articles till the last fortnight of his life. Though subject to spells of acute pain he found writing, "just sitting to it," an anodyne. Both the *Times* and the *Sunday Times* were newspapers that he wrote for occasionally toward the end.

When no longer an editor, Spender found compensation in writing authoritative books, especially biographical ones. He wrote the lives of Campbell-Bannerman, Asquith, the first Viscount Cowdray, and Sir R. A. Hudson. His *Life, Journalism and Politics* and *The Public Life* are largely autobiographical. The *Changing East* contains reflective impressions of travel. *Fifty Years of Europe* and *The Government of Mankind* have been acclaimed as scholarly historical studies. Of his reprints of newspaper articles the most popular were two volumes of *The Comments of Bagshot*. He died in 1942. His widow died five years later. There were no children.

Now we may ask ourselves: If Jowett had lived to see Spender's achievements, would he have counted him among the brilliant successes he so much admired? Would he have been proud to recall his efforts to guide the young man's ambition? I hope he would. Picturing the old pupil to ourselves we may not see him with garlanded brows and badges of honor on his breast. He was a modest man. Three times he declined a title. But when invited to be charter president of the Institute of Journalists in its Jubilee year, 1940, he replied, "I consider the invitation to be the highest honor paid to me in my professional life. I need not tell you how much I appreciate it, or how gladly I accept it." He was happy to have the warm admiration of his profession, regardless of party favoritism.

We must bear in mind that, as head of a tiny staff, Spender was not merely a writing editor. He watched all departments, ruling with a gentle hand. A characteristic criticism of his appeared on the editorial notice board after the issue of a news placard bearing the words:

DISGRACEFUL
COLLAPSE OF
ENGLAND

Every Englishman would know that this referred to test-match cricket. Spender's notice said, "Epithets imputing moral obliquity must not be applied to cricketers when they fail to score." This was kindly meant, but errors by England players still invite the scorn of critics.

He was fond of foreign travel and greatly enjoyed being a member of Lord Milner's mission to Egypt in 1919–20 to inquire into the causes of serious trouble and the form of constitution which, under the Protectorate, would be best calculated to promote peace, prosperity, self-government institutions, and protection of foreign interests. Spender also served on two Royal Commissions, that on divorce and matrimonial causes in 1909–12 and that on the private manufacture of armaments in 1935–36. He gave valuable help in all these investigations.

This independent thinker made some mistakes, but he never charged furiously around blind corners. Exceptionally well informed, exceptionally judicious, he achieved two reputations— one as an editor, one as an industrious author. His books will long be valued as source material for scholars. We may regret that in spite of all his gifts and virtues he never presided over a much more widely circulated newspaper than the *Westminster*. All journalists who knew him and saw his work, evening after evening, looked up to him with invariable respect. In my mental portrait gallery of famous editors I place him alongside C. P. Scott.

Courtesy of Katharine Garvin (Mrs. Gordon)
Photograph by Reginald Haines

J. L. GARVIN

6

J. L. Garvin

The man who set a new pattern

of Sunday papers

James Louis Garvin (1868–1947) made on the educated readers of his time an impression deep with admiration and wonderment. Those of a later generation may be surprised at his influence. It was the influence of a powerful, original, fighting mind. A single, well-remembered sentence of his indicates the character of the man. Fortunes were being made by newspaper and magazine proprietors who sought to give the public what the public wanted, especially news of violence and, in politics, for the most part tame party loyalty rather than thoughtful independence. Garvin announced a different intention. As editor of the *Observer*, the oldest of Britain's national Sunday newspapers, he said, "I mean to give the public what they don't want." He meant to improve the public taste, to go deeply into the issues of statesmanship rather than the swashbuckling of partisan bigots, and to make the paper an instrument of independent political power. He also wanted to deepen the public interest in literature and the arts. He fulfilled these intentions with almost meteoric success for many years.

Early in his career, in 1908, Lord Esher described Garvin privately as a sort of inferior Stead, without Stead's originality and divine fire. There were strong resemblances between the two journalists. Both were largely self-educated, fluent and fiery writers, intensely patriotic, and able to get information from excellent sources. Both, contending for a strong navy, had secret help from Admiral (Lord) Fisher. Stead was blamed for "Government by newspaper." Garvin excited gibes at "Government by sensation mongers," though these might have been aimed with equal or more appropriateness at Stead. Both men were proudly self-confident individualists. They demanded their own way and broke with their proprietors. It may be that in some respects Garvin had not Stead's often eccentric originality or divine fire. But he achieved a remarkable personal ascendency among educated readers. As biographer of Joseph Chamberlain (though he did not live to finish the work after the publication of three volumes) and as editor of the revised *Encyclopaedia Britannica* of 1929 (he also edited the supplementary volumes for the preceding edition, the thirteenth) he showed intellectual powers that Stead, with all his talents, did not display. I should not say that Garvin was an inferior Stead. They were among the creators of the modern press, alike in prominence even in an age of great writing editors, but with different kinds of success. Stead is best remembered for his journalism of exposure in fighting the white slavery of what he called Modern Babylon. Garvin's most remarkable achievement was in creating a new pattern of Sunday newspaper for the educated reader.

Garvin was born of Roman Catholic parents at Birkenhead on Easter Sunday, April 12, 1868. When the boy was two years old his father, an Irish laborer, was lost at sea. The widow, also of Irish blood, had a hard time in bringing up her children. James went to a Catholic school in Birkenhead and having an excellent voice became a chorister. Some of the doctrines taught, especially one of hell fire, impressed him as incredibly narrow. A time came when he fashioned for himself a mystical Christian faith outside the tenets of the Church. As soon as he was old enough, James worked in Liverpool as a newsboy for the *Liverpool Daily Post*. It was this, as he told his daughter and biographer Katharine in later life, that gave him a craving for the romance of journalism.

He had a firm Victorian belief in education as the way to independence. Buying cheap books of fairy tales, including Hans Andersen in French, he taught himself that language. Later he learned German and Spanish. The family moved across England to Hull, where an elder brother had a teacher's post at a Catholic school. James worked as an invoice clerk and in his spare time read omnivorously. He wrote letters on politics, especially on Irish Home Rule, Radical reforms, and Imperialism, for the local daily, the *Eastern Morning News*. The editor, no other than J. A. Spender, afterwards the famous editor of the *Westminster Gazette*, welcomed the letters, thinking they bore the stamp of a scholarly politician. He invited the correspondent to call on him. Garvin did not accept at first, fearing that revelation of his callow youth would rob him of the joy of seeing himself in print. But when he was twenty or so he made no more excuses, but called at the office and was shown up to the editor's room. Spender, a handsome figure then about twenty-six, looked up, said, "Excuse me, I'm expecting someone else," and through a speaking tube told his secretary to send up Mr. Garvin. The youthful visitor explained that he was Mr. Garvin, whereupon Spender flung his hands high above his head in astonishment. But the conviction formed quickly that, however boyish in appearance this pale, light-haired caller with his large, pale gray-green eyes, commanded exceptional knowledge of politics and literature.

Oddly enough Spender wrote of Garvin in the *Eastern Morning News* on July 1, 1912, "I had not the pleasure of seeing him in the flesh, when I was in Hull, but I am glad that I had the good sense to publish his letters." Katharine Garvin, in her memoir of her father, says she cannot confirm or deny the story of the interview at Hull, but is sure there is some ground for it. There is indeed. My father, who was for many years a contributor to the *Eastern Morning News*, and who obtained for me in 1902 at that office in my native city my first staff appointment, had no doubt about the meeting of the two celebrities-to-be in the old office in Whitefriargate. Then in 1945 Wilson Harris, telling the story in his life of J. A. Spender, said he had the details from Garvin. This seems to me decisive. Whose memory should we rely on, that of an editor who had received, at the time we speak of, perhaps hundreds of callers or that of a journalist describing his first interview with an editor whose approval might start him on the career he longed for?

In 1889 the Garvins moved to Newcastle upon Tyne. James, we may be sure, cast one longing ling'ring look behind as he saw Hull fading in the smoky distance. "Hull, sir," he said to me with real affection at 10 Downing Street when in the Second World War we were going into a conference with Winston Churchill— "Hull, sir, is where I effloresced, if indeed that be the word."

Newcastle brought Garvin the journalistic chance for which he longed. First he served a coal-exporting business as a correspondence clerk. When a chance to join the *Newcastle Chronicle* as a proofreader occurred, he eagerly took it, for this paper, edited by Joseph Cowen, was one of the greatest provincial journals. Cowen, eloquent and able, was expected to become as great a Radical leader in North-East England as Joseph Chamberlain was in the Midlands. A great inducement to Garvin was permission to write editorials for nothing. Very quickly Cowen decided that the young man should be a special writer, doing editorials and occasional reporting engagements that called for unusual descriptive and narrative ability. One of Garvin's earliest successes was when he accompanied Charles Stewart Parnell's coffin to Ireland and described the funeral with all the pathos and hero worship of a fervent Home Ruler. Here was a man who could write with impassioned sincerity, a glow of humanity, and picture-creating phrases. When twenty-six, Garvin married a beautiful Newcastle-Irish girl, Christina Ellen Wilson, with roots in the West of Ireland, by whom he had a son, who was killed in the First World War, and four daughters.

Like almost all young provincial journalists, Garvin began to think of seeking his fortune in Fleet Street, especially after he became a contributor to the *Fortnightly Review*. This was edited by W. L. Courtney, who was also chief dramatic critic and literary editor of the *Daily Telegraph*, the paper that joined with the New York *Herald* to send Henry Morton Stanley to find Livingstone in darkest Africa in 1871. Offering his first article to Courtney, one on the future of Irish politics, the confident young provincial stipulated that if it was accepted it must be used at once and placed first in the *Fortnightly*. Most editors would have

reacted sourly to such a demand, but Courtney recognized the
merit of the article and did as Garvin suggested. It was probably
not long before he suggested that Fleet Street was the proper
place for his contributor and he ought to join the *Telegraph*.
Garvin, though ambitious, felt no need to hurry. He was studying
the foreign press, to which the *Newcastle Chronicle*, with an
international outlook, paid watchful attention, and was reading
systematically, in more than English, history and books of travel.
He deemed it would be time at the age of thirty to descend on
London, equipped to storm the heights. Meanwhile, he was
making a name as Calchas in the *Fortnightly*.

He joined the *Telegraph* in 1899 as an editorial writer and
special writer. His first editorial, beginning "The Boer with his
hat and his stick" was returned with the edict, "Nothing must
ever begin with 'The.'" It seems odd that this rule, now a standard instruction on almost every newspaper, had not been imposed at Newcastle. There is nothing ungrammatical in starting
an article with "The," but it would look annoyingly monotonous
if almost every article in the paper began that way. Rather than
have it used too often, editors prefer that it should not be used
at all to start an article. Garvin's descriptive talent led to his
being sent to India in 1903 to report the Durbar. This was a kind
of journalism in which the *Telegraph*, rich in spacious and many-
colored word-painting, excelled in those days before we had instant pictures of what was happening on the other side of the
world. India made a lifelong impression on Garvin.

He left the *Telegraph* staff in order to edit the *Outlook* and
support Joseph Chamberlain's Tariff Reform campaign. His chief
rival was the *Spectator*, a great Unionist weekly review which still
defended Free Trade. He was now coming to the great venture
and great triumph of his life. Lord Northcliffe, naming him the
greatest journalist in the country, made him the editor and manager with a fifth share of the highly respected, little-read and
potentially powerful Sunday paper, the *Observer*. The partnership promised well, with plenty of capital and management skill
on the part of the senior partner, plenty of talent on the part of
the other, driving ambition on the part of both. Could there be
clashing ambitions? That was the danger. We must consider what
the senior partner's motives were.

When Lord Northcliffe, then Sir Alfred Harmsworth, Baronet, bought the *Observer* in May 1905, he had been phenomenally successful with the cheaper kind of newspapers and magazines. He had hoped to show his ability to excel on higher levels of journalism. The oldest of London's Sunday newspapers, with a sale well under five thousand copies, clearly made no appeal to the masses, but Harmsworth considered its circulation one of the most influential. He believed both the circulation and the paper's influence in politics as a high-class organ of opinion could be greatly increased.

He knew his acquisition of this kind of journal made Fleet Street scoff, but he had a Napoleonic belief in his power. About the same time he took over the *World* for its social prestige, thinking it might be made a rival to *Country Life*. He bought an interest in *Vanity Fair*, a high-class social weekly. He also financed an effort to make the *Manchester Courier* a powerful antagonist of the *Manchester Guardian* and to win from the *Yorkshire Post* the title of "the leading Conservative organ of the North." These enterprises showed, as did his gaining the proprietorship of the *Times* in 1908, how eagerly the founder of *Answers* and *Comic Cuts* hoped to wield power in the most influential circles of all.

It may be doubted whether he had any dreams of eminence as a Cabinet minister. His failure to win a parliamentary election at Portsmouth had convinced him that he lacked some of the qualifications of an M.P., such as a far-carrying voice for public meetings and an aptitude for close debate. But he may have thought that some day, though not in the Cabinet, he could dictate to the Cabinet. He probably knew then, as he certainly did later, that an editor of the *Times*, Thomas Barnes, was described by Lord Lyndhurst in 1834 as "the most powerful man in the country."

Northcliffe's foresight inspired another motive for exploiting high-class papers. He had made rich profits from the rising wave of readers with elementary education, made compulsory in England by an Act of Parliament in 1870. Great educational and social changes were now in ceaseless progress, though not always on the surface of events. Probing indications of the future,

Northcliffe had probably as unwavering a vision as Garvin of the coming expansion of the educated classes.

So, ready to face losses on the paper at first, Northcliffe put his faith in Garvin and helped him to make a still more telling impact on public opinion. At one time he had a notion that if he added Garvin to the editorial council of the *Daily Mail* that favorite paper of the man in the street would gain political weight. But Garvin, like Northcliffe himself and all great editors, had no love of committee discussions. Editorial councils tend to produce an inconclusive crop of hasty suggestions of no great value. Never at a loss for an incisive quotation, Garvin cited Chatham's dictum, "I will be responsible for nothing but what I direct."

All going well with his long-cherished ambitions, he started his famous editorship of the *Observer* early in 1908, the year in which Northcliffe, by gaining control of the *Times*, was to fulfill an ambition he had nursed since boyhood. To make the *Observer* pay meant a long, tough struggle, but with the Northcliffe resources of finance and management behind it Garvin had a most enviable opportunity to display his many talents. The great showpiece, the attraction to which every reader must be induced to turn, the key to journalistic and political victory, was to be the editorial. Garvin began by plunging into the dominant and most difficult question of the day's Anglo-German naval rivalry. On this subject, with his friend Admiral Fisher helpful in the background with information, he wrote as one having authority and commanded earnest attention. His articles were not only important; they looked important, more important than any others elsewhere. They had the appearance and the weight of an institution. In larger type than their old-fashioned, closely set predecessors, they ran to several wide columns, led into action by a band of well-phrased headlines and marshaled into sections, each with a trenchant subheading. The articles moved forward with regimental splendor and a glittering array of weapons—steely phrases, poetical quotations, historical parallels, citations of heroism, analogies from science, experience of foreign lands—all the resources of an almost encyclopedically full mind.

How could anyone keep up such a flow of militant, scholarly

persuasion? A woman on my staff who had been Garvin's secretary told be of some of his methods. He would start on his Sunday article perhaps as early as Thursday in the well-stored library at his home, Gregories, Beaconsfield, twenty-eight miles from Fleet Street. The first draft would be comparatively plain, arguing a case with little attempt at literary decorations. Off it would go to the printer. Perhaps a night intervened before a courier arrived with the proofs. By this time Garvin's ever active mind had recalled appropriate Shakespearean quotations and discerned new points to develop. He would insert so many balloons of fresh matter and turn so many plain phrases into sword thrusts of rhetoric that the article had to be reset. This process of expansive revision went on till the article had been set several times and occupied the greater part of the editorial page.

I have spoken of Garvin's weekly article as the showpiece of the paper, but this did not stand out as its only conspicuous attraction. Garvin kept a stern eye on the whole paper, and made it one of first-rate exposition and criticism in many subjects. Now on the crest of the wave, with the *Observer* net sales moving from a few thousand toward two hundred thousand, he enjoyed success as never before.

Garvin's first great political achievement in the *Observer* was when, armed with inside information from Admiral Fisher about Admiralty policy, he proclaimed the need to face Germany's naval challenge. Fisher wrote to him, "You are Jove now and the 'Times' will take a back seat."

The budget campaign of 1909 enabled Garvin, though writing anonymously, to stand in the forefront of politics not merely as a commentator after the event but as a prophet, creator and director of public opinion. He waged a furious campaign against socialistic finance, the weakening of the navy, and the possible breakup of the Empire. The sole remedy, he argued, was Tariff Reform. He implored the Lords to throw out a Lloyd George Budget. There were many side issues and personal dissensions in the controversy, but no one then active in politics as I was, can forget the fiery power and insistence on essentials with with Garvin led the Unionist side of the campaign against the astute and, as many said, demagogic appeals of David Lloyd George.

When King Edward VII died in 1910 the *Observer* proposed a "truce of God" and a constitutional conference between government and opposition. Such a conference having failed, Garvin wanted the Lords to take action for the reconstruction of the second chamber. To settle the long-lasting Irish trouble he proposed federation for the British Isles. Max Beerbohm hit off his power to impress by a cartoon, "Mr. Garvin giving Ideas to the Tory Party," in which the editor of the *Observer*, with large, staring eyes and hypnotically swaying arms, had put nine frock-coated leaders under a receptive spell.

Northcliffe, with his unmatched experience of what makes for journalistic success and sometimes of what makes for journalistic failure, sent Garvin many useful suggestion, which Garvin expressed gratitude for and treated on their merits. He was more independent than most of the Chief's editors and did not forget that he had been appointed to give a lead, not to follow Northcliffe's political notions, or those of the *Times* or the *Daily Mail*. But Northcliffe by 1911 had been chief proprietor of the *Times* for three years and was accustomed to exercising far more influence in the political world than he had done as proprietor of papers and magazines for the masses.

A break with Garvin came in 1918. The editor remained faithful to Joseph Chamberlain's principles of Tariff Reform and Imperial Preference. Then the Canadian-American Reciprocity Agreement changed the situation. William Maxwell Aitken, M.P., afterwards Lord Beaverbrook, who spoke with intimate knowledge of Canadian economics and politics, held that the Reciprocity Agreement favored Canada and that a British preference on foodstuffs would not now help the Dominion; so it would be best if the Unionists dropped their proposal for what were condemned as food taxes. The sequel was a *Daily Mail* editorial headed "The End of the Food Tax." It stung Garvin. He had no intention of dropping Imperial Preference. He thought there was no fear of losing Canada. He stood firm. Northcliffe wired to him, "Either you get out or I do."

It was a sad end to a partnership which had profited both. Northcliffe had had in Garvin an adviser with exceptional knowledge and judgment in political affairs. Garvin had been able to transform an ailing Sunday paper into a new kind on which his

heart was set. Northcliffe did not behave harshly. He had his
name taken off the list of *Observer* directors. If Garvin could
find someone to buy the paper, well and good. Otherwise he
would buy Garvin's shares. Few proprietors would have behaved
so generously, but in spite of differences of policy the two men
had a warm affection for each other. Dr. A. M. Gollin, who has
had exceptional opportunities to study the relevant documents,
says in his scholarly work *The Observer and J. L. Garvin, 1908–
1914*: "The 'break' in 1911 reflects credit on both men; Garvin
really did take his professional life in his hands when he defied
the Chief on a question of principle; Lord Northcliffe's motives,
though more complex perhaps, were equally worthy." It has
often been suggested that Garvin scored a great victory over the
Chief, but Dr. Gollin has put the conflict and its sequel into a
much truer perspective.

Garvin found William Waldorf Astor, afterwards Lord Astor,
willing to become sole owner of the paper, with Garvin as editor
of both the *Observer* and the *Pall Mall Gazette*. Garvin accepted
the double task with enthusiasm. He increased the influence of
the Sunday paper as war with Hitler became an increasing threat.
He gave the evening paper more of the substance and deliber-
ative character of a quality morning paper. But giving an evening
paper more intellectual sustenance than it had had hitherto did
not enjoy much success. In 1915 Astor sold the *Pall Mall Gazette*;
in 1923 it was incorporated in the *Evening Standard*.

As part of the Astor Press the *Observer* continued to be a
newspaper of weighty influence, not least in the chancelleries of
foreign governments. Garvin did not always enjoy the close cooperation with ministers that enabled him to forecast what
Cabinets meant to do. He could not give his new chief the accurate detailed information which had so delighted Northcliffe. But
for a long time Liberal critics credited him with access to State
secrets about which, in fact, he could only guess. Once more he
plunged into the subject for which as a young man he wrote for
United Ireland. But he did not now strive for Home Rule, as in
the days of his old hero, Charles Stewart Parnell. He advocated
federalism and encouraged Sir Edward Carson's stormy policy for
the defense of Ulster against the feared subjugation by Southern
Ireland.

The crash into war with Hitler in 1939 changed many problems and thrust forward new ones. Garvin had been loath to embark on any foreign policy that might expose us to attacks for which we were not well prepared. When convinced that Hitler meant conquest by arms if he could not achieve it by blackmail Garvin flung himself into a passionate struggle for stronger means of defense and a more efficient system of ministries. His *Observer* articles during the war helped greatly to hold public opinion steady. Educated readers tried to keep in step with his opinions, believing that here was a mentor with matchless inside information. Opponents made fun of his expansive, rhetorical style. They even accused him of hysterical exaggeration. But it was the style of a master of argument and ceaseless study of literature, for which the *Observer* offered an almost ideal vehicle.

Astor did not always admire his editor's independence. He did not support the view, after we had many setbacks in the war, that Winston Churchill, as prime minister, should retain the post of Minister of Defense and that Beaverbrook, who had done so well in accelerating the production of desperately needed airplanes, should return soon to the War Cabinet. Having objected to these views, and being known not to share them, Astor felt that his editor had abused his power. A famous editorship came to an end on February 28, 1942, when Garvin's contract, due for renewal, was not renewed. He told the press, "I live only to prosecute the war to a successful conclusion." Privately he said, as he often said, "When you're bitter you're beat."

He had many offers from other papers for his work. He chose to work for Lord Beaverbrook's *Sunday Express*, because he was given complete freedom to voice his opinions. But it never seemed the right place for his rich, allusive prose. It seemed so much out of keeping with the terse, snappy style of the rest of that exceedingly popular paper. After less than three years Garvin happily rejoined the *Daily Telegraph*, where he must have felt very much at home. His last article in that paper appeared a week before his death in 1947.

Garvin's life story is a heartening one for journalists, and not young journalists alone. He showed how a youth starting with pathetically few social advantages could discipline and train his mind to make him the equal in culture, and more than the equal, of men with the highest academic opportunities. Who could have been a better choice as editor of the *Encyclopaedia Britannica?* He became one of the great leaders in Unionist politics when these were most usually swayed by men with aristocratic territorial influence or the power derived from success in industry. Above all, in the rapidly changing world of journalism he thought out a new and better kind of newspaper. Here his creative gifts found their richest fulfillment. What he added to the range, depth and quality of his Sunday paper is still there and has permeated others. I cannot believe that these rich elements will ever disappear. We have learned to value them so much.

7

William Berry, Viscount Camrose

Who rejuvenated a dying giant

More than one example is recorded in the story of the British press of an editor who has taken charge of a new newspaper that seemed doomed to die in infancy and, warding off the immediate danger, has transformed it into a viable and progressive publication. To William Ewart Berry, first Viscount Camrose, however, belongs the unique distinction of taking over a once-dominant newspaper whose daily sales had eroded from a healthy two hundred thousand to a perilous eighty-four thousand and of regenerating it so skilfully as to raise that figure to a million, and with the trend still upwards. More also: he performed that feat with complete loyalty to his pledge, "Never under my control will the paper change its character in an attempt to force a rapid increase in the number of its readers."

Such is the history of the *Daily Telegraph* between the years 1927, when Lord Camrose took control, and 1954 when he died.

The retired Colonel who founded the *Daily Telegraph* in 1855 knew so little about newspapers and their economics that when his paper was only a few months old he was obliged to trade away his ownership to one, Joseph Moses Levy to liquidate his debt to Levy for printing. As a printer of newspapers Levy was more knowledgeable. Also, he had become the proprietor of the *Sunday Times*, in which capacity he had been studying with admiration the New York *Herald*, then pioneering a new style of journalism and prospering on a charge of two cents a copy. Levy's wisest decision, however, proved to be the early transfer of his son, Edward, age twenty-two, from his post as reporter on the *Sunday Times* to the editorship of the *Daily Telegraph*.

A fair assessment of the genius and the achievement of Edward Levy (who later changed his surname to Lawson) can be made by switching from the years of his eager adventuring in the mid-nineteenth century to a day in November 1913 when Lord Northcliffe and Robert Donald led a party of newspapermen to the country home of Edward Lawson, first Lord Burnham, to congratulate him on his eighteenth birthday. There, Northcliffe presented an illuminated address, signed by two hundred and fifty editors and other journalists, in which the veteran was described as the "Father of the Press" and the "doyen of his profession."

It follows that, at eighty years of age, the recipient of this tribute, had already shed much of his day-to-day responsibility as editor in chief. Gradually, his son, Harry Lawson, had been taking over. Three years later, in 1916, Harry Lawson succeeded to the Burnham barony on the death of his father, and also to the control of the *Daily Telegraph*. Proprietorship of the *Sunday Times* had been sold a long time previously.

Educated at Eton College and Oxford University, and strongly attracted by politics, Harry Lawson had been elected to the House of Commons soon after graduation, and had moved to the House of Lords on the death of his father. The new Lord Burnham had proved himself a conscientious deputy for his parent at Peterborough Court (the traditional name of the *Telegraph*'s slice of Fleet Street). He was also a prudent administrator, an excellent writer of political editorials and a genial chief, but he was never a dedicated journalist.

At the time he succeeded his father, the First World War had run only half its destined course, and was to claim the New Lord Burnham's attention as a Colonel of Yeomanry for a further two years. The incidence of the war was most unfortunate for the future of the *Daily Telegraph* because the paper was ripe for the

Courtesy of the *Daily Telegraph*

WILLIAM BERRY, the first Viscount Camrose

kind of challenging overhaul that the most successful of enterprises is liable to need at the close of a long term of paternal proprietorship.

When the claims of the army and politics abated, Burnham
made some desirable changes, but concern for tradition limited
their scope. New plant improved the appearance of the paper, but
the retention of long columns customary in the Victorian era,
still left the *Daily Telegraph* looking old-fashioned. Burnham did
succeed, however, in persuading the managing editor, Sir John
Le Sage that, at the age of eighty-six, with nearly sixty years'
service to his credit, he could retire with dignity. Thus the way
was cleared for Arthur Watson, young enough to have served as
an artillery officer in the war, to bring a modern mind to the
problems of editorship. Still, much remained to be done, and
much more capital expenditure to be undertaken.

Procrastination ended in 1927 when Burnham was invited by
the prime minister to serve on a distinguished commission of
inquiry into the future government of India. Acceptance would
entail at least two years' detachment from the paper and, having
regard to the measures necessary to arrest its declining fortunes,
Burnham realized that he could not accept this call to a task of
statesmanship without selling the *Daily Telegraph*. Family pride
made the decision hard to take, but given the right successor, the
Daily Telegraph of the future could continue to be an institution
in which the family could take a pride. But who was the man
likely to ensure to the *Daily Telegraph* the kind of future
merited by its past? After consulting only his nephew, Colonel E.
F. Lawson, who was on the business side of the paper, Lord
Burnham sent a message to Sir William Berry.

By 1927, the family aspect of the British press had become
further pronounced by the rise, since the turn of the century, of
the Berry brothers—William and Gomer. Their father, a retail
businessman of Merthyr-Tydfil in South Wales and a local worthy
(in the sense of being an alderman and a justice of the peace) had
three sons, all of whom were destined to become peers of the
realm. The eldest, who became Lord Buckland and who died
soon after ennoblement, found his career in the mining industry.
The second, William Berry (Lord Camrose) who was to serve in
almost every branch of newspaper activity except the mechanical,

says in an autobiographical interlude in his book, *British News-papers and their Controllers*, "I started my journalistic life at the age of fourteen on a local paper called *The Merthyr Times.*" After five years' graduation in that office he came to London and worked on various papers until, at the age of twenty-three, he launched the *Advertising World*, evidently the first periodical of its kind in Britain. Probably the fact that he found the necessary capital, and the circumstance that his elder brother was engaged in coal mining, provided the cause, later in his life, of his being accused by the Communist *Daily Worker* of having derived a fortune from coal. That suggestion Camrose repudiated totally, saying that such connection as he had with companies outside the press were not made until after he and Lord Kemsley were well established in the newspaper world. Neither he nor Kemsley, he asserted, made money out of coal. On balance they lost money. "Lord Kemsley and I in association with our elder brother (Lord Buckland) invested a considerable sum to keep going some col-lieries near our native town of Merthyr-Tydfil. We succeeded for a while but lost money in the effort. After Lord Buckland's death we invested further money in one of these companies. It is still there, 1947, after nationalization of the mines. No dividend has been paid and the capital value receivable from the Government is not likely to show a profit. In other words, we would have been richer men today if we had never made an investment in colliery enterprises." This repudiation leaves no room for any other con-clusion than that the Berry brothers' success as proprietors was due to their possession of the skill that is demanded for the pro-duction of successful publications, and prudence exercised in the financial administration of their properties.

Gomer Berry (Lord Kemsley), four years younger than his fraternal partner, was reputed to be more strongly attracted to the advertising side of newspaper development and the direction of their business affairs. Their partnership, so long as it lasted, suggested a fortunate combination in which journalistic talent of the elder brother was supplemented by the commercial aptitude of the younger. Undoubtedly, William had the journalistic flair essential to the success he achieved; but it was not the kind of intuition that made Northcliffe a successful innovator, nor was William Berry's period so favorable to the proliferation of new publications. Rather, he had sound journalistic experience, and the knowledge of readers' reactions that enabled him to avoid misjudgements and to correct wrong trends, which made him just the man to nurse the *Telegraph* back to leadership. His success with the *Sunday Times* had proved that.

The *Sunday Times*, for some years before the Berry brothers bought it, was notable chiefly for having survived for nearly a century and not by reason of its prestige or profitability. R. D. Blumenfeld has recorded that the paper was offered to him in the 1890's for five thousand pounds. In 1914, it was owned by Hermann Schmidt, a German who had taken British nationality, but there must have been German money invested in it, because by 1915, when the Berrys acquired it, the paper had passed into the possession of the government organization for disposing of enemy assets. T. P. O'Connor who was "Father" of the House of Commons and could have qualified for the same paternal standing in Fleet Street, having first entered it from Ireland forty-five years earlier, said the Berry brothers bought the *Sunday Times* for twenty thousand pounds; but even if that figure implied some progress in recent years, any possibility of making it a successful newspaper could have been discerned only by men who had exceptional journalistic aptitude and courage.

Camrose was to admit that initially its sales were less than eighty thousand. Twenty-two years later, they had risen to 556,700. Far from having lowered its standards to achieve that growth Camrose, as editor in chief, and his able editor, Leonard Rees, had expanded and improved its service of foreign, home, and sporting news, and had developed the reputation of the *Sunday Times* for its attention to literature, music, drama, and art, so that it was able to command as contributors, critics of the highest authority in those spheres.

An indication of the progress of the *Sunday Times* during the first seven years of the Berry regime, and of the status attained by the brothers, is afforded by a contract made between them and the then prime minister, David Lloyd George. It was described at the time as the "biggest deal in the history of publishing" and concerned the war memoirs that Lloyd George had promised to write in the near future. This news disclosed *inter alia*, that Camrose had by then acquired a controlling interest in the old-established book-publishing house of Cassell & Co. The contract provided that, for a payment of ninety thousand pounds, Lloyd George assigned to Camrose in respect of the memoirs the serial and book rights in the British Empire and the United States. Shortly afterwards, however, a major political crisis developed in which Lloyd George lost office and, being unexpectedly in need of an income, he made directly a contract with a news organization in the United States to write topical articles for a period of two years. This step was prejudicial to the earlier arrangement with Camrose and his American associates, and by mutual agreement that deal was called off. But the experience proved an instructive rehearsal for a transaction of even greater magnitude later in the century, when Camrose made an arrangement with Winston Churchill for control of the rights in that epic work, *The Second World War.*

It illustrates the capacity of the Berrys for delegating responsibility that even while engaged in the task of eliminating the lifelong inferiority complex of the *Sunday Times* and raising the paper to leadership of the quality class, the brothers were engaged also in acquiring provincial newspapers (mostly afternoon papers) deployed about the United Kingdom from Aberdeen to Bristol which eventually were grouped with the *Sunday Times* under a proprietary company known as Allied Newspapers. Even so, notwithstanding his considerable ability as an organizer and his cool handling of financial situations whose magnitude might "rattle" some hardy men of commerce, Camrose was essentially a professional journalist. He retained to the end the liveliest interest in those aspects of newspaper work that mattered most to the youth who worked his way from the *Merthyr Express* and a succession of other newspapers to a Fleet Street desk, within five years.

As an editor in chief, he was just as critical of the work of editorial writers as of reporters and subeditors; but unlike Northcliffe, he was never savage, impulsive, or even inconsiderate of the distracting conditions under which, inevitably, difficult assignments had sometimes to be carried out. Those with whose work he found fault, accepted his correction without resentment because they recognized that what he expected of them was reasonable and right. He would scrutinize critically, whenever possible, every line of an edition, to maintain a high standard of subediting, an aspect of a newspaper that can easily degenerate without vigilant and sustained supervision.

Personally, Camrose never aspired to be a stylish writer. His published work reflects his characteristically clear thinking and dispassionate mode of expression. He did not favor "writing editors" and set down the commercial failure of the *Westminster Gazette* to Spender's editorship. "Spender," he declared, was "a brilliant writer, but more than one newspaper has been ruined by the brilliant writer placed in the editor's chair." In Spender's own concept of the *Westminster,* Camrose saw the editorials exalted above the primacy that should always belong to news. The *Westminster*'s reputation as a vehicle of news suffered so consistently that even when it was converted into a morning paper under a different editorship, the new capital provided by its principal shareholder still failed to redeem its situation. This, wrote Camrose, was "another example demonstrating that unlimited money, without the necessary knowledge and experience, cannot make or sustain an efficient newspaper."

In choosing Camrose exclusively as the man to whom the future of the *Daily Telegraph* could safely be committed, Lord Burnham had clearly made the correct decision. "Camrose was the man he wanted," wrote his nephew Colonel E. F. Lawson, the only person who was in Burnham's confidence at this crucial juncture in the paper's history. "It is probably equally true," says Lawson, "that the *Daily Telegraph* was the paper Camrose wanted. Certainly, no transaction of this magnitude could ever have gone so smoothly. It was, in the full meaning of the phrase, a gentlemen's agreement." In fact, only two meetings between the two men were necessary for agreement to be reached on all the vital points: and the terms were accepted by Camrose's partners to the deal—his brother Gomer (Lord Kemsley) and Lord Iliffe, proprietor of a famous Midlands daily newspaper, the *Birmingham Post,* and of a prosperous group of periodicals on one of which the youthful Northcliffe learned what little of journalism that was not bestowed on him at birth.

Did Camrose pay a fair price for the *Daily Telegraph,* seeing that there was no "auction" of the paper? Colonel Lawson says, "It was fair and proper, having regard to the large sums Lord Camrose had to spend . . . for capital improvements which were required immediately to enable the paper to hold its own in the fierce competition in Fleet Street." That Lawson's judgment was sound is attested by the fact that one of the first decisions taken by Camrose was to confirm the Colonel in his office as general manager of the paper. Later, his part in the regeneration was recognized by appointment as managing director.

Always, when it becomes known that a newspaper is to change hands, fears assail members of the staff. The personnel of the *Daily Telegraph* was particularly sensitive in this respect. Security of tenure had been a conspicuous advantage of service under the Burnhams, as witness the record of Le Sage. Moreover, the recent growth of groups and combines in the newspaper industry, and the tendency of family proprietorship to diminish was, in the 1920's a disquieting development. In the provinces this rationalization had been accompanied by the amalgamation of several newspapers in which journalists were particularly liable to suffer by being rendered redundant. For the mechanical staffs, there was always the wide field of general printing, offering alternative employment, for in that sphere men who had served under the exacting conditions of newspaper production were rightly regarded as exceptionally efficient in their craft. For journalists, however, there was no such alternative. The growth of broadcasting had, as yet, developed only a small need of journalistic service.

The proprietor-designate of the *Daily Telegraph*, realizing what would happen when the news broke, arranged that on the eve of his assuming control, a meeting of the entire staff should take place, not on the *Daily Telegraph* premises, but in a public hall close at hand. Here, with Arthur Watson, the managing editor, in the chair, and Lord and Lady Lawson in the audience, Camrose addressed the gathering. Understandably, it was an emotional occasion. Camrose's account of it says, "Lord and Lady Burnham were both in tears . . . and a number of the staff were in the same condition. To many of them the future seemed black, as they had no knowledge of what violent changes the new proprietors might have in mind. Happily there were none of that character, and those made were gradual and not drastic at any time." The effect of this introductory gesture can be gauged by a remark made to the present writer by a senior member of the editorial staff on the morrow of the meeting. "Seemingly," he said, "the new proprietors are not the ogres some people had suggested." Soon, the editorial staff was further heartened by the news that Arthur Watson had been confirmed in office as managing editor, and, in fact, the happiest collaboration existed between Camrose and this so excellent journalist until Watson's retirement twenty-three years later.

His earliest inspection of the *Telegraph*'s premises convinced Camrose that, even with the existing plant, the production of the paper was impeded by the character of the building and the complexity resulting from piecemeal extensions in the past. He outlined the kind of structure needed for a much more productive future and, having reconciled himself to the formidable expenditure involved, he handed over his plan to Colonel Burnham with whom he discussed the scheme. With his mind relieved of that problem, whose practical solution would occupy at least two years, he turned his attention to the organization of the staff, which could be amended without delay.

The Burnhams had never been fastidious about the staffing structure, or about the designation and functions of the key people. Camrose preferred precision and also the pattern of editorial responsibility, well understood by journalists generally, that had become conventional in national newspaper offices. Arthur Watson's impressions of early contacts with the new proprietor are instructive, in the light of what was achieved in the next twenty years.

"It quickly became apparent," noted the managing editor, that he had not come into control as a financier but as a journalist. . . . He took more delight in forging the paper as he thought it ought to be than in its commercial success, but he would not have thought his editorial work to be well done . . . had not financial success attended it. . . . Of the basic character of the paper he approved. . . . He therefore desired no revolutionary changes. . . . Quality was, from the first, his guiding principle." He was "insistent upon a wide news coverage by his own staff. . . . He had a news tape machine on his own floor and was frequently in touch with the news editor over the office telephone to know what was being done. . . . As journalists must, Lord Camrose tackled his newspaper in his first waking moments, and he had a secretary at his house to whom he dictated his criticisms and suggestions for transmission to the office."

During the first two years of the new regime no spectacular changes were made in the appearance of the paper, and the price remained at the "unpopular" level of twopence. Regular readers, however, could hardly have been unaware of an enlargement and improvement in the news services, resulting from an augmentation of the staff and of a better editorial structure. Also, the standard of subediting was, to journalists, noticeably higher and the typography more sensitive. Yet, unheralded though these improvements were, the decline in the sales of the paper which, at the date of the take-over were about eighty-four thousand, had ben arrested and, taking an upward turn, had risen to one hundred thousand.

In the meantime, building operations had gone ahead and had been extended beyond the mechanical and publishing side to the remainder of the premises. The site area had been increased by an additional half acre, affording an extended frontage and giving the *Daily Telegraph* ultimately the most impressive newspaper building in Fleet Street. Indeed, the new façade, in the classical, pillared style, was so imposing that there were critics who said it needed for its full appreciation the spaciousness of Trafalgar Square. Still the familiar public clock that jutted, high up, from the old offices had a successor in the same position as though to assure the doubtful that, believe it or not, here the *Daily Telegraph* was still located.

Most of this, of course, had been achieved by capital expenditure, but the time was at hand the better *Daily Telegraph*, to which these changes were preparatory, would soon justify the optimistic spirit now prevailing in the transformed Peterborough Court.

Problems arising from the transitional stage of the building, were numerous. To maintain in one half of the premises efficient editorial operation and mechanical production, while the other half was being rebuilt, led to exasperating situations at times. The fact that the paper came out punctually, without any evidence of the overnight tensions, was of itself a tribute to the cooperation of the staff. Colonel Lawson, being responsible for the physical reconstruction, ensured that by constant improvisation the nightly tasks of the staff were facilitated. The imper-turbable Arthur Watson adapted editorial processes to the changing environment, and Lord Kemsley (Gomer Berry) directed the reorganized advertising department, notwithstanding that he, like his elder brother, had daily obligations to their considerable newspaper activities outside Peterborough Court.

On an appointed weekend in February 1930, the Saturday issue appeared in its customary size. But on Monday, its readers found the *Daily Telegraph* much easier to handle. Those two extra inches, each way, that had caused the *Telegraph* to be regarded as old-fashioned, had disappeared for good. "The day of the tall newspaper, as of the tall folio, is gone," said an editorial devoted to the new look.

A more significant change was effected eight months later, when the price of the paper, and the income from sales were halved. The new plant was now in operation, capable of turning out forty thousand copies of a forty-paged paper each hour. The editorial staff had been uplifted by the year's transforming processes. Morale was high. Camrose, however, cool and confident though he appeared, was conscious that something of a gamble was involved. No exact precedent existed to suggest the extent to which readers of the "popular" penny papers would be drawn to the *Daily Telegraph*. Unlike their familiar purchase, the *Telegraph* offered no extraneous attractions such as free insurance, gift schemes, and high-prized crossword competitions, but simply a very good newspaper relying solely on the quality and volume of its contents. There was, indeed a crossword, but the satisfaction of solving it was the winner's only reward.

The immediate response was encouraging. From the 100,000 mark, the sales rose to 175,000. In the next month, March, the figures continued their upward course to 200,000—twice the sale recorded before the price was changed. Thereafter, taking the results on the same day in May of each year, the sales rose steadily from 274,250 in the year 1932, to 353,648 in 1934. In 1397—ten years after the Camrose era opened on the low level of 84,000—the sales of the penny *Telegraph* had ascended to 565,262.

The price had been halved, but the quality of the contents had been improved and in much the same way as Camrose

had raised the appeal of the *Sunday Times*. There was a better
service of news from all quarters. More space and more discriminating attention was accorded to women's interests. What the
Telegraph staff had always called "cultural" features, despite the
disfavor with which the adjective might be regarded by readers,
showed a sharpened awareness of changing tastes; and even sport,
for which the paper had always enjoyed a good reputation, had
shown itself capable of improvement.

Northcliffe had said during the years of its decline that there
was nothing wrong with the *Telegraph* but anno Domini. That,
by and large, was what the new policy was intended to correct.
Camrose favored the kind of signed, editorial-page articles that
were related to the news of the day, rather than the reminiscences
of celebrities whose fame was of yesterday. Nevertheless, excep-
tions were made and during the early years of his control. The
memoirs of two prime ministers who held office during the First
World War, (H. H. Asquith and David Lloyd George) were, in
part, serialized on the editorial page.

The year 1937 was marked by another event which is likely
to merit reference in the history of the British press for all time—
the purchase by Camrose of the *Morning Post* and its subsequent
integration with the *Daily Telegraph*. As its last editor, H. A.
Gwynne, explained in a valedictory article,

> The *Morning Post* is the oldest daily newspaper in England. We
> have behind us the memories and traditions of more than a
> century and a half. We have been an influence in the social and
> political life of our country through generation after generation;
> and we have had an honourable and remembered part in all the
> moving history of those many years.
>
> A journal which is old enough to have recorded the American
> Declaration of Independence, the guillotining of King Louis and
> Queen Marie Antoinette, and the Battle of Trafalgar, may claim,
> and may feel itself to be, not a mere piece of mechanism, but a
> living, sentient organism, with a soul of its own.

More than thirty years after the amalgamation, the memory
of the *Morning Post* was still saluted by adding its name to the
title of the *Daily Telegraph* on the front page of every issue.

Reasons for failure to pay its way were numerous, one being
that successive proprietors for most of a hundred years had not

made viability the primary condition of their support. As an organ of opinion it had moved from a moderate Conservatism to a position too far to the right to please the middle-class reader. Its predeliction for "strong government" led the early ninteenth century poet, Thomas Moore, to depict a Tory Home Secretary beginning the official day with

> His table piled with tea and toast,
> Death Warrants and the *Morning Post*.

No doubt this aspect of the paper's story had been over-emphasized by partisan critics and had impeded its progress in the twentieth century, but deservedly or not, the "image" of the *Morning Post* as an organ of the landed aristocracy, and its small advertisement columns as the best media for those in search of the perfect butler, handicapped it to the end.

At the time of the amalgamation, the sales of the *Post* were about 100,000: Seven months later, on the May day fixed for purposes of comparison, it was seen that the *Telegraph*'s figure had risen from 565,262 in 1937 to 662,730. Evidently, the readership of the *Post* had been acquired almost totally. A more significant indication of recorded progress is that by May 1939, the sales of *Telegraph* were up to 763,557 which, contrasted with the figure immediately before the "marriage" with the *Post*, showed a gain of almost 200,000.

So notable a rise in circulation was not the only gain accruing from the amalgamation. Although the *Post* could not afford an editorial staff of generous size, its standard of professional competence was high. Camrose, with characteristic consideration, ensured the pensioning of those members who were of an age for retirement. Thus, those men who joined the *Telegraph* were doubly acceptable in that they represented an injection of youthful enterprise as well as reinforcement of talent.

Another major event occurred, also, in the same year. The three men who, ten years earlier combined in the purchase of the *Telegraph*—Lords Camrose, Kemsley, and Iliffe—decided to separate. A three-way division was agreed. Camrose, as his share, took the *Telegraph*, the *Financial Times*, and the Amalgamated Press (consisting of the large periodical business that was North-cliffe's first achievement and sold eventually to the Berry brothers by Rothermere). In the sector that went to Lord Kemsley was the *Sunday Times*, but for some years after the rearrangement of ownership, the London edition of that paper continued to be printed, by contract, at Peterborough Court. Fleet Street gossip at the time seemed well founded when it presented a Camrose deeply disappointed by losing control of a paper for whose success he was so largely responsible. The explanation, however, seems to be that, after the most careful consideration, no equitable division of the properties between the three partners could be found that would leave Camrose in possession of both *Daily Telegraph* and the *Sunday Times*. Still, there was the future of the *Telegraph* on which Camrose's abundant energies could now be concentrated.

Now and again, the editor in chief contributed an article about the progress of the paper, telling readers in an intimate but always a modest manner, something of his aims and principles. At this juncture when the *Telegraph* had become his chief preoccupation, he posed the question, "How high could the Telegraph climb?" He confessed soon afterwards that he did not feel confident enough to answer his own inquiry; but by June 1939, he wrote, "Nowadays, the growth has gone so far that I am not alone in thinking that the round million a day is the figure to which we may reasonably aspire." At the same time he reaffirmed his determination that no ambition for increased sales could ever be allowed to influence in the slightest, the policy and character of the paper—a wise statement, which would be of greater interest to readers than the statistics of the circulation department for, after all, the reader chooses his newspaper because it satisfies his own tastes and interests. At that moment the figure was 736, 557 and, as it had been rising at a rate of 100,000 a year, the attainment of the "round million" may not have seemed far off.

The year was, however, 1939, the month was June. Ten weeks later the Second World War began.

Anyone who had experience of conducting a newspaper during the First World War could be under no illusion about what was coming his way on a repetition of that catastrophe. Lord Camrose had the knowledge; but the problems he purchased in acquiring the *Sunday Times* in 1915, were those of a newspaper with a meager sale, published only once a week. The *Telegraph*,

which some three-quarters of a million readers expected to receive six times a week, was a problem that far outran his earlier
experience of wartime publishing; and the most formidable
aspect of it was the supply of newsprint.

In the last year of peace, British newspapers used 1,250,000
tons of newsprint, most of it imported, and therefore brought
over the seas at the peril of men's lives from submarine activities.
On the outbreak of World War II, government restrictions on the
use of newsprint meant that the number of pages of every paper
had to be reduced by half. In the following year, the penny
papers had to be cut to six pages, and papers of higher cost to
shrink proportionately, and in 1941, to four pages. Members of
the newspaper proprietors organizations were in continuous consultation among themselves and with the government, to get the
best supply they could and to ensure an equitable distribution
among themselves. Later, the proprietors formed a nonprofit-
making company, which, by arrangement with the government,
became the sole buyers and distributors of newsprint.

The *Daily Telegraph* was in a somewhat anomalous position.
It was in the penny classification but the number of its pages
made it comparable to the higher-priced papers. There was, however, a factor that the management considered might fairly be
urged to ease the *Telegraph*'s situation. The newsprint used at
Peterborough Court was of a heavier (that is, a thicker) texture
than the kind commonly consumed. As its manufacturers were
associated with the *Telegraph* by the directorship of Lord Camrose, it was soon ascertained that the firm could produce the
paper in a lighter weight. That made possible the production of
the slightly larger issues appropriate to the status of the *Telegraph*
as a quality newspaper. A time came during the long war when
the thinning of newsprint to a degree that would have been
totally unacceptable in prewar days became general. While journalists marveled at the technical ingenuity displayed in this effort
to produce the maximum supply of copies consistent with what
the government ordained, they were not proud of the thin, flimsy
sheets on which so much was crowded as to render them almost
marginless.

During the early period of hostilities, which became known
as the "twilight war," relatively mild restrictions coupled with

technical contrivance resulted in a larger output of smaller papers. The sale of the *Telegraph* rose to 920,000. But sterner times
came with the fall of France and the diversion of the enemy's air
assault to Britain, inaugurating that ordeal of sixty consecutive
nights in which London was the target of heavy bombing raids.
Arthur Watson has left on record a glimpse of his editor in chief
at this period. "Lord Camrose," he wrote, "sat alone in the proprietorial rooms, contemptuous of air raid warnings, wrestling
with the problem, as Government restrictions closed down upon
Fleet Street, of preserving the special character of the *Daily
Telegraph* in face of the order to cut down to four pages. To
strengthen his case he increased the price to three-halfpence,
against the penny at which the 'popular' papers were sold, and
fought tenaciously for the right to print six pages most of the
week, with an occasional four. He won, but only at the cost of
some 180,000 copies daily to bring the consumption of newsprint
within the ration . . ." Ultimately, Camrose's sacrifice of sales to
his ideal of an adequate newspaper, was much heavier than at the
time of Watson's observation. Between June 1940 and August,
1941, the sales were cut deliberately from 920,000 to 637,000.

As Watson noted, with the protraction of the war, his chief
sought refuge from personal anxieties by involving himself more
and more in what he formerly regarded as details delegated to
others. Nor was this without importance, because active service
with the armed forces depleted the staff, taking particularly the
younger men. Lord Camrose's eldest son, Seymour Berry, had
been embodied with his Territorial regiment on mobilization in
1939, and his second son, Michael, had taken the same course.
So, too, had the general manager, Colonel E. F. Lawson, destined
to return eventually to the office as a retired major general.

Camrose, though he neither aspired to political office nor
showed any desire to become a public figure, was always available
for such service as he could render when called upon. If he felt
he had something to contribute to a debate, he spoke in the
House of Lords, always characteristically to the point. Early in
the war, he undertook an *ad hoc* duty to survey what, at the time,
was one of the government's oddest improvisations, the Ministry
of Information. Harold Nicolson's published *Diaries* tell of encounters with Camrose in select assemblies close to the heart of

events; and Kenneth Young, editing Churchill's correspondence with Beaverbrook, brackets Camrose with Brendan Bracken and Lord Cherwell as among the "real intimates of Churchill." Such companionship with men most closely concerned in the direction of the war may never have been obvious in the news columns of the *Telegraph*, but undoubtedly it was valuable in guiding public opinion through the medium of its editorials; for as an intelligent organ of opinion it ranked with the *Times* and such regional dailies as the *Manchester Guardian* (then still based upon Manchester) and the *Yorkshire Post.* In the mid-war period, Wilson Harris, editor of the *Spectator*, surveying the condition of the Press, wrote, "The *Telegaph* has steadily advanced in circulation and prestige, holding a unique place between the *Times* on the one hand and the popular papers on the other, and combining successfully many of the virtues of both."

But at this time and for some years still to come, the supply of copies of the *Telegraph* was not equal to the demand; hence the streamer across the facade of its Fleet Street building,

SHARE YOUR TELEGRAPH WITH A FRIEND

One of the problems created by newsprint restriction concerned advertising. Of course, the space for displayed advertisements was inadequate and, so long as the proportion of editorial contents in relation to advertising was strictly regulated, nothing could be done to alleviate that grievance. The small advertisements were likewise affected, and this aspect of the paper provided cause for particular concern. From an early date the *Telegraph*, as the pioneer of small advertisements with box numbers attached, attracted and held the lion's share of them.

What made the problem acute was that, as the war continued, shortages of a wide variety of articles increased. The man who wanted a lawn mower, for instance, had no hope of buying a new one because the makers were fully occupied in the manufacture of tanks. Also, as more and more men were called for service with the armed forces and unfit men directed to war work, staffs were mostly in dire need of reinforcement. Thus, in the *Telegraph* office, small advertisements awaiting publication piled up, with the result that the time lag between receipt and publication might be a month or more.

From one of its executives came the solution of the problem. Divide the daily output of the paper into two editions, A and B, and limit the appearance of each advertisement to one edition. Then mix the editions before distribution. Thus, while the advertiser would have his need made known in only half the number of papers than heretofore, it would be subject to only half the delay by which it was previously handicapped. The scheme proved acceptable and, for the great majority, relief came sooner than it would otherwise have done. After all, with a daily printing of over six hundred thousand copies, to have your need made known to some three houndred thousand gave substantial hope of some helpful replies.

The day when such problems would disappear was farther away than was generally anticipated. Complete removal of restrictions on the printing of newspapers did not come with Germany's capitulation, nor even a year later. In one of his progress reports to his readers, published in September 1946, Lord Camrose directed attention to the larger paper published that day. "As from today, every daily paper increases its number of pages on three days a week. Little enough, it is true." All newspapers, he said, were selling more copies than they did before the war (a situation only possible because they had been made pathetically small, and the available supplies of newsprint had been spun out to achieve that result). Still, there had been some increases in the ration and thus the *Telegraph*, too, had been able, while maintaining its larger size, to print more copies. In the final paragraph, Lord Camrose disclosed the number of that very issue "ordered by the public." It was 989,131.

In fact, that "round million" on which he had set his hopes was attained in April 1947, but an economic crisis then in the offing led, in July, to a reimposition of restrictions because devaluation had dictated a reduction in dollar imports. The *Telegraph*'s sales fell back to the nine hundred thousand level. Though they rose subsequently by some eight thousand, a process of "freezing" circulations delayed the day when the round million, when reached, would not be undermined by further government intervention.

The day came in 1953; and press freedom in that respect was fully restored. The future was clear for the paper to go as high as its merits would take it, and Lord Camrose, confident that so long as it presented itself as an example of good journalism, and scorned to increase its sales by gifts, competitions, free insurance, and the like, the *Daily Telegraph* could dominate the British press.

In that belief he died in 1954, at the age of seventy-five.

8

Arthur H. Mann

*Fearless editor of the abdication
and appeasement crises*

When Arthur Henry Mann became editor of the *Yorkshire Post*
in December 1919 after the First World War, both Fleet Street
and the readers of the paper felt surprise. The new chief differed
conspicuously from his predecessor in the old-fashioned office, the
core of it once the flat where the proprietor lived over the shop,
at the corner of Albion Street and Bond Street, Leeds.

J. S. R. Phillips, whose large, ancient and flat desk Mann
took over, had a name as a writing editor, but he was also widely
known as a genial personality. He readily accepted invitations to
speak and deserved the enthusiastic applause he received. A story
he told against himself was than an unimportant society in a
small West Riding town invited him to an annual dinner and
when he wrote accepting and asking on which toast he should
peg his speech the reply came that he was not on the toast list—
the mayor and other local men of mark would provide all the
oratory wanted.

All kinds of people thought well of him. On a visit with
other British editors to the Kaiser his knowledge of German made
him spokesman for the guests. He told a story that made His Imperial Majesty laugh heartily. At the newspaper office Phillips

was devoted to his colleagues and they were devoted to him. He toiled as hard as anyone in the First World War that took away so many of his fellow workers. In those grim days he worked himself to death. He left behind the memory of a beloved editor—a tribute that not many editors receive in the jungle of journalism.

Mann, coming from the editorship of the London *Evening Standard* at the age of forty-two, had some admirable qualities, obvious or latent. But he was no public speaker, no linguist, and he knew little of Yorkshire. He had no love of conferences and of talkative persons who put forward proposals purely as a basis for discussion, purely, so to speak, to be kicked around. He enjoyed the role of reclusive autocrat in touch with the country's great leaders. With ordinary people he was strangely shy.

During his editorship, a Lord Mayor of Leeds, with some of his expenses allowance still left toward the end of his term of office, decided to invite members of the local press to luncheon and so began a custom honored every year since. Mann as the senior local journalist took it to be his duty to propose the Lord Mayor's health and praise his achievements. I was then editing the *Leeds Mercury*, a morning journal, which many years before surrendered to the *Yorkshire Post* its position as the leading paper of the county. Mann more than once told me he hated having to speak. If he gave me a signal would I please rise and propose the toast? He knew that that would be no trouble to me. However, whenever it came to the point Mann felt he must not evade his duty. I waited for his signal in vain. His speech was always a discriminating tribute, not without lighthearted touches, but delivered with a somewhat apprehensive air. When C. P. Scott of the *Manchester Guardian* died the British Broadcasting Corporation asked Mann to broadcast an appreciation. He could not but accept, since like all editors he had an intense admiration for the man who had made a provincial newspaper a world force. He prepared an excellent script, rehearsed it with Philip Fox, manager of the BBC's Leeds studio, and read it with a nervousness which many listeners probably attributed to emotion at the loss of an old friend.

What, then, were Mann's qualities that outweighed those in which he did not compare well with his predecessor? The chairman, who appointed him, the Honorable Rupert Beckett, then a

Photograph by the *Yorkshire Post* Studio

ARTHUR MANN

leading banker in the City of London, where he later presided over Westminister Bank, told me how the choice was made. The acting editor on Phillips's death, James Sykes, declared himself too old to carry on indefinitely. Mr. Beckett and his brother, Sir Gervase Beckett, advertised the vacant post. They were delighted when they found the editor of the *Evening Standard* had sent in an application. This paper with its well-informed London Diary was favorite reading with both. They invited Mann to call on them. They were now even more delighted to have made two discoveries. The editor himself collected most of the exclusive pieces of news that appeared in the Diary. He enjoyed the friendship and trust of Tory statesmen, just as J. A. Spender in his *Westminster Gazette* days acted almost as a Liberal minister without portfolio, giving counsel and gathering information. Then the two brothers, tall and commanding in appearance themselves, were impressed by Mann's seignorial presence. Dignified, thoughtful, and modest, he looked as if he would be more at home in a British embassy than in a feverish newspaper office with its thundering rotary presses, rattling tape machines, and constant telephone calls. The Becketts were sure that this was the man for them. How could he fail to maintain the quality of the *Yorkshire Post* and enliven those dignified columns with a new alertness to what was happening behind the scenes at Westminster? If he seemed slightly cold and aloof in contrast with the warmhearted Phillips, did this not betoken a good disciplinarian?

So Arthur Mann went to Leeds under encouraging auspices and set about improving a rather stodgy provincial paper. He proved to be all that Rupert Beckett and his brother hoped for. He did not make changes with a bull-at-a-gate onrush, but gently gave the paper broader scope in accordance with the spirit of a postwar era. There were not wanting the usual local know-alls who assured him that the *Yorkshire Post* did not need to change like all the jumpy popular papers. They took the line that it was a special institution for a special community and could only be changed at its peril. Mann, who had had much experience of journalism, in the provinces and in Fleet Street, knew how often and how exaggeratedly that plea of a special case could be used. Certainly there were veteran readers who condemned the most useful changes. The editorials had appeared without headings.

It was assumed the reader would want to read them, just as he would want to read the London Letter, though it had no side-headings to catch attention. Mann adopted the universal modern method of headings large and small. At once fogyish veterans dispatched protests to the new editor, asking scornfully whether he thought they could not tell by reading it what an editorial or or a London note was about. Mann smiled and went on slowly brightening the look of the paper.

Arthur Mann was the eldest of thirteen children of a Warwick alderman who led the local Conservative party and was an honorary freeman and twice mayor of the town. Arthur gained a reputation as a cricketer at Warwick School, captained the school team and scored a century against King Edward's School, Birmingham. He began his journalistic career with the *Western Mail* of Cardiff, and for a time played cricket for Glamorgan. Next he went to Birmingham, first as a member of the staff of the *Birmingham Daily Mail*. Then he edited the *Birmingham Dispatch*. Next he went to Fleet Street as London editor of the Manchester *Daily Dispatch*. This paper had a strong popular appeal in the North of England, especially among the textile workers, but had nothing like the prestige of the *Manchester Guardian* or *Yorkshire Post*. Perhaps to rival their reputation for inside knowledge of the political world, Mann made a great feature of the London Letter. At that time London Letters enjoyed in the provincial press a popularity that his since declined. Lord Northcliffe once enlightened me on this subject. At his behest I made some suggestions, which I thought might improve the then leading popular paper, the *Daily Mail*. I thought something in the nature of a gossipy, highly personalized London Letter, entitled 'It seems to me" would be attractive. "Young man, don't be foolish," said Northcliffe with a frown. "Readers want hard news. The *Daily Mail* gives them hard news. Provincial London Letters are mainly stuffed with rubbishy guess-work and rumor-mongering which no editor would disgrace his news columns with." Though I did not agree with that sweeping judgment it had some truth within its exaggerations. But Mann's London Letter in the *Daily Dispatch*, a generation or more ago, did give readers a flattering sense of being in the know about affairs of much moment. His experience in building up the feature helped him later to improve the *Evening Standard* with the warmly appreciated Londoner's Diary.

Mann had charge of the *Yorkshire Post* for twenty years. As Mr. Beckett and his brother Sir Gervase expected, the new chief improved the paper not merely through his contacts with national leaders but by showing a remarkable quality of independent leadership. This manifested itself in two memorable chapters of history, his part in the abdication of King Edward VIII and his staunch denunciation of the policy of appeasement toward Hitler when the führer was planning world war. But Mann's first acts of editorship were devoted to making the *Yorkshire Post* a little more attractive to the eye. When he decided on a whole picture page, by no means a brand-new innovation in even the serious press, old fogies accused him of descending to the level of the trivial and sensational papers. Soon the beauty of many of the pictures, especially large ones showing Yorkshire landscapes, captivated the most censorious. Another feature that Mann began, though not till 1928, had its critics at first. Under the title, "This World of Ours," chosen from a large number submitted by the journalistic staff, it mingled wit, wisdom, and learning in a playful miscellany. F. A. Rice, who had edited *The Granta*, the Cambridge undergraduates' journal, took charge of the new feature over the signature of Northerner. He usually wrote the more fun-producing paragraphs. As a relief in a largely political organ the feature quickly won general favor. H. W. Metcalfe, who succeeded Rice as Northerner, kept up its agreeable character. He left the paper to serve in the Royal Navy when the Second World War was about to darken the world. Mann despaired of getting a contributor with the talent of a Rice or a Metcalfe, dropped "This World" for the time being and longed for the day when Metcalfe would return to his column after serving with the Fleet Air Arm. Metcalfe never did. When the aircraft carrier *Eagle* was sunk he rescued three of his comrades and was mentioned in dispatches. In 1943 he was killed. By this time Mann had retired from the *Yorkshire Post* and I succeeded him. I resolved to restore "This World," but what difficulties and disheartenments I inflicted on myself! My chairman had a fixed belief that no one could ever equal poor Metcalfe. Every week he used to come into my room with a gloomy, "I don't like your Northerner II at all. Can't you get somebody better?" I had thirteen men trying their hand one after another, and at last hit on a most worthy successor to Rice and Metcalfe in Andrew Weir. He still uses the signature Northerner II, one I chose because after the memorial tributes to Metcalfe so many readers thought of him as the original Northerner, though he was himself the second.

Mann's supervision of the *Yorkshire Post* was fairly close, considering that guidance of its editorial policy he held to be his chief responsibility and considering, too, that he was editor in chief of a group, and kept a watchful eye on the *Leeds Mercury*, the *Yorkshire Evening Post*, the *Doncaster Chronicle*, and for a time the declining *Yorkshire Weekly Post*. He was especially interested in sport, sometimes altered his racing tipster's predictions and devised for the *Mercury* an attractive cricket forecast competition. His relations with his editorial writers were much more sympathetic than those with his subeditors and reporters. When I came to Leeds to edit the *Mercury* a former editorial writer of his, Arthur J. Cummings, warned me that I might find him coldly austere. I did at first, but as we lived for a long time in the same residential club and usually had breakfast together, I soon found him much friendlier than I expected. One of the earliest questions he put to me concerned the main page of the *Yorkshire Post*. Passing it over, he said, "Tell me, as a Northcliffe man, what do you think of the choice of news for the main page?" I replied, "Speaking purely from the point of view of a Northcliffe man, I should say the page is overweighted with politics and is destitute of sex." Mann smiled wryly and never asked me that question again. But he did like to be told of the Northcliffe rules for makeup.

I had to be careful of my candor. Mann had the sensitiveness of a very shy man. Collin Brooks came from Liverpool to be one of his editorial writers, and being a man of ideas, a novelist, an economist, and much else he became most useful. Mann relied on him for exchanges of political gossip. But when Brooks wrote a novel in which Arthur Mann seemed to be portrayed as a youngish colleague whose manifest duty was to make Mann's ideas clearer, the editor in chief was not amused.

Mann's best friend during his earlier years was his chairman, Rupert Beckett, who found him a keen companion at golf (sometimes on Scottish holidays), bridge, and poker. Moreover, Mann, like his banker chairman, was a born true-blue Tory with rampant contempt for predatory traits he suspected in nearly all Socialists. At first, when briefing leaders on controversies within the Conservative party, he showed a preference for balanced editorials. Later, especially when a former *Daily Mail* colleague of mine, Charles Tower, joined his staff as chief editorial writer, Mann began to favor philippics. Tower, trained at the public school of Marlborough, and at Oxford in classics, and on the *Morning Leader* and *Daily Mail* in international affairs, especially those concerning Germany, had a trenchant style. There was good reason for his hatred of German expansionism and violence. With a view to describing a wild scene in Berlin in 1914, he was watching closely when a blow from a policeman's truncheon crippled him for life. With firsthand knowledge of certain aggressive qualities in the German character, he never let Hitler's treacheries deceive him in the mid-thirties. Unhappily many Britons and Americans did let themselves be misled for a long time by Nazi propaganda and promises.

Before the Hitler menace rose to its bloody climax, Mann's fearless character and deep knowledge of political life showed itself in the abdication excitement that arose late in 1936. As the stories about King Edward VIII and Mrs. Wallis Simpson spread, I discussed them several times with Mann. American and other foreign papers, which I was getting at the office and from friends abroad, felt no compulsion to be reticent about a royal romance. We knew how strongly the prime minister, Stanley Baldwin, felt about the constitutional proprieties. Editorial editors were deeply concerned about the fast-approaching crisis. I had ready to print some most readable details from one of my correspondents, Elizabeth Craig, who had married an American journalist, Arthur E. Mann (no relation of my editor in chief, Arthur Henry Mann). She saw a good deal of London society life, and was a trustworthy witness who did not credit every rumor that was on the wing. Were we right to hold back so important a story when it had spread so widely through the world? Would not one of the popular London papers startle the country with it before long? Ought we not to print a discreet version of it? I told Mann I was sure Northcliffe would have refused to be silent whether the government wished it or not. My friend, Sir James Baillie, vice-chancellor of Leeds University, wondered why we stayed reticent. "We cannot any longer accept the Stuart maxim, 'The King can do no wrong,' " he said when he and I talked it over.

Mann thought premature publicity by a single British paper might cause an explosion of outraged loyalty. The King inspired much admiration and affection. The nation might rally to his defense as it did to the defense of our most renowned soldier when the *Daily Mail* attacked him for the shortage of suitably powerful shells in the First World War. It had one contents bill for all editions, bearing the words, "Kitchener's Tragic Blunder." This shocked the public, who remembered how Kitchener of Khartum crushed the khalifa at Omdurman, brought the South African War to a successful conclusion, and recruited a million men to fight the kaiser. The Service clubs in Pall Mall forthwith banned the *Mail* and what was at that time another Northcliffe paper, the *Times*. Members of the London Stock Exchange burned copies of the two papers, raised cheers for Kitchener, jeers for Northcliffe. There were angry demonstrations at the Baltic Exchange in London and the Cardiff Coal and Shipping Exchange. *Daily Mail* sales dropped by 238,000 copies. As a soldier in the French and Belgian trenches who knew how severely we were handicapped by lack of effective shells such as the enemy had, I welcomed Northcliffe's brave and patriotic denunciation. He acted rightly, but for a time he paid heavily. Might there not be similar penalty for a paper that censored the King?

Probably not if the press acted as one. Leading editors held that until the Church of England or the government took some official action, the gossip going around was simply gossip, indeed much of it scandalous tittle-tattle. If it became known that some official move would be made soon, then the whole of the press meanwhile could join in a sort of gentlemen's agreement on silence. Though I doubted whether Northcliffe, who had died fourteen years before, would have sheltered in that way behind official authority, anxious editors were saved from the fear of being scooped.

On December 1, 1936, at the *Leeds Mercury* office, I picked up our evening paper and saw a significant statement had been made by Bishop Blunt at a Bradford diocesan conference. He said the benefit to be derived by the people from the King's coronation, then being planned, would depend in the first instance on the "faith, prayer and self-dedication of the King himself." The King, he went on, would abundantly need divine grace if he were to do his duty faithfully. "We hope that he is aware of this need," the bishop added. "Some of us wish that he gave more positive signs of such awareness."

Meaningful, well-considered words, I thought. Was this the Church's cool and careful signal to the press? I walked the short distance to the *Yorkshire Post* office. Mann was in or near London. Finnerty, the veteran news editor, held the fort. "This could be the signal," I said, pointing to the bishop's address. Finnerty looked blank "Signal? What signal? How do you mean?" I explained and asked for every effort to be made to get into touch with Mann quickly. Before long he came on the phone and I told him what the bishop had said. Mann replied with his usual calm, "Right, the Church has made a move. Let the P.A. circulate our editorial—yours too." P.A. meant the Press Association, the great British news agency working closely with Reuters and exchanging news with agencies in many parts of the world. Both the *Yorkshire Post* and the *Leeds Mercury* had prepared their editorials for use as soon as the great topic could be discussed publicly. They were telegraphed to all morning papers in the British Isles and cabled to many countries abroad. Very few papers failed to emphasize the phrase, "We do not accept the Stuart doctrine, 'The King can do no wrong.'"

Other British newspapers followed the lead of the *Yorkshire Post* and *Leeds Mercury* or perhaps made a similar decision on their own initiative. The London papers held their peace for another day. But further silence was no longer possible on so vital a question. The King's wish to marry Mrs. Simpson and keep his throne had some powerful supporters, among them Winston Churchill, but on the other side were the prime minister, the archbishop of Canterbury, and our most reputable newspapers. When the conflicting voices ceased, and the throne passed to another, I heard from a leading politician that Winston Churchill remarked sadly, "Edward would have got away with it but for that fellow Mann."

A rumor spread that Stanley Baldwin inspired Mann's pub-

lication of the famous editorial. Baldwin did not; Mann used his
own judgment. It was said Mann consulted many other papers
before deciding to publish. He did not. As usual, he relied on his
own judgment. It is said that he aimed to scoop the London
papers. He had no such aim, no such expectation. When he
ordered the *Yorkshire Post* and *Leeds Mercury* editorials to be
wired to the Press Association for general circulation, he assumed
that all morning papers would accept the bishop's pronouncement as a signal for action and would send their editorials on the
subject to the P.A., as was then the custom after all big debatable
events.

Would it not be one of the most extraordinary accidents in
British history if purely private and unofficial animadversions by
a bishop upon the monarch and a provincial editorial had caused
him to lose his throne? I think Winston Churchill was for once
wrong. Edward VIII, or rather the Duke of Windsor as he now
is, says in *A King's Story* that he hoped to settle his problem one
way or the other by private negotiation with his ministers, but he
found the Bradford bombshell, as he called it, shattered the hope.
It seems to me incredibly fantastic to suppose that the Church,
Parliament and the press would have remained silent and inert
in so momentous a crisis while the King and ministers settled
affairs in secrecy. The "Bradford bombshell" reverberated immediately in Leeds, though not in Printing House Square, and
Arthur Mann's firm response greatly strengthened his reputation.
The views he so speedily expressed became those of the great
mass of the British people.

He deserves even more credit for a campaign in which he
encountered furious opposition from fellow Conservatives. These
included many readers of the *Yorkshire Post*. Giving up the
Guardian was a Northern reader's habit that never deterred C. P.
Scott from doing what he considered right. Nor did his own
readers' protests or falling away ever tempt Arthur Mann to yield
on a question of conscience. Long before I heard anyone else say
it, Mann declared to me, "Hitler is a thug, surrounded by thugs.
We should be mad to thrust his word." He never departed from
this view. The *Yorkshire Post*, early in the events that threatened
world peace, declared: "We may recognize fully the sense of
national worth and capacity which Hitlerism has inspired in

Germans. We should not deny the contributions which a fit and confident nation can make to the progress of the world." Germany's choice of government, in Mann's view, was not our concern, but he argued that her racial and religious intolerance offended public opinion in this country. If there were to be peace between the two nations there must also be frankness; and Germany should show her willingness to take part in League of Nations' methods of international cooperation. The League must combine strength with elasticity. There must be united resistance to aggression, but such resistance should be accompanied by evidence of the desire to find remedies for legitimate grievances. Collective deliberations and collective decisions were needed. We could not swerve from that policy without damaging our prestige and without plainly betraying those countries which had so far gone with us in pursuit of League policy. These doctrines were steadily and repeatedly enunciated while Hitler was building up his strength for blackmail or war. Mann urged that a vigorous policy of rearmament must be our reply to the signs of ruthless German expansionism.

In the light of events from 1933, when Hitler became chancellor and 1934, when he abolished the presidency which the aged Hindenburg had held and proclaimed himself führer, it may seem strange that the views of the *Yorkshire Post* on Nazi policy, British rearmament, and the League of Nations met with much resistance. In that resistance, frequent use was made of the word appeasement. Neville Chamberlain, the prime minister who succeeded Stanley Baldwin in 1937, long believed that Hitler could be pacified by concessions. When Mann went to see him once to plead for swift rearmament, he had a chilly reception. Chamberlain presumably believed that the editor's outspokenness hindered efforts to come to reasonable terms with the fuhrer. He may have thought that for the leading Conservative paper in the provinces to oppose the leading policy of a Conservative prime minister was a sort of treachery. But Mann, loyal to a Conservative philosophy, put patriotism before a placatory plan, which he believed must fail.

Some of his opponents at home believed he was unduly influenced by Winston Churchill, whom they regarded as too militaristic. This was not so. Mann thought for himself and had not always been supported by Churchill, notably on India's future, as he was in the appeasement crisis. Some thought Mann paid too much heed to the opinions of Anthony Eden, who had married a niece of the chairman of the *Yorkshire Post*. Again, the answer is that Mann, as everybody who knew him appreciated, relied on his own judgment, though the two men often exchanged views and usually agreed. I have even heard it suggested that Mann denounced Hitler's anti-Semitism because Leeds contained a large number of Jews and their support was valuable to the paper. This suspicion is baseless. Mann detested any inhuman policy, whether it victimized readers of his or not.

I said to him one day as war approached in 1939, "Thank God the appeasement nonsense is finished. We probably roused the nation and the government to rearm in time. But we shall get no credit. When war does come our leading articles will be forgotten. The heroes of the day will be the sailors, the soldiers, the airmen. Our part will be ignored." "I know," said Mann, "but what does that matter?" My fears were not groundless. When the expected war began its cruel course there were readers who reproached us and asked, "Why did you not warn us of this?" As if we had not warned our readers all through the appeasement period!

Mann chose to retire when the directors resolved to merge their two morning papers and issue the combined paper at the price of a penny, since he regarded such a paper with considerable misgivings. "We one and all wish him well," said the chairman. Mann would never accept a knighthood but was made a Companion of Honor in 1941. After much useful public work, including five years as a governor of the British Broadcasting Corporation, he settled into a contented old age at Folkestone with his wife. I am grateful to have known him as my mentor, my chief, and my friend. Never shall I forget his dignity, his integrity, his meditative serenity, his dislike of the slipshod or hasty. He inspired editorials in which every phrase was telling, every sentence carried weight. It was as though he kept himself poised and tense to strike the decisive blow for the policy he believed in. In venerable old age he had the right to remember how he did his country and the cause of freedom much service. He had trained many journalists in responsibility.

Courtesy of the *Daily Express*

R. D. BLUMENFELD

9

R. D. Blumenfeld

*Fleet Street's leader from the
American Midwest*

Ralph D. Blumenfeld (1864–1948) has a distinction unique
among those editors of British daily newspapers who met successfully the challenge, which in the early years of the twentieth
century was presented by a literate public of vast proportions,
brought into existence by enlightened legislation on education
passed in 1870.

Had not natural modesty and a fine sense of humor forbidden it, "R. D. B." might have exclaimed, *Veni, Vidi, Vici!*

Born of American parents at Watertown, Wisconsin, and
having been trained in journalism there, and in Chicago and New
York, he arrived in London in 1897. He was no immigrant, seeking an opening in British journalism. He came on an assignment
that might have satisfied the immediate ambition of any eager
American reporter. He was the duly accredited London correspondent of the New York *Herald*.

During his first few years in London, he was entrusted with
increasing responsibilities, and the course of his career suggested
that its climax would be reached in the editorship of the *Herald*.
So highly did his proprietor rate R. D. B.'s potentialities that,
six years after his arrival in London, he was ordered back to New

York to supervise the erection of new headquarters for the *Herald* group, and then to assume office as business manager of the whole enterprise. His enthusiasm for such a future, however, was not great. He acknowledges in his published *Diary* that he was unfamiliar with the duties of a business manager and what he had seen of them did not entice him.

After a year in New York, a yearning to return to London was heightened by a curious proposal. He was invited to undertake the formation of a company in Britain to manufacture typesetting machines, which were then coming into use in the United States. He accepted, but such was his love of journalism that, notwithstanding the claims of "a great manufacturing business," he found time to contribute to many American newspapers and "frequently acted as a Special Correspondent."

The business of introducing typesetting machines must have been more congenial to Blumenfeld than he suggests in the published story of his career. His father, David Blumenfeld of Wisconsin, was rather more than the editor of a small community newspaper; he was proprietor and printer, too. Thus, the young Ralph received his early training from his father, with the result that when in later years he was called upon to lecture to British journalists, he could claim with some pride that, as a reporter, he had often taken his copy to the composing room and put it into type, and could still do so if need be.

Whimsically, he might even tease an audience of experienced journalists with questions such as "What is a hair space?" "What would you do with a mutton quad?" or "How would you set a hanging paragraph?" Among the qualifications desirable in an editor, he attached importance to a knowledge of typography and an understanding of the technical processes involved in making a newspaper. An editor without that equipment, he contended, was at the mercy of printers and printers' foremen.

Arthur Christiansen, R. D. B.'s most outstanding successor in the editorship of the *Daily Express*, depicts in his book, *Headlines all my Life*, the editorial staff turning out the paper when the general strike of 1926 stopped all printing. Christiansen, then a young and newly joined reporter, describes how the editorial men set about the various mechanical processes, and how "Blumenfeld, the venerable, dignified and much-feared editor-in-chief, took off his black coat and wrapped a white apron round his middle to become Head Printer for the day." This inherited aptitude for printing explains how it was that R. D. B., notwithstanding his ardent affection for journalism and his dislike of managerial chores, found a mechanical typesetting business tolerable for six whole years.

Even when Joseph Pulitzer, visiting London during that period, tried to enlist Blumenfeld for the New York *World*, he received a dusty answer. An invitation to lunch was followed by a long drive around London in a Victorian carriage in the June sunshine, during which, says *R.D.B.'s Diary*, Pulitzer bombarded him with questions about the *Herald*'s interior arrangements . . . "He was obviously bent on getting inside information, and I was bent on not telling him, even though I am no longer a *Herald* man."

Pulitzer sensed this stonewalling and remarked, "You are not very communicative. I expect when you've joined the *World* you will be more so."

To that, the embarrassed guest retorted, "Excuse me, Mr. Pulitzer, I have never said I would join your staff. I do not want to do so." The proprietor of the *World*, with natural resentment, asked, "Why not, please?" Then came the decisive answer, "Because I choose not to be on the *World*—at least not at present." With that, according to the *Diary*, Pulitzer sat up straight, lifted his walking stick and poked the coachman in the back, saying, "Stop, please. This gentleman is getting out here." And that, says R. D. B. "is how I didn't join the *World*."

That refusal may well have been due to his admitted dislike of the ways of Pulitzer's *World*, or it might have been that, shortly before the drive, Blumenfeld had been talking with another proprietor. At that period an incident of considerable significance in Blumenfeld's career occurred when he called at Carter's hairdressing establishment in Fleet Street. Carter's was just the kind of place toward which R. D. B.'s affection for English tradition would direct his patronage. Its premises shared the antiquity of that enclave of chambers and tree-shaded courts inhabited by lawyers and judges, known as the Temple. Carter's was dedicated to the care of the legal cranium in more senses than one. In addition to keeping the lawyers' hair in good order, it specialized also in the valeting of their top hats, ironing them to a superb gloss that proclaimed fastidiousness and prosperity. Journalists, too, might be seen there if they were well known and therefore prosperous. Some indeed wore top hats, for tolerance of sloppy dressing did not begin until the 1914–18 war imposed austerity.

According to one version of what occurred when the barber began to operate on his hair, R. D. B. heard a voice from the next chair inquiring, "Blumenfeld, when are you going back to your proper job?" The voice was easily recognizable as that of Alfred Harmsworth, later Lord Northcliffe. The result of the talk was an understanding that the wanderer would return to the fold for at least a meeting with the Chief in the *Daily Mail* office.

Thus it was that R. D. B. went back to his "proper job," never to stray again. No man was better equipped than Northcliffe to detect that R. D. B. was born for journalism, so no risk was entailed in his going straight from his typesetting salesmanship to the post of news editor of the *Daily Mail*. For the wrong man, that could have been a hot seat, but R. D. B. has left nothing on record to suggest that it was other than an entirely happy experience. What Northcliffe thought of his work can be deduced from Northcliffe's reaction when, after two years, he told the Chief that he wished to resign.

Blumenfeld wanted to join Arthur Pearson, a rising star of the press at that time. Pearson, having given Northcliffe a brisk, competitive run in the periodical field for several years, sought to extend the contest to daily journalism by challenging the *Daily Mail*, whose four years' career had been a story of unparalleled success. Encouraged by a wing of the Conservative party, Pearson launched the *Daily Express*.

The new paper was no pale reflection of the *Mail*. It had its own individuality, well calculated to arrest and retain the attention of the broad mass of the population. It merited success because, as R. D. B. was later to testify, Pearson had qualities that entitled him to "a great place in modern journalism." But, at the time Pearson embarked on his bold enterprise, he had involved himself in politics, for whose sophisticated ways he had no natural aptitude. These activities occupied time that would have been better rewarded had he devoted it to his newspaper. Then, his sight began to fail, and its deterioration could not be checked. He was destined soon to become totally blind.

Obviously, he needed Blumenfeld who, moved by Pearson's courage and cheerfulness in adversity more than any other consideration, felt he must respond. "I had long been observing Mr. Pearson," says R. D. B. "He was the most lovable man I had met for many years, and I felt terribly sorry for him; so I decided to throw in my lot with the *Daily Express.*"

When this was explained to Northcliffe, the Chief agreed warmly about Pearson's personal qualities, but such sentiments could not deter him from delivering the warning he felt bound to give to R. D. B. "You will break your heart trying to get that newspaper on its feet," he said. "It has no chance." To match the achievement of the *Mail* it would need a million pounds spent on it. "And Pearson hasn't got it. You will be back here in six months." Still, Blumenfeld chose to become editor of the *Daily Express.*"

Certainly, the paper needed more capital. After much hard work, with good results, all that R. D. B.'s journalistic enterprise could do was not, of itself, sufficient to win the kind of circulation enjoyed by the *Mail*. As he diagnosed the trouble a few years later, "The situation was, my good ship *Daily Express* was strong enough in hull and frame and steering gear, and all that, but short of steam. Like the Mississippi steamer of note, she was under-powered and over-whistled. Every time the whistle blew, the engines stopped." Observing the struggle of the *Express* to catch up with the *Mail*, Northcliffe might well remain confident of seeing his former news editor coming back like a prodigal son, even though the six months of his prediction had been long exceeded.

What, then, was the secret of the lively survival of the *Express* during those lean years in which it carried the handicap of inadequate capital for improvement of plant and expansion of services? Sidney Dark, who served as a reporter under R. D. B. both on the *Mail* and the *Express*, explained it in a reminiscent work in the 1920's saying, "Blumenfeld is a most accomplished journalist. No man ever had a keener nose for news or a better idea of how to present it."

Moreover, his zest for the newspaper extended to all the stages of production. He toured the mechanical departments of his paper with keen interest and enthusiasm while the work was in full swing, deriving new stimulus from the scene. He wrote: "I have often observed that revitalising effect on men who were once connected with my trade. . . . We hear of the traditional war horse which prances and pirouettes on hearing the sound of the guns. You should see Mr. [Rudyard] Kipling in the composing room!"

After one such visit, Kipling gave him a book, on the flyleaf of which the visitor wrote an inscription that explains, in part, why the *Express* under Blumenfeld succeeded after such an expert as Northcliffe had predicted it must fail. Having inscribed the book "To R. D. B., from Rudyard Kipling," the journalist-turned-poet continued:

> *Who once had served to the sultry hour*
> *When roaring like a gale,*
> *The Harrild and the Hoe devour*
> *The league-long paper bale*
> *And has lit his pipe in the morning calm*
> *That follows the midnight stress;*
> *He has sold his heart to the old black art*
> *Men call the Daily Press.*

Although by this time Blumenfeld had spent the greater part of his adult life in England and had assimilated himself to his environment in a remarkable way ("He is the most English thing I know," wrote Dark, *"Plus royaliste que le roi"*), he could view the British scene with a sense of detachment due to his American origin, and his unfailing sense of humor prevented his assessments from being overwhelmed by his affection and admiration of British traditions and ways.

In that detachment, he had an advantage over Northcliffe. His British rival, developing a sense of power from his immense success, became increasingly Napoleonic in attitude and impulsive in his judgments. On political issues the *Mail* could be pompous, and its view of public figures could be colored by Northcliffe's personal antipathies which, inevitably, were not always shared by all its readers. So, for the man in the street who did not wish to begin his day oppressed by the inherent wickedness or incompetence of his leaders, the *Express*, with its liveliness and optimism, could be more to his taste than the *Mail*, even though the typography of the *Express* was less versatile and its newsprint a trifle inferior.

During the First World War, however, control of imported newsprint limited drastically the size of newspapers. For the less wealthy journals, that development cushioned the impact of competition and put an end to extravagant enterprises like the promotion of air races, and expeditions to Arctic regions, that provided exclusive news for their Fleet Street sponsors.

Long accustomed to austere conditions that made superior journalistic resource the chief means of competing with rivals, Blumenfeld's *Express* was adept in making the best of the restrictive conditions that now affected all newspapers. But already the editor, now virtually the proprietor, discovered a likely source of the additional "steam" that his otherwise happy ship required.

In his round of professional and social engagements R. D. B. had been introduced to a young Canadian who, though only thirty-one years old, had made a fortune in his homeland. Setting an example that was to be followed down to this day by other wealthy Canadians, Max Aitken had come to Britain to relieve the boredom of moneymaking by living in a more variegated society and, perhaps, by entering Parliament, to get closer to world affairs.

Aitken's desire for a seat in the House of Commons, was by no means the limit of his interest. At their first meeting, says R. D. B., Aitken "stupefied" him with a torrent of questions. "He lifted the top off my head." At their second encounter, Max predicted, " 'You and I are going to do great things together.' I did not agree." Still, they continued to meet frequently; and by his unending interrogation and his visits to the *Express* office, Aitken picked up considerable knowledge concerning the production of newspapers. Also, his one and only parliamentary election showed that, by winning so difficult a constituency, he had an instinct for successful publicity.

There is evidence that Aitken's election to Parliament had not diminished his intention of entering the newspaper world, for Waldorf Astor, proprietor of the *Observer*, heard that this thruster was engaged in negotiations for the *Express*, the *Globe*, and the *Evening Times*. But Aitken was notorious for his ability to talk on two or three telephones simultaneously, and the political line was engaging most of his attention at that time.

Chief among his political friends was Bonar Law, by birth a Canadian but by ancestry and upbringing a Scot. Law was one of the ablest and most respected of Conservative ex-ministers. As the Conservatives were now in Opposition and in a mood to change their leader, Law was being named as the most suitable successor.

Lloyd George described Law as "honest to the verge of simplicity." Asquith found him "meekly ambitious." Aitken perceived that while scrupulous honesty would commend this rather dour but warmhearted man to the public, feebleness of ambition would be fatal to his chances in the inevitable jockeying for position that would precede the ultimate selection.

Aitken had a superfluity of ambition. He had, too, a gift for swift tactical maneuver and an audacity, masked by urbanity, that was proof against rebuff. He attached himself to Bonar Law in such a way that, in a field of three runners, Law succeeded. On the basis of his long observation of the Opposition front bench, Lloyd George declared, "The fools have stumbled on their best man." But the "stumbling" had been ingeniously directed.

Claims that Law was virtually unknown before Aitken brought him forward are manifestly absurd. All the same, Law's "stage manager" did not go unrewarded. By Law's promotion to the leadership, Aitken's prestige within the party was enhanced, and it seemed inexpedient for him to proceed, for the time being, with his plan to make himself a national figure by exploiting the financial relationship he had now established with the *Express*.

The outbreak of war in 1914 deferred Aitken's plan still further, for there was only one course that could properly be taken now by a Conservative M.P. who was a fit man, age thirty-three. With the arrival in Britain of the earliest contingent of the Canadian army, Aitken was installed in it, by action taken in Ottawa, as record officer to the force; and when the first division of Canadians moved to France, Lieutenant Colonel Aitken went too, as the official "Eye Witness," whose duty was to write descriptive dispatches that would be made available to all Canada's newspapers. Kenneth Young (in *Churchill and Beaverbrook*) says

"It was his first essay in writing for the public. His self-tutelage by books and his friendship with such men as Kipling and Blumenfeld of the *Express*, stood him in good stead."

Being able to return to London from time to time on political duties, Aitken played a well-documented part in the operation to remove Asquith from the premiership in favor of Lloyd George, for which service he had reason to expect ministerial appointment as head of the Board of Trade. For once, the millionaire's luck was out. After a lesser appointment had been proposed and declined, he accepted a peerage. With it, he took over (choosing to serve without salary) a new post- as Minister of Information which, being a wartime improvisation, disappeared at the end of the war. Then it was that R. D. B.'s friend, now ennobled as Baron Beaverbrook, turned toward Fleet Street and began to write his name in the history of the press. But still in the editor's chair was Blumenfeld, who was to remain for a further fifteen years.

Before taking up the controlling interest offered to him by Blumenfeld, the new Lord Beaverbrook consulted Lord Rothermere, brother and financial adviser of Lord Northcliffe, by whose death Rothermere was soon to become proprietor of the *Daily Mail*. It is significant of the potentialities of the *Daily Express* at that time (and also of R. D. B.'s success in keeping the paper afloat despite its shortage of capital) that Rothermere advised Beaverbrook to accept the offer; and acceptance followed.

If the future of the *Express* had not been well considered by R. D. B. in drawing up the terms of the offer, the ship might have foundered, even with the generous addition of steam that Beaverbrook supplied. It might have broken up from having two captains on the bridge. Happily, there was an understanding that maintained Blumenfeld's authority as editor.

It was a compliment to the goodwill enjoyed by the *Daily Express* that Beaverbrook, who was planning a Sunday paper that would be his own sphere of interest, decided to call it the *Sunday Express*. Had the daily paper's pulse been so feeble as to make its expectation of life precarious, the new proprietor would hardly have handicapped his brainchild by proclaiming its relationship to the *Daily Express* so plainly.

Postwar Britain, inevitably, showed social changes that affected the trend of newspapers. Increasingly, the workaday world was locking its doors on Friday night until Monday morning, and so, too, was officialdom. Thus, many prolific sources of news that were flowing freely on five days of the week yielded nothing for publication on Sunday, when ironically the population had more leisure for reading than on any other day. Logically, the corrective lay in presenting features that attracted attention, contributions that appealed not only by their subjects but by the distinction of their authors.

An instructive glimpse of what happened as the *Sunday Express* made its debut in 1919, is afforded by the published diary of the then Dean of St. Paul's Cathedral, Dr. Inge, one of the most courageous and controversial figures of the day: "The *Sunday Express* has employed me to write a series of short articles, offering me a magnificent remuneration." And a month later: "The *Sunday Express* has paid me £230 for eight short causeries on things in general, and pressed me hard to continue writing for them every week, indefinitely."

Such was the effect of the policy Beaverbrook inaugurated for the new paper. The right contributor confronted by the incentives of generous payment and freedom to air personal views, could almost always produce work that arrested attention and provoked widespread discussion.

Not everything that was attempted at the dawn of the Beaverbrook era was so easy as that. In the first few years, the new paper lost a good deal of money, which was not an experience to which Beaverbrook was accustomed. The important change, however, was that the financial "steam" necessary for a policy of expansion was now available, and it was enabling the *Daily Express* to achieve the results that Blumenfeld's conduct of the paper had long merited, but which were denied previously by financial stringency.

At the time R. D. B. had brought into his newspaper the man who had predicted, "You and I are going to do great things together," the sales of the daily paper were no higher than 350,000 copies a day. Within three years, the figure had increased almost threefold. Inevitably, such growth necessitated new printing plant, not only to meet an unsatisfied demand for the paper, but to enable the pages to be multiplied to accommodate the increased volume of advertising that was offered.

On the editorial side, too, more journalists were engaged. Blumenfeld had always contrived to maintain a staff which, though small, was highly talented. In theory, the *Mail* should have had a monopoly of the best men. But there is something of the artistic temperament in most journalists. Both Northcliffe and Blumenfeld were journalists in every sense; but Blumenfeld had the better understanding of the breed's characteristics. Moreover, he was equable, with a sense of humor that never quite deserted him even in a situation in which indignation was not only justifiable but almost righteous. Northcliffe could be as moody and savage as he could be generous; he fluctuated between extremes.

Thus, there were good men who preferred Blumenfeld as a taskmaster. They knew well what he wanted. To express appreciation and encouragement when those tonics were merited, was instinctive in him. It is significant that almost the last words he uttered were spoken to those who lifted him gently to his bed after a seizure—"You managed that very well."

Christiansen has written that R. D. B. was "much feared," but that impression, as he explained later in his book, was made by an incident in this young subeditor's earliest years, when the news of Lindberg's Atlantic flight had been badly presented. "I had never handled news of this magnitude before," says Christiansen, and two senior men who were on duty were out of the office. The subsequent inquest was "terrifying." When R. D. B. demanded, "Who was in charge?" the accusing finger was pointed at Christiansen.

"Sack him," said the editor in chief sharply; then, characteristically, seeking to say something in extenuation, Blumenfeld added "He's too good looking to be of any use."

The penalty might have stood, had not John Gordon intervened. Gordon, whose name will always be associated with a later distinction as editor of the *Sunday Express* in an outstandingly successful period, was always a frank and bold witness. One statement alone in his evidence before the first Royal Commission on the press, "We all know it to be true that whenever we see a story in a newspaper concerning something we know about, it is more often wrong than right," will ensure his name something like immortality in the history of British newspapers. Gordon came to the rescue, mindful of those two seniors who were absent from their posts, and he proceeded to argue that "it was ridiculous to sack the office boy when the blame lay higher up the ladder."

Thus Christiansen survived to become one of the men who set a new and distinctive style which was followed generally in the presentation of news in the best-selling newspapers. Nevertheless, his reprieve might well have followed from R. D. B.'s own review of the case.

By such episodes in the story of Blumenfeld's career the character of the man can best be illustrated; for, in the editor of a widely read newspaper, as in a statesman, character is certainly not less important than aptitude for the daily duties and ability to cope with the problems for whose solution he is responsible.

A comparison of their respective positions published in 1930, shows the *Daily Mail* enjoying a circulation of 1,845,000, and the *Daily Express* running closely behind with 1,693,000. The political policy of the *Mail* was defined as "Independent, right-wing Conservative" and the *Express* as "Independent Conservative, Anti-collective security—Favours high Tariffs."

Politics had become an obsession with both newspapers (or, more precisely with their proprietors). The differences in their policies were as nothing by contrast with the tie that bound the two men—namely, their hostility toward the leader of the Conservative party, the former prime minister, Stanley Baldwin. The causes of this joint vendetta are of no importance today, save that the dregs of the controversy show a tendency to drip into history and biography.

The conflict reached its climax when the ex-prime minister, in the most vigorous speech of his career, declared in 1930, "The papers conducted by Lord Rothermere and Lord Beaverbrook are not newspapers in the ordinary acceptance of the term. They are engines of propaganda for the constantly changing policies, desires . . . personal likes and dislikes of the two men. What the proprietorship of these papers is aiming at is power; but power without responsibility—the prerogative of the harlot throughout the ages."

Where Blumenfeld stood in this tempestuous, political interlude, is hard to discover. He appears to have said little about it, and, as yet, no definitive biography exists. He had known Baldwin even longer than he had known Beaverbrook, though never intimately. In 1930, he was still editor of the *Daily Express*, but his authority had been compromised by the creation of an office of "Managing Editor," filled by a Canadian protege of Beaverbrook named Beverley Baxter who, by 1929, had been elevated to the rank of "Editor-in-Chief." Whether that maneuver had anything to do with Blumenfeld's resignation in 1932 is not quite clear. He was then sixty-eight and had been editor of the paper for thirty years, a record that exceeds the normal qualification for retirement from the exacting demands of daily journalism. Still, R. D. B. remained, to the end of his life in 1948, chairman of the *Daily Express* company.

It is plain, however, that when Beaverbrook's political ambitions became paramount, his early prediction that he and R. D. B. were going to do great things together, ceased to be valid. The concept of a newspaper as accepted by Max Aitken in 1910 must have been different from the idea expressed in evidence given by Lord Beaverbrook to the Royal Commission on the Press in 1947–49. The Commission's report says that "Lord Beaverbrook, when asked what was his main purpose in running his papers, replied 'I run the paper purely for the purpose of making propaganda, and with no other motive,' and he added that the propaganda 'was in support of policies which he himself considered important rather than in support of one political party.' "

If, in 1910, he had cherished any such notion, it seems certain that R. D. B., with the knowledge which he always exhibited of the country's political history and traditions, would have told the future Lord Beaverbrook that the only hope of achieving political aims in Britain was to support the party whose principles and outlook were consistent with such aims, maintaining all the time a reasonably good relationship with the leaders of that party. He might have added that it would be crass folly to try to create a new party by newspaper propaganda *plus* the oratory of the proprietor, stumping the country as though he were an elected political leader.

What happened to the relationship of the two men in the decade between 1922 and the retirement of the embarrassed editor, can be deduced from passages in the biographies of some contemporaries. Thus, the memoirs of Lady Byng, wife of Field Marshal Viscount Byng of Vimy, neighbors of R. D. B. at Dunmow, Essex, make reference to "Mr. Blumenfeld of the *Daily Express*, who became a great friend because he was an honest man in journalism, having many a row with the proprietor of his paper on questions of ethics, which he often disliked."

Corroborating that evidence of something more than a slight rift in the lute, is the diary of Sir Ronald Waterhouse, private secretary to three successive prime ministers. In January 1928, returning from the French Riviera to London, Waterhouse encountered R. D. B. in the Blue Train and they talked far into the night about Bonar Law, Baldwin, and Beaverbrook.

Says the diary: "Blumenfeld had known and admired Baldwin greatly, but failed to understand his 'fickle friendship' or 'the callous way he casts away an inconvenient colleague.' " R. D. B., is further reported as telling Waterhouse, who was then serving Stanley Baldwin, "Nowadays, whenever S. B. sees me in the Carlton Club, he cuts me." The diarist describes Blumenfeld as being "not only distressed but genuinely hurt by this reversal of congenial contact."

Back in London, Waterhouse reported the substance of this conversation to the prime minister in an effort to repair the breach; but, he notes, "Baldwin found it impossible to countenance 'a man who has sold his soul,' meaning to Beaverbrook."

It may well be that J. L. Garvin was right when he described Baldwin's attitude to Beaverbrook as "against every dictate of common sense." Certainly, one would have expected him to appreciate that a man caught in a dilemma produced by conflicting loyalties—between the obligations of a friendship and his contractual duty to a partner—merited a more charitable judgment than he pronounced at that time.

What happened to the *Daily Express* after Blumenfield's retirement is a necessary pendant to the Blumenfeld story. The paper continued to go ahead, its sales mounting to a point where they were second only to those of the *Daily Mirror* which, being a tabloid, was in a different category. Yet, in relation to the sole motive with which Beaverbrook entered the newspaper world, he failed. Toward the end of his life he admitted that failure with deep disappointment. Millions of people bought every issue of the newspapers he controlled. They liked them because the news was lively, timely, and enterprising. The feature articles were generally excellent, being the work of writers outstanding in their respective fields. Of that rare species, the talented cartoonists, the *Express* outbid its rivals for the best. The reading public lapped up what they enjoyed and ignored the political content whose publication was the chief purpose for which Beaverbrook became a newspaper proprietor.

In an obituary study of the proprietor's career, Sir William Haley, then editor of the *Times*, said explicitly that Beaverbrook was not a journalist. The claim Beaverbrook made before the Royal Commission on the Press, implying that if he did not wish to use the newspapers for political propaganda he would not own newspapers, was described by Sir William as "the attitude of a politician, not of a journalist." Nevertheless, Haley conceded that he influenced journalism. "He worked through journalists—Blumenfeld, Baxter, Christiansen and others. . . . He had to give them their heads to retain their zest."

It is noteworthy that Christiansen, recalling in retirement his own editorship of the *Express*, wrote, "For a medium that changes so much with the public mood, it is surprising that the method of producing a newspaper changes so little, as little in fact as Blumenfeld's desk. That great man laid down the method for the *Express*, and it has been followed by the editors of the paper ever since." Describing the daily editorial conference with its survey of the day's events and all that flowed from that review, Christiansen declared, "the system is the same now in its essentials as it was when I first sat behind that desk." Therein, of course, is evidence that R. D. B. did not allow the turbulence of the world's doings in each new day to obscure the sound, fixed principles of editorial construction of a newspaper.

An interesting reflection by the retrospective Christiansen is that "Editors do not always get the credit for increasing the circulation." Inevitably, that conclusion raises the question of how much credit is due to R. D. B. for the transformation of the *Express* between 1902, when he became its editor, and 1932 when he retired. At the outset, the paper's circulation was so poor that Northcliffe predicted death within six months. Thirty years later it was perhaps the most prosperous of all British daily newspapers. R. D. B.'s achievement was that, on meager capital and by journalistic talent alone, he had raised the paper from a condition near extinction to a point at which, still lacking capital, it survived for several years against competition of wealthier rivals. The paper's soundness in that respect was proved by its remarkable response to the financial injections it received when Lord Beaverbrook became its sponsor. The potentialities were there, and the even livelier journalism, which his younger successors introduced, proved to be entirely in harmony with what readers expected of the *Express*. The innovations were natural developments of the paper's established character.

Despite the claims that the *Express* had always made upon its editor's attention, R. D. B. had never been insensitive to the well-being of journalism as a profession, or cold toward the educational and benevolent activities of its organizations. In 1927 he felt able to accept an invitation to become president of the profession's senior organization, the Institute of Journalists. It was an office that had been filled by many distinguished journalists, but it was by no means a merely decorative position.

Blumenfeld brought imagination, purposefulness, and wit to the routine chores of presiding at meetings, even though he disturbed some of the Founding Fathers by a marked tendency to be empirical rather than constitutionally correct. He cut corners, deflated the long-winded, and caused controversy to dissolve in laughter.

He made his year particularly notable by attracting from the Carnegie Foundation an invitation to take a party of journalists on a tour of the United States. The invitation stipulated that the participants were to be, for the greater part, journalists whose location or duties were such that they had little or no contact with Americans in Britain. It was such a party that he led for most of a three months' tour across the American continent. Later, a party of American journalists, selected on a similar basis, visited Britain, and R. D. B., though no longer president of the

Institute, ensured that the same, intimate Anglo-American contact was maintained in Britain as the British visitors had experienced in the United States.

In that kind of company he was at his best as a speaker, and
his fund of appropriate reminiscence was rich. It was on an occasion of that kind, though not an Institute party, at which he told
with great effect of an experience of his early days in London.
Having leased a house, his name was entered automatically on
the electoral register, and equally automatically, though unknown to him, he became liable to jury duty. Thus, the day
came when he was summoned to discharge that obligation at a
session of criminal trials.

He realized that the summons was irregular because he was
an American citizen; but he thought it might be interesting and
probably yield material for a story for his paper, if he left events
to take their course. He complied with all requirements up to the
point at which his squad of "twelve good men" was being led by
an usher toward the guarded door that opened on to the jury box
of one of the courts. Then, feeling that the joke had gone far
enough, R. D. B. told the usher that he doubted whether he was
qualified to be a juryman because he was not of British nationality.

"What are you then?" asked the usher sharply, hand on door-
knob.

"American."

"Same thing," ruled the usher. "Get inside!"

One may well suspect there was a sequel. But wisely, R. D. B.
ended his speech at that point. "Same thing!" It was a happy
thought to leave to the echoes at an Anglo-American party.

In fact, Blumenfeld took British nationality in 1906. In my
experience the question of his status in that respect rarely arose.
When it did arise among journalists, most of those present did
not know the answer, nor did they care if anyone enlightened
them on the point. It was of no consequence. He was a fine
journalist who won the affection of the profession because he
"loved the brotherhood." Undaunted by formidable competition,
he enlivened Fleet Street with the better qualities of American
journalistic enterprise and thus, to our lasting advantage, left his
distinctive mark upon the British press.

Courtesy of the *Daily Express*

LORD BEAVERBROOK (flanked by Lord Thomson
left, Lord Rothermere right) addressing a dinner party given in
his honor by Lord Thomson in May 1964. This was his last
public appearance

10

Lord Beaverbrook

Edward VIII's code name
for him was Tornado

When Lord Beaverbrook died in 1964, at the age of eighty-five, those who knew him well passed different verdicts on his astonishing career. Some reckoned him the greatest journalist since Northcliffe. Lord Thomson of Fleet entitled him the great professional. Lord Rothermere summed up thus: "Beaverbrook was forty when he entered Fleet Street to learn his trade the hard way. He made a flat on the top of the *Daily Express* building and worked day and night learning the job of how to run a newspaper. He would have succeeded in any kind of work which he took up." But Sir William Haley, editor of the *Times* when Lord Astor of Hever was the proprietor, said Beaverbrook was not a journalist. Why not? "He came into journalism with a fortune made elsewhere. He entered British politics and bought the *Daily Express* for political purposes. He was always a politician."

Some held Beaverbrook to be a cruel tyrant of an employer. Others praised his generosity and compassion. One journalist named him a Pedlar of Dreams; when King Edward VIII and Mrs. Simpson arranged a code for their messages they called him Tornado; somebody denounced him as a maker of mischief. One man described him as a buccaneer and pirate, another as meticulously honest, another as wicked but generous.

Can these different estimates of character be reconciled? I think they can. Nor would I deny to Beaverbrook the name of journalist, which I have no doubt he would have claimed. Surely a man can be both a journalist and devoted politician. Many journalists exercise strong influence as politicians, nationally or locally. But it must be admitted that Beaverbrook started his journalism as a rich proprietor, not as a hard-driven reporter.

Let us look at the salient facts of his career and see how they moulded his character and his journalism. William Maxwell Aitken, the future Lord Beaverbrook, born at Maple, Ontario, on May 25, 1879, was the son of a Presbyterian minister who had emigrated from Scotland. The family soon moved to Newcastle, New Brunswick. Here the boy grew up among lumbermen who came with logs down the river Miramichi. He loved the song of the sawmill. He loved talking to the fishermen and watching the ships arrive from Liverpool and Glasgow. At school he was a wild imp of mischief, but, said the master, a born leader of men from the day he left the cradle.

His father often spoke of Scotland, and the lad dreamed of making his way in Britain. Why not in the United States? No; for historical reasons, expressed in the United Empire Loyalists, New Brunswick was imbued with pro-British rather than pro-American sentiment. Young Aitken tried various jobs—as a clerk in a bank, an insurance salesman, and so forth, but he found life a hard struggle. The luck turned when he became secretary to John L. Stairs of Halifax, Nova Scotia, president of a steel company and a bank, and with a hand in many local interests. If a secretary to a rich man shows ambition and enterprise, he is likely to become a rich man himself. Young Aitken did. Canada's rapid commercial development helped him. He was right in the swim. He was in touch with wealthy men, won their confidence, and when they started a holding and investing company, the Royal Securities Corporation, he became its managing director.

Stairs knew well what money had been made in Canada and the United States in the provision of electric light and power as the horse-and-buggy era changed into one of streetcars and trains. Looking further afield, he dispatched Aitken to look for similar scope in the West Indies. Two years there tested his prowess. The results were good—good for Stairs, good for Aitken, good for the

West Indies. Stairs died soon after Aitken returned to Halifax. When the estate was wound up, fifty thousand dollars went to the young man.

In 1906 he married into one of the oldest families of Nova Scotia. Gladys Drury, daughter of a future general who had fought in the South African war, was a both gracious and firm personality. In the following year Aitken moved to Montreal, there to become a stockbroker and to carry out more mergers, in his own words, than any man in Canada, before or since. The time was ripe, politically and industrially, for big amalgamations. Tariffs were reducing the power of foreign competition, enabling mergers to obtain monopolistic or near-monopolistic conditions at home. Aitken was as quick as anyone to see what advantages there were in the cutting out of both foreign and domestic competition. His merger that is best remembered, because it lives in controversy, made a vast combine of cement companies. As cement is a prime need when a nation is in the midst of a building boom, this combine assured rich profits.

Sir Sandford Fleming, an important railway engineer and head of a cement concern, helped with the flotation by becoming honorary president of the new Canada Cement Company. Later he resigned and accused Aitken of making excessive profit for himself, and over-capitalization. Aitken undoubtedly did very well out of the merger. But his version of the break with Fleming had it that Fleming wanted him to buy up his cement company, the Exshaw, at an excessive price. Aitken refused, thinking it would not be sound business.

Young Max Aitken, with plenty of money coming in, liked to spend it on members of the family. His father, with such a generous son, was able to retire from the pulpit. He had been a painstaking and eloquent minister who brought up a family with all the care and thrift that we associate with the manse. It must have been a life of mental stress, for he once astonished his son by admitting he could not wholly believe the evangelical gospel his congregation paid him to preach. Now he changed. Religious doubts need no longer be repressed. He warmly thanked Max for his kindness. Max thought he was being thanked for providing his parents with a luxurious holiday. "No," said the Reverend William Aitken, "it's not for these comforts [a hired car and so forth] that I am thanking you. I am grateful beyond telling that I will never have to preach another damn sermon."

A millionaire, self-made, at the age of thirty-one, Max looked for a political career in Britain. He had so large a self-perpetuating fortune that he need no longer face the heart-in-the-mouth hazards of large-scale speculation. He prepared to indulge in the excitement of political battle and the rewards of statesmanship. He had been to England two years before to sell Canadian industrial bonds. He then met Bonar Law, who was also from New Brunswick and also son of a Presbyterian minister. Bonar Law does not seem to have been attracted to him at this first meeting. Circumstances now were different.

Aitken talked politics. He showed himself a sworn champion of tariffs and Imperial Preference. He was an amusing talker when he set out to be, whereas Bonar Law was not. There began between them one of the strangest, firmest, and most fruitful friendships in politics. Aitken was odd-looking, with his large head, unruly hair, wide, wide grin, and often twinkling eyes— just what the cartoonists were to like. His voice was much more distinctively Canadian than Bonar Law's. He talked, but also listened. He could be excellent fun. His energy seemed inexhaustible. Bonar Law was his exact opposite. He loved his armchair, his pipe, and playing bridge.

Aitken could make friends quickly. Not only Bonar Law but R. D. Blumenfeld, Wisconsin-born editor of the *Daily Express*, who taught him to play lawn tennis, and those brilliant young Tory leaders—Winston Churchill and F. E. Smith, later Earl of Birkenhead—took to him at once. Other influential men welcomed his companionship.

Before 1910 ended, the newcomer sat in Parliament as Member for Ashton-under-Lyne, having won it from the Liberals after an exciting and picturesque campaign in which he declared as the greatest issue of the day the solidarity of the Empire. Probably no other candidate deemed that question so urgent. Aitken chose the subject he knew best. At that time some votes in some constituencies were undoubtedly rewarded with money. How? Mr. Alan Wood, writing what he claimed to be the true history of Lord Beaverbrook, tells that, according to one story at Ashton-under-Lyne, "doubtless somewhat exaggerated," one lady used to

knock at door after door with the appealing formula: "Good
morning, I'm doing some canvassing for Mr. Aitken. Could I
use your lavatory, please?" After an interval the pulling of a
chain would be heard, the lady would emerge, she would express
her thanks, and as some appreciation would leave a pound on the
kitchen table. The pulling of chains would be heard in leisurely
progression all down the street. However, such a careful man as
Max Aitken would enjoy professional help to avoid the pitfalls
of British election law, and I imagine the story is much exaggerated.

To become an M.P. at the first attempt, especially in a constituency where the pronunciation of "cotton" as "caaton" was
at first mystifying, must be considered a signal achievement. Soon
Aitken was unpaid private secretary to Bonar Law, and once
again to be secretary to a man of high position proved a stepping
stone to astonishing success, including a knighthood in 1911.

Aitken's progress as a political figure in the lobbies of the
House of Commons—he was more effective there than when on
his feet in the chamber—showed a sudden spurt. Arthur James
Balfour, leader of the Conservative opposition, was induced,
partly by hostile pressure in his own party, to give way to somebody else. Almost in retirement, he eagerly gave much of his time
to philosophy and literature. Austen Chamberlain and Walter
Long were powerful contenders for the leadership. But rather
than split the party they gave way to a third candidate, no other
than Aitken's hero, Bonar Law. The two friends gave each other
invaluable help. Aitken imbued Bonar Law with driving force.
Bonar Law, a future prime minister, certified, as it were, Aitken's
impeccable character.

Inexhaustibly active, Aitken increased his political useful-
ness. When Britain clashed with Germany in the First World
War he went to the western front as "eyewitness" (a kind of
official war correspondent) with the Canadian army. He was not
as severely repressed as British correspondents were by the professional soldier's ingrained fear of disclosures that might help
the enemy. He shared Northcliffe's view that "This war cannot be
run in the dark" and his fear that "We shall lose this war by
secrecy."

He was made a baronet in 1916. The following year brought

Asquith's fall from office and the possibility that Bonar Law, as leader of the Conservative party, would become prime minister. Though Bonar Law was invited by the King to form a government, Lloyd George's claims to the war leadership of the country, as Aitken realized, were insuperable. Lloyd George, safely in supreme power, asked Aitken to go to the House of Lords to represent two or three important departments. The youngish politician, perhaps in two minds, accepted. To be ennobled, to possess yet another trophy of wonderful success, to choose the Canadian name of Lord Beaverbrook—all this must have been pleasing to a man who had been severely assailed in his native Canada and now had every right to hold his head high. But the time when a peer could be prime minister had gone. Lord Beaverbrook could never rule from 10 Downing Street. So ambitious a man could not fail to regret the chance he had sacrificed. He regretted it for the rest of his life.

When, in February 1918, Lloyd George made him head of the Ministry of Information, Beaverbrook proved to be a master of propaganda. This appointment excited some criticism, but Lloyd George replied that Beaverbrook was a man of great and exceptional organizing ability, and the first man to realize the propaganda value of films. Later Stanley Baldwin, a future prime minister, attributed to Beaverbrook a combination of "rare vision" and "ability to master details." Lord Northcliffe was to describe him as "one of the straightest men in the country."

A week or two before the war ended, Beaverbrook, who had had an operation for an enlarged gland in his neck, resigned his ministerial post. Though always deeply involved in politics, he was not again to be a minister until the Second World War, when as a stimulater of aircraft production he electrified all Britain. That was more than twenty years later. Now, one phase of his career ended; another began: though he remained the incessant politician, we see him as a press lord, battling against the *Daily Mail* of the long all-powerful Lord Northcliffe, the Napoleon of Fleet Street.

Although he had made friends with Blumenfeld and other leading editors, Beaverbrook, toward the end of the First World War, started his control of the *Daily Express* with the odds against him. Northcliffe was nearing the time when he could use the slogan, "Daily Mail—Million Sale." That newspaper's achievements were on everybody's lips. A jest about the paper by a comedian would make a music hall audience roar with laughter. The *Express*, bright though it was, with that American innovation, news on the front page, rarely sold three hundred thousand a day. Blumenfeld told Beaverbrook he could have the controlling interest for £17,500. That sum seemed small, but what would the paper's losses amount to before it started to pay its way? Northcliffe, probably without any ulterior motive, told Beaverbrook the paper would lose for him every penny he had. But Beaverbrook, if an amateur at first with no grip on the complexities of the newspaper industry, and his experienced henchman and teacher, Blumenfeld, were potentially a strong combination. Northcliffe rebuked me when I, a *Daily Mail* man, said the *Express* seemed to be mainly a typist's paper. "Young man," he warned me with a frown, "the *Express* is our greatest danger. Beaverbrook is learning fast." Sometimes he jeered at the *Express* as the Imitative Press, but there is such a thing as imitating a good product and then surpassing it.

Beaverbrook, believing it would pay to run his presses seven days a week, a sound principle, started the *Sunday Express*, but for a long time it added to his burdens. When a strong-minded Scotsman, John Gordon, became its editor and held that position year after year, it found a welcome place in an overcrowded field. His chief, duly grateful, helped Gordon to become probably the wealthiest salaried journalist in the Britain of our time. Beaverbrook had also excellent editors for the morning paper after the redoubtable Blumenfeld retired, first the Canadian Beverley Baxter and then Arthur Christiansen. In the art of displaying news attractively Christiansen had rivals but no equal. He left it to Beaverbook to dictate political policy whenever his chief wished to do so—and that was very often—while he himself became a supreme artist in makeup. The title of his autobiography, *Headlines All My Life*, indicated one of his main skills. As general manager Beaverbrook long had a Canadian, E. J. Robertson, a quiet, courteous, most able man.

The usual picture of Beaverbrook as a newspaper owner learning the hard way is of a man of kaleidoscopic moods, shifting breathlessly from sneers to flattery; bubbling with joy, and then shaking with rage; using three telephones at once; sending down to the staff below his office flat an unending stream of ideas, reprimands, praise, and instructions; now dealing with some paltry matter Northcliffe would have scorned to bother with; now swiftly dictating the line to take on a suddenly predominant issue. Artistic license sharpens and colors this picture. But no doubt Beaverbrook put all the energy he could into improving his newspapers, thought fast, and—a man of histrionic temperament—had many changes of mood. He could lash a man with contemptuous words, and a little later apologize for being unjust.

Despite what Northcliffe said in his office communiqués, Beaverbrook was not primarily an imitator. He stamped his personality on the *Express*—an exuberant, observant, fighting personality. He was not bound by stiff conventions. The finances of the oil world, the romances of making a fortune, the perplexities of international statecraft were to him neither sacred mysteries nor profane. He had them probed in simple English and with an air of masterly understanding. His readers gained the comfortable feeling that they were well informed. They might be gray-haired clerks bent over ledgers all day long, or junior girl typists with milk and a bun for lunch, but they had their notions of grandeur, fairy tales of wealth. Their morning paper colored their daydreams. Was not life an unpredictably romantic adventure? Did not young secretaries sometimes marry millionaires? Did not handsome legacies astonish the most unexpectant persons? Was not the world throbbing with events that made you exclaim, "Well, I never! Just fancy that!" And how silly the people in high positions often were! The *Express* went for them properly.

If your turn came—and you never knew, did you, in such a changing world?—you would show your better sense. If ever you read the *Times* you felt small and insignificant, under the rule of learned people who seemed always to be saying, "These great problems are not so simple as you think." But the *Express* did make them simple. You felt Lord Beaverbrook with his deep faith in Britain and her Empire thought just as you did. It made you feel three inches taller. Yes, the *Express* had its critics. So had the Empire. The cynics were always ready to snap and yap at what was fine and great. They could not understand why Beaverbrook pointed out the mistakes of the British Council, the favoritism the State showed to the Cooperative movement, and other inflaming thorns in his flesh. But Beaverbrook refused to be silenced. He went on and on, fighting all the time. He loved fighting. One of his maxims is said to have been: "I *always* dispute the umpire's decision."

Still the *Daily Mail* kept ahead. It had immense prestige. It had done so much to help to win the First World War. We who had been soldiers in the shell-battered trenches, while our German opponents were safe in deep dugouts, were grateful to it for the reforms it forced on our commanders. It was still to us the soldiers' friend. In 1922, the year of Northcliffe's pathetic death, with a mind deranged, it was selling 1,784,000 copies, with the *Express* standing at almost a million fewer, 793,000.

In that year Beaverbrook bought from Sir Edward Hulton his *Evening Standard* and provincial papers, kept the *Standard*, and sold the provincial papers to Rothermere for as much as he had given Hulton for the whole mixed bag. The *Standard* was the surviving evening companion of a once powerful morning paper for which W. E. Gladstone had a great respect.

Beaverbrook went vigorously into the task of improving it, notably with bookish articles by Arnold Bennett, whom he had put in charge of British propaganda to France in the First World War. Later he attracted from the *Star* the incomparable cartoonist, David Low. Among writers for the paper were H. G. Wells and Dean Inge. Even readers who disliked the quirks, somersaults, and personal gibes in the editorials, which day after day reflected Beaverbrook's own mind, became attached to a paper with such a galaxy of talent.

Beaverbrook showed his political power in 1922 by helping to topple Lloyd George and to put Bonar Law in 10 Downing Street. At last we had a declared policy of tranquillity after Britain's disasters, delusions, and dissensions. But the new prime minister had little peace. A victim of throat cancer, he died after being prime minister for only two hundred days. This was a heartbreaking blow to Beaverbrook, who, whatever his weaknesses might be, could be a staunch friend. Five years later he had to endure an even more shattering blow in the death of his wife at the age of forty-two.

When in 1929 Stanley Baldwin's government suffered defeat and made way for Ramsay MacDonald's second government, it seemed to Beaverbrook the right moment for launching his Empire Free Trade Policy, embodying much that he had been revolving in his mind since he first took an interest in Joseph Chamberlain's tariff policy. He conducted the campaign with ruthless astuteness, though the policy presented difficulties in a fast changing world. How could we expect the British Dominions to let our exports of machinery monopolize their markets when they had begun to manufacture for themselves? If we were to do their manufacturing in return for our imports of food, how were we to enable our own farmers to flourish? Was protection for our agriculture feasible? Would the nation put up with taxes on food? Such questions as these arose immediately, as in the great days of Joseph Chamberlain's crusade.

Many citizens came to look on the struggle not as a campaign for strengthening our economy when our commercial and military power dwindled, but as an onslaught by press lords to overwhelm an annoying rival in politics, Stanley Baldwin. To the impartial observer, each side seemed to be daubing the other with abuse. Baldwin spoke of quickly acquired newspaper fortunes and power going to the head like wine, driving Rothermere and Beaverbrook to dictate, domineer, and blackmail. He accused the pair of behaving like prostitutes—"They wish to exert the traditional privilege of the harlot throughout the ages, that of power without responsibility," a phrase suggested by Rudyard Kipling.

Beaverbrook could hit back just as hard. This is what he said when Baldwin's approval of Empire Free Trade wavered: "Mr. Baldwin is the champion of all backsliders. We believe we have brought him to grace; we lift up our voices in a hymn of rejoicing; and we have hardly got through the first line of it before we see him crawling down the aisle again."

When I went to see Baldwin, a poor rheumatic cripple in his old age, to give him information about his distant relatives, the Kiplings in Yorkshire, he looked back sadly on his career. Thinking of accusations that he had been a poor guardian of national defense in a time of growing peril, he asked, "Do you think history will vindicate me?" But in the thirties his reputation stood

high. He seemed to have got the better of his chief press adversary
in the encounter just briefly described. Nor was another remarkable success far off, Edward VIII's abdication. Beaverbrook strove
hard to stave it off with what the King termed "Max's natural
belligerence." But the King was less concerned to stay on the
throne than his champion would have liked. He let the crown go
without a fierce struggle.

While these political activities were afoot, Beaverbrook, the
most powerful leader of the press after Northcliffe's death,
worked himself and his staff as hard as he could. Competition
stimulated his pugnacity and enterprise. He picked for his editorial staffs men in whom a mass public could delight. John
Gordon, with his exposures of political trickery and treachery
and of bureaucratic tomfoolery, became a much appreciated
Defender of the Little Man. A favorite of another kind, whom
death denied many years of success such as Gordon enjoyed so
deservedly, was Viscount Castlerosse, an Irish grandee of ponderous girth who always reminded me of Thackeray's disquisi-
tions in *Vanity Fair* on how to live on nothing a year. He had
what you might call financial worries, except that they never
seemed to worry him. He lived a gay and expensive life and
vastly amused Beaverbrook. With his chief's encouragement and
help Castlerosse wrote outspoken society gossip for the *Sunday
Express*.

A reckless newspaper war in the thirties, especially in the
morning paper field, called for Beaverbrook's fighting prowess.
He responded eagerly. One trusty weapon was his wealth. His
Express could stand higher costs. Some rivals were imperiled by
them. The *Daily News*, the *Daily Chronicle*, the *Daily Herald* all
suffered increasing pressure. Julius Salter Elias (later Lord South-
wood) developed a system of gifts for those who would give an
order for the *Herald*. No longer was that old standby, insurance
for the subscriber—he need not be a reader—the inducement.
Elias's legions of canvassers offered silk stockings, fountain pens,
cameras, and what not. The cost to the papers became monstrous.
It had to stop. Elias was bluntly told that other proprietors would
do everything they could to force up his already menacing costs if
he persisted with what were called free gifts. It was agreed that

these were to cease, that nothing below cost should be offered to subscribers, but that canvassing, free insurance, and competitions should go on.

However, Elias badly wanted to buy more readers. He thought of an ingenious method to get around the agreement. His company, Odhams, published popular books on a large scale. These included a dictionary, the *Home Doctor*, and so forth. Why not offer these cheap books at cost price to those who would order the *Herald* for ten weeks? Then he would be offering attractive inducements without breaking faith with his competitors. That was *his* idea.

The plan worked and he developed it by offering a complete set of Dickens in sixteen volumes. Fleet Street became enraged. "Elias," Beaverbrook declaimed, "this is war—war to the death. I shall fight you to the bitter end"—and with this threat he plunged an imaginary sword through his foe's body. Elias fought on. The *Express, Mail,* and *News Chronicle* (the *Daily News* and *Daily Chronicle* had merged) offered new readers their sets of Dickens as promptly as they could and at much expense. Even this beloved genius did not suffice. Canvassers began to bestow on eager recipients overcoats, mackintoshes, boots and shoes, ladies' underwear, tea sets, mangles, mincing machines. Were old readers chagrined at seeing a shower of gifts for new readers? Not at all. The faithful old reader of the *Mail* would subscribe to the *Express* and collect his reward. His neighbor the faithful old reader of the *Express* would subscribe to the *Mail* and collect *his* reward. For ten weeks they exchanged papers, and everybody was happy. Everybody perhaps except the circulation seekers, who found the cost of their war mounted to menacing heights.

The *Express*, livelier than ever in makeup and tone, with a brilliant news service, pushed its circulation ahead of the *Mail's.* The *Herald* did even better for a time. Its gifts enabled it to claim to be the first paper in the world to reach a sale of two million copies a day. But the gifts were its undoing in the race. It had to skimp its news services to keep on. The *Express* sent special correspondents to hunt exciting news all over the world. It enjoyed scoop after scoop. It had not yet to face the competition of the tabloid *Daily Mirror* as transformed by Harry Guy

Bartholomew's notions of what would appeal to the entertainment-loving masses.

The *Express* was no longer termed, as it had been by Northcliffe, the Imitative Press but the Sunshine Press, for it sought to radiate encouragement and confidence in the multitude of "little men" who made it prosper. Beaverbrook called on them to enjoy peace with a good heart, and on May 23, 1938, printed this message: "There will be no major war in Europe this year or next. So go about your own business with confidence in the future and fear not." He added: "Provide us with airplanes, anti-aircraft guns, and ammunition. Develop our own Imperial resources and give our races prosperity and happiness at home." The public fastened on the assurance, often repeated, that there would be no war. Did Beaverbrook believe this or was he, as some thought, trying to create a climate of opinion to encourage advertising in his newspapers? I believe his faith in continued peace was sincere. The outbreak in 1939 of a war of bloodshed, the Second World War, put an end to the competitive extravagances of the circulation war. Now Beaverbrook was again to be a minister and by his ruthless driving force startle the country.

Not that he had ever lost his interest in politics and power. He never ceased to practice those secret persuasions, which the censorious describe as intrigues. Much of what he said in print or in advice to politicians had not only the ring of sincerity but the backing of exceptional business experience. Certainly he could change his mind with a speed which many critics regarded as a sign of utter irresponsibility. But his faith in the Empire and his hatred of war, his scepticism about the League of Nations, his belief that we alone could not hope to police the world, made sense.

When that man of destiny, that man who by the mercy of God could lead Britain into greatness—Winston Churchill—replaced Neville Chamberlain as head of the government, he appointed Beaverbrook as Minister of Aircraft Production. There could have been no more suitable post for Beaverbrook and no more suitable man for the post. He had nothing of the gentle English creed of loving the game beyond the prize. He wanted to win at any cost, by whatever means, not by copybook maxims but by brutal, slave-driving discipline for those, however eminent, who wanted to play weekend golf when defeat faced Britain if she did not get more airplanes. All his primal instincts came into action. He was a man of war.

His genius for persuasion won over the housewives. They cheerfully gave up their saucepans to be turned into Spitfires and Hurricanes. (The Spitfires we talked of then were not golf balls, nor were Hurricanes the hundred-miles-an-hour storms with sweet feminine names.) No one ever wanted power, or a fortune, or the love of his loved one more than Beaverbrook wanted the airplanes that were to win the Battle of Britain.

The impetus he gave to aircraft production provided the climax of his political career. In later ministerial posts he became furiously quarrelsome. He termed Ernest Bevin a "blundering ass." He seemed to think even less of "that miserable little man, Attlee, who can't even control his own party." In plain English, he became impossible. Even Churchill, so often his stimulating crony and confidant, could stand his conduct no longer. Reconciliation came after a while, for Churchill was a generous man, but Beaverbrook's days of political power were over. He still inspired his newspapers with his own explosive hatreds. He opposed with slashing lustiness our seeking to join the Common Market. Appearing before the first Royal Commission on the press, he made a fine impression of frankness and desire to be fair. I felt that he was becoming a Grand Old Man in the familiar British fashion.

As it may be thought I have an undue bias in his favor, let me tell how he showed me a remarkable and continuing kindness. When I was editing the *Yorkshire Post* the Churchill government asked me to help in thwarting the Communists' efforts to get university meetings to pass resolutions in their favor. These, though induced by tactics that will appear, were acclaimed by the *Daily Worker* as momentous revolutionary victories. A mission entrusted to me was to debate with Mr. D. N. Pritt, Q.C., who had been expelled from the Labour party for writing in support of the USSR. He had become an extreme leftist and was now denouncing the supposed iniquities of the British press. We had a large and vociferous meeting of University of London students. For a couple of hours or so we on the government side were

clearly in the majority. A Conservative office-bearer at my side
assured me that we could not lose. Then students began slipping
out, perhaps to study, perhaps to anticipate the closing time
ordained by the licensing laws. Communist speakers still held
on in the spirit of a filibuster. The prompter at my side began to
look forlorn. He tried to get the vote taken, but the Communists,
an ever eager proportion of the dwindling audience, objected
with a synthetically furious passion for free speech. When their
victory was certain by a sweeping majority, they agreed to a
count of hands and noisily made the most of it.

I noticed there stayed to the end a remarkable number of
busily writing recorders. But except in the *Daily Worker* the
meeting won from the press nothing but a brief item or so. A day
or two later a cable reached me from the West Indies. It brought
me warm thanks from Beaverbrook, in almost biblical phrases,
for my fairness to his papers and my general defense of the press.
Those busy shorthand writers had sent him a verbatim report of
everything I said about him and his papers. The *Daily Express*
offered some rivalry to the *Yorkshire Post* in our own mass circulation area, but when acting as spokesman for the press I
should never have thought of trying to belittle a rival. Ordinary
decency would have prevented such an attack on such an occasion. But Beaverbrook seemed truly grateful, and on many occasions had me warmly praised in his papers.

A letter of his I especially valued was one that wished well
a scheme of mine for saving persons innocently involved in some
tragedy or other exciting event from being pestered by a horde of
news hunters. It seemed to me as chairman of the Press Council
that with the significant increase in reporters this problem of
pestering, owing to force of numbers, would become still more
acute and unless remedied would harm the reputation of journalism. Provincial papers often make friendly arrangements to keep
down the number of reporters putting questions to a harassed
victim and then share the information gained. Could some such
scheme be arranged for the London Press? Beaverbrook encouraged me to continue my crusade. But a difficulty I could never
overcome was that Fleet Street news editors would not agree to
any self-denial in a suddenly arising case lest they should rob
themselves of exclusive news.

My last message from Beaverbrook came only a few days before he died. It was to thank me for something I had written for *World's Press News,* an account of the birthday dinner given in his honor by Lord Thomson of Fleet to 658 guests. This was the most representative gathering of men controlling, working for and profiting by the press that London ever saw. Once again, the old warrior surprised us all. Word went around from his friends, people who should know, that he was probably too frail to appear. At best, we were assured, he would look in for five minutes. I thought I saw his second wife, the former Lady Dunn, whom he married a year before, quietly come in as if to await his appearance. Suddenly there arose a piercing fanfare from Royal Air Force trumpeters, and there with a smiling, cherubic Lord Thomson of Fleet stepped an even more broadly smiling Beaverbrook, not looking at all frail but bright-eyed and eager to spot with Christian name greetings his close friends in that great Hail-to-the-Chief audience. He rejoiced to see the Mounties, the feathered Indian braves, and the stage-set of the Old Manse at Newcastle, New Brunswick, where he lived as a child—surprises planned for him by the ever-resourceful Roy Thomson. The old man joined cheerfully in singing "Land of Hope and Glory," put in the program at his own request.

Would he make a speech? Indeed he did, one of his best, his Canadian voice resonant, genial, persuasive. He did not attempt the peacock plumage of an Edmund Burke's oratory or the elaborate, almost Virgilian metaphors of the fifth Lord Rosebery, whose son sat near him; but gave us intimate, man-to-man talk, swinging from grave to gay, from lively to severe, with flashes of autobiography, character analysis, fragments of history, legpulls for his host, warm praise for the mass of journalists so "vitally important and bitterly maligned." The frequent smile emphasized insistence that the journalist must be a man of optimism. Above all, he spoke of himself as always an apprentice—an apprentice to finance, to politics, to Fleet Street, to industrial production in wartime. In a touching surprise curtain line that suggested the faithful Calvinist, he wondered what he would be apprenticed to next.

Yes, he had been an apprentice to Fleet Street and became one of its great leaders in the Northcliffe tradition. He was a master of our craft. Even Sir William Haley, no admirer of some of Beaverbrook's fighting methods, said: "The *Express* newspapers were constantly on the attack. The people and things to be attacked were often ill chosen. There was always something to engage the reader's attention. The reader might sometimes be enraged; he would never be bored. He was continually entertained."

Beaverbrook will not fade into a legend as the years pass, and more monsters disport themselves in the Fleet Street deep. His books will remain as a memorial. Such works as *Politicians and the Press, Politicians and the War,* and *The Decline and Fall of Lloyd George* show his gifts as a historian of his own time and his mastery of an emphatic, pithy, often biblical style.

Now, finally, back to the question whether Beaverbrook, so much a politician, deserved the title of journalist. He ran papers from a political motive. They enabled him to conduct ("quite frankly and legitimately," as the Royal Commission on the Press reported in 1962) such campaigns as those for British Empire ideals and against Britain's joining the Common Market. His campaigns roused opposition and met with some signal failures, but he conducted them with lusty zeal, enjoyment, and journalistic aptitude. Sir Andrew Caird, of the *Daily Mail*, was fond of telling me, "Repetition is the soul of journalism." Beaverbrook never forgot that maxim when campaigning. He drove in his points with hammer blow after hammer blow. He did not turn his newspapers into dull propaganda sheets. He had a Northcliffe's keenness for news and spent vast sums on reporting events all over the world.

Beaverbrook also developed journalistic features such as those with a names-make-news basis. Whether he or his henchman, Christiansen, invented the maxim for his reporters, "Get in on the inside," it bore the stamp of his own methods in many spheres. Though he did not revolutionize journalism as Northcliffe did, where Northcliffe left off he carried on in a bold, pioneering spirit. He was a born businessman, he took to politics as a fox hound takes to hunting, and he made himself, by persevering experiments, a master of journalism. Some people, especially foes, may have thought of him as having the menace and destructiveness of a tornado. The metaphor did him injustice. He did not resemble a violent force of nature. He was far more subtle and had a far closer insight into character than most of his embittered rivals. Exceptional business powers and lifelong readiness to learn—and to teach—helped to make him a giant of British journalism, feared by rivals and affectionately admired by most of those he drove as hard in the service of his newspapers as he drove himself. A touching tribute was paid to him by his son and heir, the Honorable John William Max Aitken, who had a most gallant record as a fighter pilot in the Second World War. This Max thought his unique father should be the one Lord Beaverbrook. He himself is content to be known as Sir Max Aitken, Baronet.

11

Sir William Haley

The editor who changed the face of the Times

When in 1952 it was announced that Sir William Haley had resigned from the office of director-general of the British Broadcasting Corporation to become editor of the *Times*, many eyebrows were raised, for he had established the reputation of being the strongest and, by any test, the most successful ruler of Broadcasting House since the redoubtable creator of the BBC, John Reith. Moreover, he had just inaugurated auspiciously the most important extension of British broadcasting since its foundation, by taking experimental television out of the cold storage to which it had been consigned on the outbreak of war in 1939, and integrating a full service of viewing into the BBC's output.

There was no evidence that Haley at the age of fifty-one had tired of the work, nor had he ever been known to exhibit symptoms of distaste for the considerable powers with which the office of director general is vested.

Seen in terms of magnitude, he was renouncing control of Britain's most intensive medium of communication with a potential audience of some twenty-five million, in order to edit a venerable newspaper whose daily sale was about 230,000 copies. His explanation was ideally simple and, for dedicated journalists, it sufficed. "You must remember," he said, "that I'm a journalist. I've always regarded the editor of the *Times* as the head of my profession."

Thus was the mystique of the *Times* demonstrated again. To those who knew the history of the *Times*, Haley's choice recalled particularly an event nearly a century earlier, when the prime minister, Lord Palmerston, offered the then editor, John Thadeus Delane, "a high place in the Civil Service" at a time of life when he might well have begun to see something increasingly attractive in a less exacting occupation. Explaining his rejection of the offer, Delane wrote, "My whole life is bound up with the Paper. I must either work for it or not at all."

To appreciate the achievements of Sir William Haley in his fourteen years' editorship of the *Times*, it is necessary to envisage the institution called "The Paper" as it existed when he became its editor. Such a perspective requires an awareness of the restrictive influence that could be exerted on the editor's independence by the tentacles of tradition; and a consciousness of such factors as the hereditary element in the ownership, the standard of scholarship prevailing among the senior staff, and the level of intelligence assumed in its readers. Then, despite the air of altruism pervading the proprietorship, commercial viability lost none of its usual importance; the annual accounts were considered realistically. The enlistment of talented writers for its staff had still to be accomplished in face of a strict rule of anonymity. As expressed by John Walter III, the *Times* required "absolute devotion." Exceptionally gifted men were expected to accept the rule without complaint for a lifetime of service, with never a by-line for their encouragement.

There still lingered at home and abroad a belief originating in the nineteenth century, despite frequent repudiation, that the *Times* was the mouthpiece of the British government. This fiction drew sustenance from the fact that the policy of the paper had been always to recognize that the government of the day had the practical task of carrying on the nation's business and should receive general support in acknowledgement of that responsibility. Nevertheless, that restraining influence had never prevented the adoption of a critical attitude toward the actions of the secretary of state for foreign affairs when criticism seemed to

Courtesy of *The Times*

SIR WILLIAM HALEY

be warranted; for which reason no such minister could be indifferent to the view of the *Times*.

When in the early years of the twentieth century, misfortune
and financial stringency compelled a sale that brought Northcliffe into the position of chief proprietor, the paper felt the
installation of a new, electrifying influence. "I don't know how
you will make it succeed," said the managing director, Moberly
Bell, who had been Northcliffe's staunch ally in the deal, "but
I am sure you will." For himself, the new chief proprietor saw
the operation as "getting the barnacled-covered whale off the
rocks and safely into deep waters." He did not specify the means
to that end. The situation was that the Walter family still had
a minority holding; but that apart, Northcliffe had declared himself devoid of any desire to impose his will upon the *Times*, and
had endorsed the well-recognized independence of the editor.
Nevertheless, he found that the staff recognized the inevitability
of change if the sales were to be lifted from the perilous level of
twenty-eight thousand copies.

In practice, this understanding meant that when something
in Northcliffe's abundant flow of suggestions did not offend
against the well-established principles of the *Times*, the editor
proved amenable, and Northcliffe gracious. Anything to the
contrary had no future, though the chief proprietor might try
repeatedly to insinuate it by devious means. There were moments
when, frustrated, he recalled that the *Times* office occupied the
site of an ancient monastery and he railed in derision at "Ye
old Black Friars." Still, the Friars, hurt and silent, adhered to
their familiar ritual.

It was hardly to be expected that eventually they would
commemorate his good works in such a stained glass window as
that which glows in Volume 4 of the official *History of the Times*.
In the serene aftermath of Northcliffe's turbulent existence, it
was possible for the historian to see him as "the saviour of *The
Times* . . . unquestionably the greatest popular jounalist of his
time," and to perceive that "his deep respect for the public weal
and healthy public opinion made him supreme in his time, as it
had Barnes and Delane in their day. Like them, he was a journalist in the old and true sense of the word. . . . *The Times* was
not his creation, but he re-created it. Yet he never felt at home

Courtesy of *The Times*

WILLIAM REES-MOGG

in it. He did not learn the lesson that in the office of *The Times* personal power, whether of the proprietor or editor, must be limited. The quality that gave the paper its distinction was not conferred by one man; it was the contribution of a society."

With Northcliffe's death in 1922, his interest as chief proprietor of the *Times* had inevitably to be sold. A formidable bid by Lord Rothermere for his brother's place was overcome partly by the determination of the reigning John Walter to eliminate any suggestion of a continuance of the Northcliffe influence, and partly—perhaps chiefly—by the skill with which the negotiations for the sale were handled by the paper's managing director, Sir Campbell Stuart. After some tense moments, Northcliffe's interest was bought, jointly, by the Honorable John Astor and John Walter V, for £1,580,000, of which Astor provided by far the greater part and thus became chief proprietor.

Although Major Astor, thirty-six years old, was a director of the *Observer* (the Sunday newspaper of which his elder brother William Waldorf Astor was proprietor), he was not intimately involved in the *Observer*'s control. On graduating at Oxford, he had chosen a military career. After serving with distinction throughout the First World War, he retired from the army and was turning toward politics when he was invited to join John Walter in opening a new chapter in the history of the *Times*.

By nature he was a quiet, clearheaded man in whom thought preceded speech; in some ways the antithesis of the impulsive Northcliffe. He was destined to acquire a unique place for himself in the newspaper communities of Britain and the Commonwealth. He gave his patronage and his wise counsel to so many societies of the press that he was once styled "The Squire of Fleet Street," and when in 1956 he was raised to the peerage as Lord Astor of Hever, the event was accorded such general acclaim in the journalistic community as is rarely evoked by the bestowal of an honor on a newspaper proprietor.

On his becoming chief proprietor of the *Times* he expressed complete agreement with Walter's view that the traditional code and practices of Printing House Square should be restored to full vigor. That necessitated the dismissal of the then editor, Wickham Steed, because he, though long in the service of the *Times* had, on promotion to the editorship by Northcliffe, so permeated the paper with his patron's personality and policies as to make the *Times* simply an echo of the *Daily Mail*.

His place was filled by recalling Steed's predecessor, Geoffrey Dawson, who had resisted Northcliffe's pressure to the point at which, in 1919, he could endure no longer the chief proprietor's endless exhortations and imperious directions that disregarded the independence of the editor as previously understood; and resignation became the only honorable course. Eleven years earlier when Dawson as editor of the Johannesburg *Star* was spending a holiday in England, Northcliffe had met him and resolved in his own mind that Dawson should be the next editor of the *Times*, though the post was not to fall vacant for four years. Dawson seemed eminently the *Times* type of person. From Oxford University, with a Fellowship of All Souls to certify his intellectual quality, he was selected to be one of a group of young civil servants to restore the ways of peaceful administration in South Africa after the Boer War. From that task he passed to the editorship of Johannesburg's daily *Star*, with appointment as the *Times* resident correspondent added thereto. Soon after Northcliffe had installed him at Printing House Square, the editorship seemed to fit him like a glove, and throughout the testing time of the First World War his relationship with both the chief proprietor and John Walter was never seriously disturbed. But with the end of hostilities and the emergence of postwar political problems that agitated the overactive mind of Northcliffe whose general health had suffered a decline, tension developed between th two men and ended in a breach that was never repaired, thereby demonstrating, according to Northcliffe's biographers, that "membership of a university *corps d'elite* was no guarantee of sensitiveness to latent tragedy."

The restoration of Dawson in 1922 resulted in his continuance in office for a further nineteen years. Toward the end of this extended term he steered the *Times* through the two most critical years of the Second World War. For him, it was a more difficult period than any phase of the earlier war by reason of the nightly aerial bombardment of London, in the course of which the *Times* building was hit and grievously damaged. In January 1939 he had expressed a wish to retire, but it was not until October 1941 that office conditions were favorable to a change, and he was able to retire to one of the Yorkshire dales. There, after only three years of retirement, he died.

As Dawson's editorship passes into history, there is an increasing tendency to censure him in ever stronger terms for the support accorded by the *Times* to Chamberlain's policy of appeasement. In the context of this work such criticism is relevant only for any instructive light it may cast on the dual function of editorial opinion, which must sometimes interpret the government to the people and sometimes represent popular opinion to a government that is acting contrary to public feeling. A dictum of Printing House Square insisted that the *Times*, or any other newspaper, should be "not an organ through which the government should influence the people, but an organ through which the people should influence the government."

Dawson was conscious of the strong sentiment prevailing at home and in the Commonwealth that arose from the concept of the 1914–18 conflict as "a war to end war." It led to a conviction that to contemplate another war would be a betrayal of more than a million men of Britain and the Commonwealth who had sacrificed their lives that war should cease to be an instrument of policy. He was highly sensitive also to the possibility that a British government might embark on a foreign policy in which war was a hazard, and that the Dominions, disapproving, would proffer no military help.

Dawson might well have been impressed by an incident in 1936, when the then prime minister, Stanley Baldwin, addressed in Westminster Hall a contingent of four thousand Canadian veterans who were returning from a pilgrimage to their battlefields of 1914–18. Baldwin told them, "If Europe and the world can find no other way of settling disputes than the way of war— even now, when we are still finding and burying the bodies of those who fell twenty years ago—the world deserves to perish." As the prime minister finished that statement, said the *Times* report, "There was silence for a minute. Then the stillness was shattered by a great burst of cheering."

Even so, events were to prove that Dawson was wrong in his judgment, by which the great influence of the *Times* was exerted in favor of conciliation when conciliation was no longer a realistic policy. In this, Barrington-Ward, as deputy editor and an editorial writer, supported his chief without demur, though the reasons for their harmony might be dissimilar.

Experience of combatant service in the First World War was a major factor in Barrington-Ward's life, and affected his outlook profoundly. After taking his M.A. degree at Balliol College, Oxford, he graduated as a barrister and then moved toward making journalism his profession by serving as editorial secretary to Dawson. In 1914, immediately on the declaration of war, and twelve months after he had joined the *Times*, Barrington-Ward enlisted, and was soon in action as an infantry officer. His quality as a soldier is attested by a record of two decorations for gallantry and distinguished service, and by his having been mentioned in dispatches three times.

At the war's end he joined the staff of the *Observer*, and as its assistant editor he resigned some eight years later to become assistant editor of the *Times*. When in 1941 he succeeded Dawson in the editorship, he was well versed in every branch of the editorial side of the office. Being one of the most industrious of men, he had found time to acquaint himself, and to be interested in, every other aspect of the paper's well-being. His term as editor was destined to last only seven years, and for more than half that period the war continued, with the common peril dictating major policy. For the remainder of his time a Labour government held office, and as its task was largely one of domestic restoration and as Barrington-Ward (according to the *History of the Times*) was a "Radical Tory," those years offered little scope for the kind of editorial proclamation that earned for the *Times* in earlier days the unofficial title of "The Thunderer." He contrived to find time to travel intensively, viewing the postwar world as an exercise essential to an understanding of new international problems. In these exertions, as in his habit of working fourteen hours a day in the office, he gave inadequate consideration to a physical constitution that had suffered in the arduous experiences of long war service in his youth. At the time of his appointment to the editorship, he wrote "for a private eye" some reflections in which he acknowledged, "My life was really forfeit in 1914 and it is the merest, the least deserved of flukes that I have survived to enjoy so much of which war robbed the pick of my contemporaries." Seven years after that disclosure, he died in South Africa, in the course of a cruise undertaken for the benefit of his health, at the age of fifty-seven.

That early termination of an editorship left a problem of succession. At the time of Barrington-Ward's death, the paper was in the capable hands of its deputy editor, Mr. F. W. Casey, a product of Trinity College, Dublin. He was a man of sound judgment, professional dedication, and natural charm, with a record of twenty-eight years' service to the *Times* in Paris, Washington, and Printing House Square. A lengthy term as editor could not be expected of him, but he filled that exacting office with distinction until his retirement in 1952 enabled Sir William Haley to receive a call to what he regarded as the headship of his profession.

Haley was right, at that time, in thus assessing the importance of the position. Whether British journalists, by and large, rated the *Times* as the best of all newspapers (and as tastes differ, some did not), there was likely to be general agreement in regarding its editorship as the most responsible command in the whole range of the press. The independence of the editor and the techniques of journalism had to be exercised within a complex of precedents and of rulings, written and unwritten, deriving from more than a century of history, and so continuously relevant to the conduct of the paper that it is scarcely possible to describe the career of any of its editors without relating also much of the story of Printing House Square. It was just because the traditions of that establishment were indeed so strong and deeply rooted, that neither the professional genius nor the tactical resourcefulness of Northcliffe could prevail upon what he thought was his own property.

Of those institutional factors, the Haley of 1952 had some knowledge gained at an impressionable age, for when just out of his teens he had served on the staff of the *Times* as a shorthand telephonist. Obviously, he had gone farther afield to prove his worth or he would not have been constructing what was popularly regarded as a dictatorship in Broadcasting House when he received the irresistible recall to Printing House Square. Obviously also, he was a remarkable man.

One of the initial educational advantages attending the birth in Jersey of William John Haley to a Yorkshire father and a

Jersey mother, was that he became bilingual, Jersey being one of the Channel Islands that William, Duke of Normandy, incorporated in the United Kingdom at the time of the Norman conquest. Other educational advantages invariable in the "standard pattern" of *Times* editors were not his. He did not graduate at Oxford or Cambridge. He was sent to a college in Jersey, though later, when he had achieved distinction in his own right, Cambridge did something toward bringing him into line with his predecessors by conferring on him the honorary degree of LL.D., with a Fellowship of Jesus College; and Haley showed his appreciation by taking as active an interest in the university and college as his duties allowed.

Long before that development, the year of his birth (1901) had become relevant to the course of his career. During his schooldays the declaration of war in 1914 came to mean that military service might be in store for him. But before he reached the appropriate age, he was already serving at sea as a wireless operator in the merchant navy. In 1919 that experience enabled him to make his first contact with journalism through the telephone network of the *Times*. He secured employment as a shorthand telephonist at Printing House Square, receiving news messages, in which capacity he was responsible ultimately to the editor, Wickham Steed, but in practice was answerable to Steed's secretary.

Following the contents of the paper each day, he perceived that much of the material he was receiving from correspondents in Europe, such as extracts from Continental newspapers and similar routine stories, was not being published; it was not sufficiently selective. Boldly, he submitted a memorandum suggesting that economy and other benefits would accrue if these messages were directed in the first instance to the *Times* office in Brussels, and there evaluated before transmission to London, thus reducing the volume to manegeable proportions and increasing the chances of publication.

His proposal found favor, with the consequence that the general manager sent for him and packed him off to Brussels to put his plan into operation. It is significant of the impression that the nineteen-year-old Haley must have created that his instructions were reinforced by authority to draw from the cashier one thousand pounds to finance the operation. Another person who obviously must have formed a high opinion (indeed, the highest opinion) of him was Wickham Steed's secretary, Haley's "former boss," as one of his colleagues described her, for she became his wife in the following year.

In 1922, when Haley was well-established in Brussels, he was "discovered" by one Frank Hall, general manager and former editor of the *Manchester Evening News*, a keen detector of talent. The young man was attracted by the reportership that Hall offered; and soon Haley and his wife moved to what was then the second most important newspaper center in the United Kingdom. In addition to its own strong local press, Manchester was the city chosen for the production of northern editions of several national newspapers. It was also the headquarters of the *Manchester Guardian*, unique in being a provincially produced daily newspaper with a national circulation and a considerable reputation abroad. The *Guardian* was, and is, owned by the same company as the *Evening News*, the predominant afternoon paper of the region.

In the space of eight years, Haley graduated from reporter to managing editor of the *Manchester Evening News*. Moreover, as he progressed it became evident to the directors of the two newspapers that he had an aptitude for organization and finance, then rare among journalists who concentrate upon the technicalities of their craft. Thus, in the year that he was appointed managing editor of the *Evening News* he was also elected to the board of the company and designated joint managing director of both newspapers. It has been set to Haley's credit that he devised the means by which the prosperity of the *Evening News* could be employed to buttress the *Guardian* at a time when its financial position made survival precarious.

Other gestures of proprietorial confidence in these exceptional gifts were made after Haley's promotion to the boardroom. He was nominated by the company for membership of the governing bodies of the Press Association (the principal agency for home news) and of the associated organization, Reuters (source of the greatest volume of foreign news). Here again his outstanding ability was so evident that when, with the coming of World War II, it was necessary to establish an understanding with the press of the Commonwealth about wartime services, Haley was asked to visit the countries concerned and to exchange views.

What he accomplished was of considerable consequence to the agencies concerned and also was regarded by the wartime Ministry of Information as a valuable achievement in relation to the ministry's functions. Having thus made a deep impression in official quarters, it was not surprising that in 1943 when British broadcasting was in need of a strong directing hand, Haley was appointed to the newly created office of editor in chief at Broadcasting House, with editorial authority over all services. In the light of after-events, it is clear that this step was but a temporary measure to enable him to familiarize himself with the structure and performance of the corporation before being elevated to the peak position of director general, in which capacity his first action was to abolish the post of editor in chief.

Thus he was responsible for the direction of broadcasting during the last two years of war, and at the war's end he was honored by being created a Knight of the Order of St. Michael and St. George, an award usually reserved for outstanding military and administrative achievements overseas, and thus signifying that his service had extended significantly beyond the United Kingdom. To that distinction, France added somewhat later the insignia of Chevalier of the Legion of Honor.

Then opened that phase in which, with Norman Collins (who later went over to commercial broadcasting), he took British television from the half-developed stage in which it had been set aside on the outbreak of war, and put it on a course that was to make viewers more numerous than listeners. That result was achieved before he relinquished his vast command over communications in favor of the editorship of a newspaper that was read by only a fraction of his former subscribers.

So he arrived at Printing House Square, in some ways the most improbable editor in the long history of the *Times*. Here for example, was an editor with a knighthood where previously the rule was that any member of the editorial staff who accepted a title or lesser honor (other than war decorations) must resign, since such marks of favor bestowed by government recommendation might signify a sense of obligation to an authority toward which the *Times* maintained an inflexible independence.

No such divided loyalty could be suspected in Sir William Haley. A close student of politics, possessing a newspaperman's knowledge of partisan operations, overt and covert, his BBC record shows that he was ever alert, and resistant, to any attempt by the three governments of his period to impair the independence of the corporation, other than by the acceptance of those restraints that wartime security demanded. Now, as editor of the *Times*, he, who had made many rules elsewhere, was subject to the complex code that had done much to make it the newspaper whose editorship represented the summit of his ambition.

The transition from a national broadcasting corporation that was young, exuberantly enterprising, striving to please everybody, to an institution whose history began in the reign of George III, and whose daily activities were influenced by the accumulated experience of nearly two hundred years, did not daunt the editor-elect. While it is doubtful whether the responsibilities of any eminence to which he aspired would daunt this unusual editor of the *Times*, he had also the advantage of having conducted a reconnaissance of the institution some thirty years earlier, and he knew how little it had changed fundamentally. He appears to have accepted serenely the situation as it existed at the time he took charge, and to have exercised his talents within the framework of the paper's traditions and, nevertheless, finding plenty of room for enterprise and improvement.

During the early years of his editorship, a lively advertising campaign by posters proclaimed the *Times* as the newspaper of "the Top People," envisaging its elevated readers as the sort of people for whom only the best is good enough. Haley, in an interview with Donald McLachlan on the eve of his retirement, did not dispute the assumption that those who read serious newspapers do so because of their greater responsibilities, and not on account of superior education. In retrospect, much of the work he accomplished in improving the paper was of a kind calculated to commend it to that section of the community, the "few but fit," by reason of its integrity and its recognizable efficiency as a newspaper.

His own personal integrity, which according to colleagues who knew him best was his predominant characteristic, was to be detected in the editorials of which, like all his predecessors except

Delane, he wrote many. The title of one of his leading articles, "It *is* a Moral Issue," became something of a catch phrase in the office, because it was so typical of the writer. In other days in Printing House Square, an editorial writer confronted by a particularly thorny subject for comment, might describe his assignment as "a three-pipe problem"; but Haley never resorted to tobacco in any circumstances. If he could find a moral issue in the topic for treatment, he had an opening for an incisive editorial. In recent times the incidence of such issues tends increasingly to confirm the prediction in 1907 of William Ralph Inge, an exceptionally luminous Dean of St. Paul's Cathedral, that conflicts between the moral and the intellectual view would divide increasingly the political world into two camps, "for there is hardly a burning question in politics that is not answered differently by the intellect and by the emotions." Even so, it would be wrong to assume that in handling such themes for the *Times* with its numerous readers in high places, it was possible simply to descant on the moral issue and to ignore the fact that, unlike the moralists, statesmen are under an obligation to devise solutions that are eminently practical, and also acceptable to communities in which sensitivity to moral factors is variable.

Haley's integrity was likewise reflected in the practice, which he introduced, of printing conspicuously corrections of errors that had appeared in the paper, a proceeding which, though it certainly would count for righteousness with the "Top People," would be regarded equally as evidence of efficiency. Errors in newspapers (even most libels) are inadvertent, probably due to haste. But when recognized by readers as errors, they are set down to slackness, an imputation that can be met only by prompt and frank correction; and on that course the new editor of the *Times* insisted by his demand for efficiency as well as integrity.

News, however, is the prime requirement of the *Times* as of any newspaper, but for the editor it entailed exceptional responsibilities by reason of the traditional reliance of the *Times* on its own sources of news of every kind. It had long maintained its own parliamentary staff, its own corps of law reporters who were qualified barristers; and, by its own worldwide chain of correspondents, it had achieved its reputation as the most trustworthy authority on foreign affairs, which sometimes told the foreign secretary of events, or foreshadowed developments, appreciably in advance of embassies and consulates.

Close supervision of the news was an aspect of editorship to which the new editor brought a volume of experience unlikely to have been matched by any of his predecessors. That experience began in Manchester, where the young Haley went as a reporter. His literary ability was more than adequate to the work; but reporters must mix and mingle with all manner of men and women, patiently, pleasantly, and receptively; and by all accounts that part of the duty did not suit Haley's temperament. He found his métier, however, as a subeditor. He could whip through urgent news stories with great facility, rearranging the facts in better sequence, improving the phraseology, applying the arresting headings and sometimes detecting clues to supplementary stories for later editions. His excellence in such essential "processing" of news soon brought him to the head of the subeditors' table.

Iverach McDonald who, at the *Times*, became his deputy, has written that, looking back on Haley's fourteen years at Printing House Square, he remembers chiefly the editor's combination of drive and his hour-by-hour insistence on the primacy of news, as well as his great sense of editorial responsibility, of power, and complete independence. This witness recalls, too, his "reshaping the paper two or three times in as many hours, if need be; writing with extraordinary speed; redoing headings and captions; getting late stories followed up hard. . . . He liked nothing better than being out in the composing room, getting the paper away and seeing the nightly miracle accomplished on time."

Haley's strong sense of the primacy of news, however, did not diminish his concern for the feature pages, in which he made many innovations. One such was an original literary feature that became widely read, and known as the "Oliver Edwards' article" from the *nom de plume* he bestowed on its contributor. It did not consist of orthodox reviewing. It was a causerie of books and authors, intimate and reflective. Haley's choice of this "by-line" is, of itself, a clue to his acquaintance with great literature, for many of the "top people" had forgotten that Oliver Edwards was a fellow collegian of Samuel Johnson at Oxford where they parted and had no further contact for forty years until they met accidentally in Fleet Street. There, Edwards, reciting what had happened to him in the meantime, mentioned various professions that had attracted him, adding. "I have tried, too, in my time, to be a philosopher; but I don't know how, cheerfulness was always breaking in."

Whether Haley intended the choice of that pen name to be a disclosure of his own disposition is doubtful (earlier, he had written similarly for the *Manchester Evening News* as Joseph Sell), for when he launched the feature he arranged for certain other members of the literary staff to take a turn in the role of Oliver Edwards, but he came to like the part so well that, before long, he took it into his own hands exclusively. All the same, he would never confirm or contradict the speculation of gossip writers who named him as the contributor, while others doubted whether the range of literary knowledge disclosed by the mysterious Oliver could be possessed by a journalist of Haley's antecedents and intensive career. Sir Linton Andrews had no doubt. He regarded Haley as the best-read man he had ever met.

The ultimate biographer of the last editor of the *Times* in its classic days will reveal that Haley was, from his youth, an omnivorous reader, and that during his most active period in journalism, reading was almost his sole form of recreation. That chronicler may reveal also, that during his years as a shorthand telephonist at Printing House Square, the young Haley, having access to the room in which the large assortment of new books was held pending review, would make his way there at the end of his period of duty at the telephones, between midnight and dawn, and would spend an hour or two browsing among the latest addition to English literature before cycling to his bachelor's lodging. Thus, the Oliver Edwards feature might be regarded as an intellectual link between his telephonic introduction to journalism and his later experience with the same newspaper when he had become the head of his profession.

Iverach McDonald, who had the distinction of playing the retiring voluntary as Sir William Haley left Printing House Square on the last day of 1967, summarized Haley's editorial achievement thus: "From his first day he set about improving the paper, bringing in many new features, getting stories and leaders [editorials] written, 'in words of one syllable' as he used to insist, getting more pictures in, getting off-beat specials written. In the end, the old format, with personal advertisements on the front page would no longer do."

That spectacular improvement (it could hardly be called revolutionary, for the *Times* was the last daily newspaper in the United Kingdom to make the change) was symbolic of constitutional changes that were even then in the making, and of a reorganization that was to bring in its train considerable departures from traditional editorial methods.

The issue of May 3, 1966 carried on its front page the principal news of the day, accompanied by a topical photograph, in place of the familiar columns of announcements of births, marriages, and deaths, advertisements for missing heirs, personal messages popularly known as "agonies," and statutory notices as dull as the "agonies" were arresting. Those contents, over which many readers with leisure spent an appreciable amount of time, were assigned to page two.

The editorial, however, remained in its familiar position. It was entitled "Modern Times" and there can be little doubt about the identity of the writer. It began with a mild apology, first quoting Richard Hooker for the truism, "Change is not made without inconvenience, even from worse to better." But the writer of the editorial, mindful of those drastic changes that lay in the near future, wished to focus attention of an aspect of change more profound than the mere side effect of inconvenience.

"Change is the law of life," he declared. "If things do not evolve, they die. *The Times* of yesterday was not *The Times* of 1916 or of 1956. Every newspaper is evolving all the time. Placing news on the front page of *The Times* is one more step along a road this paper has been treading for 181 years. Uniqueness is not a virtue if it becomes mere eccentricity. There is no future for any newspaper as a museum piece."

The closing sentences seemed to breathe defiance of the old guard by preparing that section of the readership for a future in which evolution would be accelerated. "Some people have expressed the dark suspicion," said this initial message of a changed *Thunderer*, "that one of the reasons *The Times* is modernizing itself is to get more readers. Of course it is. And we shall go on trying to get more readers for as long as we believe in our purpose."

Such was the message the *Times* issued to its readers in the spring of 1966. In the fall of that year came the more historic announcement of constitutional changes whereby Lord Thomson of Fleet, proprietor of the *Sunday Times* (and of innumerable other newspapers) had entered into the proprietorial structure of the *Times* by agreement with Lord Astor of Hever, his heir, Mr. Gavin Astor, and Mr. John Walter.

Before his ultimate departure from Printing House Square, Sir William Haley was reported as simplifying the proprietorial changes by saying that the paper had to have money pumped into it. A sum of £1.50 million had gone in already; an amount that was not to be had from the former proprietors. It had taken time to bring about the change, but he could claim to have got the process started. The circulation had already reached three hundred thousand.

By then, Sir William had relinquished the editorship to Mr. William Rees-Mogg, and had been for a year chairman of the Times Newspapers Limited, under the presidency of Mr. Gavin Astor. During that year, he had accepted the editorship of the *Encyclopaedia Britannica*. Early in 1968, at the age of sixty-six, without any ceremonious farewell from the profession he had headed, he departed for Chicago and new responsibilities. He left a record of personal achievement such as none of his predecessors could equal—director general of the British Broadcasting Corporation, editor of the *Times*, editor of *Encyclopaedia Britannica* —a truly remarkable sequence of milestones in the career of a man who merited by ability every appointment he received. He had his faults, and consequently his critics. But, as has been said, "The Almighty is a wonderful handicapper," and none can doubt that such a balancing intrusion is indeed providential.

Courtesy of the *Daily Mirror*

CECIL HARMSWORTH KING

12

King, Cudlipp, and Others

Men who promoted the Mirror to the
"largest daily sale on earth"

From any survey of British journalistic enterprise in the twentieth century the *Daily Mirror* emerges as a success story without parallel. Moreover, the paper's claim to have achieved the "largest daily sale on earth" is attributable not to massive injections of money over a long period but to adventurous editorship, exercised by men who were not, in every instance, editors.

There is a Fleet Street legend portraying how a veteran editor of Victorian vintage was reduced to a state of silent astonishment on its being proved to him that half the population of Great Britain consisted indubitably of women, nearly all of whom could read. Possibly, that mathematical fact had to be thrust upon his attention to explain why Alfred Harmsworth (Lord Northcliffe) had just announced his intention to launch a daily newspaper, designed for women by an editorial staff wholly feminine.

Northcliffe's enthusiasm for this project in 1903 seems to have been tempered by a shade of doubt until W. T. Stead was seen to be toying with the same idea. Then he moved quickly from contemplation to action—perhaps too quickly. The approach to production of the paper was not characterized by the intensive care that marked the successful launching of the *Daily Mail* seven years earlier. Had it been, some assumptions might have been proved impractical. Production of the first issue of the *Daily Mirror* was, in fact, under-rehearsed.

Though public curiosity ensured a large demand, initial inquisitiveness was soon satisfied. A drop in the sales of any newspaper immediately after its novelties have been revealed, is natural and expected; but the demand soon settles at a steady level. In respect of the *Mirror*, however, the decline continued catastrophically. In less than three months, the initial sale of 276,000 had fallen to 24,801 copies, and Northcliffe had to accept the unpalatable conclusion that, for the first time, his wizardry had failed. Misjudgment was obvious.

His decision to entrust the editorial side of the paper entirely to women had been rash, rather than courageous. It may have seemed an exciting innovation from a publicity angle at a time when higher education was producing a reserve of trained, feminine talent, much of which was languishing by reason of the conservatism of the older professions. Northcliffe had adopted total feminine staffing because women journalists had proved excellent contributors to the large section of the *Daily Mail* allocated to women's interests. Further, he registered his confidence in the ability of women journalists by appointing the editor of the women's features of the *Daily Mail* to take charge of this first daily paper for women.

The all-women rule for the editorial staff of the *Mirror* was qualified by a single exception. One male subeditor was introduced, to work at the point of contact with the printers, whose masculine vocabulary was unlikely always to be agreeable to the ears of "gentlewomen"—a term Northcliffe used frequently in visualizing both the staff and reader of the paper. The male journalist chosen for this otherwise Adamless Eden was H. Hamilton Fyfe, a young man of exceptional ability and charm, destined later to become an outstanding war correspondent and a playwright.

In his age of reminiscence, I heard Fyfe tell of some of his difficulties when working "at the stone" and generally supervising the transition of the manuscript copy to the typeset page. He had

Courtesy of the *Daily Mirror*
Photograph by Arthur Sidey

HUGH CUDLIPP

cause particularly to remember the evening when the master printer brought to light a heading containing a crude *double-entendre*. Fyfe struck out the ambiguous words and substituted a safe line. Next day he was summoned to the presence of a lady editor highly incensed by his having changed a headline she herself had written. Finding the situation too embarrassing for complete candor, Fyfe explained his action later to a married member of the staff and she, in turn, enlarged the editor's incomplete knowledge of masculine synonyms.

Although the need for vigilance in that context was everpresent, the fatal limitation in the constitution of the staff was the drawing-room-and-university background of those admirable women, so eager to justify their place in journalism. For a newspaper that had to attract a large readership from the whole range of womanhood, such gentlewomen were too restricted in their experience of life to understand the needs of the majority of women in the populous suburbs of the industrial regions.

Northcliffe's reputation as the master of popular journalism had suffered a reverse. Fleet Street was jesting at his expense, which derision was harder to bear than his loss of one hundred thousand pounds on the venture. Yet the newspaper that his financially minded brother, Harold, would gladly have abandoned, was to survive, and was eventually to achieve the largest sale of any daily paper in the world. In 1967, the *Daily Mirror* recorded the highest average sale in its history—5,282,000 copies daily.

Between those extremes of fortune, the Mirror climbed for sixty-four years. It was not a continuous ascent; nor, on the other hand, was it erratic. Sometimes the paper lost readers at a rate that other journals would find alarming (due usually to political misjudgments) and sometimes it plodded complacently along a mathematical plateau; but overall, the *Mirror*'s history discloses a truly remarkable performance. Somewhere down the years, editorial genius was at work. Who provided it?

In the record of the *Mirror*'s long haul, three names stand out conspicuously. They are, in chronological order, Guy Bartholomew, Cecil Harmsworth King, and Hugh Cudlipp. All the same, they would not be there (though almost certainly they would have shone somewhere) but for Northcliffe's courage, or obstinacy, in facing what looked like total failure. To the dismal predictions of the defeatists in his circle, and to the jests of his rivals, Northcliffe turned a deaf ear, and resolved upon that most difficult of operations—a new start.

His first measure of reform was to replace the lady editor by Hamilton Fyfe who, in turn, adapted the staff to the requirements implied by Northcliffe's revised title, *"Daily Illustrated Mirror*: A Paper for Men and Women." The word "Illustrated" was introduced because, said Northcliffe, in the course of his disastrous experience with the first *Mirror*, he had discovered that what the public wanted was a daily picture paper. That claim was distinctly hard on the *Daily Graphic* whose distinguishing characteristic since its birth a decade earlier was its policy of illustrating the news with a generous array of pictures.

The *Daily Graphic* did not prosper, but it had a loyal, middle-class readership and it carried on hopefully, looking to the day when in place of the line drawings and woodcuts, to which it was restricted, it could present good reproductions of photographs. Such a hope had been cherished by Northcliffe, also. For some time past he had employed an expert doing research work in that sphere. Even so, when the proprietor saw the earliest photographic illustrations in the *Mirror*, he pronounced them "a ghastly mess." But perseverance paid off. By retouching photographs and by the use of a special printing ink, better reproduction of photographs on rought newsprint by fast rotary presses was achieved, though the results still left plenty of room for improvement.

Sales of the replanned *Mirror* escalated at a rate that tempted Northcliffe to indulge in a riposte to his rivals. Little more than a year after the depressing day when the first *Mirror* came off the machines, the reorganized paper carried an article under his own byline, proclaiming the redemption of "the only journalistic failure with which I have been associated."

Soon thereafter he hived off the paper to premises clear of the *Daily Mail* building, and before long he assigned to his brother Harold (Viscount Rothermere to-be) the control of the *Mirror*'s finances and administration. About the same time, he engaged for its staff a journalist named Alexander Kenealy who had served on the New York *Herald* and other American newspapers and who had latterly been working in London on Blumenfeld's *Daily Express*. Kenealy's preference was for a kind of journalism more aggressive than that of Hamilton Fyfe. Its effect so accelerated the rising sales of the *Mirror*, already running at about 350,000 daily, that Fyfe's three years' editorship soon came to an end by his transference to the *Daily Mail*; and Kenealy reigned in his stead.

Although from then onward Northcliffe's interest in the *Mirror* became less intimate, the publicity attendant on the *Mirror*'s birth had made widely known his responsibility for that paper as well as the *Daily Mail*; and years after he had seemed to leave Kenealy much to his own devices, he fired a broadside at him for introducing into the paper stories that fell below the standard of good taste that he maintained strictly in the *Mail*. Nevertheless, he retained a personal regard for the man, and in 1915 when Kenealy went down with an illness that was soon to prove fatal, Northcliffe took a day off from his heavy wartime commitments to make a journey into the countryside that he might spend some hours at the bedside of his dying editor.

Northcliffe, now occupied increasingly with political aspects of the war and also with the *Times*, could give little attention to the *Mirror* which, anyhow, had always a lower place in his priorities than the *Mail*. Having fixed a figure beyond which the capital of the *Mirror* was not to be increased (though its sales continued to expand), he left brother Harold and Kenealy's successor, Edward Flynn, to take care of the paper. Its staff, however, were enthusiastically interested, encouraged by progress on the pictorial side, where audacity of enterprise in getting photographs of a world at war and improvements in the quality of reproduction were creating increased public demand, despite the competition of a new rival in the *Daily Sketch*. Confidently, the company launched a Sunday issue called the *Sunday Pictorial* (now the *Sunday Mirror*).

Among the men who had contributed to this phase of the *Mirror*'s progress was Guy Bartholomew, who had joined the staff during Fyfe's editorship. He was a complex person. Bartholomew's background was proletarian and his formal education had been scanty, making him excessively class-conscious. But he had an artistic instinct, which after some training at an art school enabled him to develop as a cartoonist. He was twenty-six when he joined the infant *Mirror*, then selling twenty-five thousand copies. When he left the paper, at the approximate age of seventy, its circulation was then in sight of five million; and he was chairman of the company.

Bartholomew had neither charm nor sociability to assist his advancement, and his temperament was sometimes incalculable. His best asset was his instinct for what was visually arresting; he could visualize news in pictorial terms. With the coming of the First World War, his yearning to enlist as an airman was frustrated by imperfect eyesight, but he was accepted as an army photographer with commissioned rank. Some of the official pictures of battles of that war, now part of a national collection and regarded as historic, were taken by Bartholomew. To get them he shirked no risk; and subsequently on his return to the *Mirror* as picture editor, the audacity he himself had shown in war was the measure of risk he expected his cameramen to accept in carrying out hazardous assignments.

Between the two World Wars, Lord Rothermere, who on Northcliffe's death had acquired the *Mirror* and its Sunday associate, decided to part with his interest. Instead of making an outright sale, he disposed of his shares piecemeal, over a period, on the Stock Exchange. Thus, before he died in 1940, his hand had been withdrawn from the two papers, but John Cowley, a former manager of the *Daily Mail* whom he had made a *Mirror* executive and, later, the Company's chairman, remained.

As early as 1931, Rothermere had written to Cowley saying explicitly that the *Mirror* and the *Sunday Pictorial* were "entirely under your and your colleagues' control." Thereafter, except for an occasional article under his own by-line, part of his restless advocacy of a foreign policy of appeasement, Rothermere made no attempt to influence the two papers. Nevertheless, the public continued to assume that Rothermere was still a force in Geraldine House, the *Mirror*'s headquarters, named after his mother.

When, in the next decade, the Royal Commission on the Press investigated every aspect of the newspaper industry, its report said: "Among national newspapers there are two companies in which no individual shareholders, or group shareholders, has control—The Daily Mirror Newspapers Ltd. and The Sunday Pictorial Newspapers (1920) Ltd. . . . The controlling interest in the *Mirror* rests with the *Sunday Pictorial* company, and *vice versa*. The practical effect of this is that the directors of the two companies can exercise absolute control." As the members of the board were all salaried employees, here was something akin to worker control.

At the time this power vacuum was created, newspapers were not prospering. The effect in Britain of the world economic crisis was reflected in statistics of unemployment showing a total of 2,859,000 men and women living on state insurance benefit that afforded just a bare subsistence. In these circumstances, newspapers suffered heavy losses in both advertising revenue and circulation. The *Daily Mirror's* sales fell almost to 700,000 against an average of 1,072,000 before the slump. Its readership had become almost exclusively middle class and the tone of the paper complacently genteel. Probably, its most popular page was that devoted to juveniles (but notoriously followed for years by nearly as many adults), the particular attraction being a feature depicting the adventures of three animal characters, "Pip, Squeak and Wilfred" by a clever caricaturist, A. B. Payne.

About midway through the thirties, employment showed a small but sustained improvement, sufficient to turn thoughts to the possibilities of a drive to recover the paper's lost ground. Though John Cowley was still in office as chairman of the company, Bartholomew had been appointed editorial director. Also, in that year the editorship of the *Daily Mirror* passed from Brownlee to Cecil Thomas. Not far behind Bartholomew in the hierarchy of Geraldine House was Cecil Harmsworth King who, in 1934, was advertising director.

King, younger than the editorial director by twenty-three years, was as his middle name proclaims, a member of the Harmsworth family, his mother being a sister of Northcliffe and Rothermere. All the same, he had not been introduced into the family business at the top level. A year in the advertising department of a Glasgow newspaper plus some experience in the same branch of the *Daily Mail,* and three years' successful service to the *Mirror* preceded his promotion to directorial status, by which time he had acquired in the newspaper world a reputation in his own right. Though differing from Bartholomew in educational background, in political attitude, and much else, he shared fully the older man's dissatisfaction with the static situation to which the paper had been brought by the circumstances of the time.

In their joint study of the measures that might inaugurate a more active and prosperous phase, both men had been impressed by the "tabloid" newspaper then forging ahead in the United States. They were as much attracted by the kind of features and the brash presentation of the news in those journals as they were by their handy size, though the dimensions of the *Mirror*'s page were already small by comparison with the majority of British newspapers.

Another change regarded as most necessary by both men, was the achievement of the larger readership that must be won. The natural British tendency to understatement had been rudely disturbed in the postwar years, but such assertiveness as developed, tended to be limited to political news and opinion. There was everywhere a certain reverence in presenting news about that ill-defined class of highly placed persons now called "The Establishment." The activities of these VIPs were accorded by newspapers generally an importance out of all proportion to the interest they possessed for the mass of readers. By contrast, matters of intimate relevance to the lives of millions were seldom reflected adequately, even in what were classed, by price, as "popular" papers. The heat with which such problems were discussed in workshops, transport cafes, public houses, and wherever women congregated did not radiate from the headlines of the kind of *Daily Mirror* as then produced.

Bartholomew and King, for differing reasons, agreed that they must work toward a *Mirror* that would be challenging, assertive. It must identify itself closely with the mass of its readers and make the millions articulate. It must publicize opinions already widely held but seldom expressed in print. It must employ the bluntness with which they were uttered, and use big type for problems that loomed large in humble homes.

Obviously, a newspaper accustomed to behave sedately in all that pertained to editorship, and retaining something of its tradition as a paper for gentlewomen, could not switch suddenly to a policy that its old regulars might resent as crudely sensational.

The kind of compromise that was adopted is to be detected in the *Mirror*'s own description of itself in the 1938 edition of the *Newspaper Press Directory*:

> The oldest established yet still modern daily picture newspaper. It gives all the news in concise form and is notable for its many pictures, brilliantly conceived and finely produced. The *Daily Mirror* is essentially a family newspaper with recognised feminine influence. Its special daily articles are rich in humanity; and its numerous strip cartoons, spread throughout the paper, assure full reader-interest on all pages of the paper.

It is not difficult to see in that announcement the collaboration of Bartholomew, who thought in terms of pictures, and of King, who was conscious of the advertising value of a strong feminine following. Aware of the middle-class appeal by which the *Mirror* had held its loyal nucleus of readers, Bartholomew and King showed a certain restraint in setting the paper toward the Left-wise political course on which they had agreed.

It was at this juncture there entered upon the scene young Hugh Cudlipp, who was to exercise the greatest influence on the development of the paper, and was destined ultimately to become preeminent in the world's largest publishing organization. Although King was quick to recognize in Cudlipp "unquestionably, the finest journalist in the country," the newcomer did not reach the *Mirror* as a result of his talent being discovered by either Bartholomew or King. He was not enticed into their service, as was Connor ("Cassandra"), their outstanding editorial writer, about the same time. Cudlipp made the acquaintance of Bartholomew and King by replying to an anonymous advertisement for "a bright assistant features editor with ideas, able to take charge," inserted by Bartholomew in the *Daily Telegraph*.

Cudlipp, then twenty-two, had begun his journalistic career very modestly in his native city of Cardiff, with such a measure of schooling as a leaving age of fourteen implies. Gathering experience first on a local weekly and then on the Cardiff *Evening Express*, he moved up to reporting on Lancashire papers and, by the age of nineteen, had shown such exceptional aptitude for journalism that he was appointed features editor of the *Sunday Chronicle*, in London.

He was the youngest of three brothers, whose father was a commercial traveller. Both his elders, Percy and Reginald, were in journalism, the firstborn being editor of Beaverbrook's *Evening Standard* at the time Hugh dispatched his answer to Bartholomew's advertisement. Reginald was on his way to the editorship of the *News of the World*, though the war was to delay his arrival. There is no evidence of family influence, however, behind Hugh's appointment to the *Mirror*. The remarkable, natural zest of the Cudlipp brothers for what Kipling called "the old black art" was all they needed to propel them.

Hugh Cudlipp never needed the aid of sophisticated processes like reader research to tell him the topics in which the broad mass of the population were interested. He knew from boyhood up, the topics and the terms in which those subjects were discussed. Bartholomew was unlikely to differ from him about these aspects of journalism, though the two men were by no means always in accord. King had instinctive confidence in Cudlipp's judgment and backed him staunchly. Thus, though Chairman Cowley and his social circle in town and country were disturbed by the headlines and contents-bills with which the *Mirror* row shocked the population into wakefulness on most mornings, the sales of the paper rose and the dividends improved. So what more could a professional company chairman desire?

The *Mirror* was now unique among daily newspapers in being free from the personal tastes and political ambitions of a controlling shareholder. As Cowley was once to remark, its ownership was just like that of the British railways in those days before nationalization. The *Mirror* and its Sunday associate existed for sale to the largest number of people they were capable of attracting. There was, however, a slight constitutional difference in the personnel of the two boards, though Cowley presided over both. While Bartholomew had the last word in the day-to-day conduct of the *Mirror*, King had that privilege in respect of the *Sunday Pictorial*.

Some two years after Cudlipp's arrival, a clash of interest between the two directors occurred. King felt the need of Cudlipp's electrifying touch on the Sunday paper, whose circulation, by a slow decline, had lost more than a million readers. Bartholomew was unwilling to let go of the man he had attracted by his small advertisement. Something like Solomon's judgment had to be applied to the deadlock. Cudlipp must choose; and Bartholomew felt sure he would opt for the *Mirror*. Personal considerations apart, to expect a lively journalist, one "with ideas," to forego the opportunity of editing a Sunday newspaper (which despite its decline still had a million readers) was to fail to appreciate how irresistible was the challenge presented to Hugh Cudlipp at the age of twenty-four. In this instance, moreover, it is clear that although he had been recruited by "Bart," Cudlipp had never esteemed the temperamental Bartholomew very highly. He had much greater confidence in and respect for King. So the young man accepted the challenge, and Bartholomew's benediction was, "You'll get no help from me—no help at all," though later he was to relent to the extent of releasing two good *Mirror* men at Cudlipp's request to serve on the *Pictorial*.

Three years later, when Cudlipp declined exemption from war service in World War II and joined the army, the downward trend of the *Pictorial*'s sales had been reversed and, in an upward climb, had gained nearly four hundred thousand readers. Little of this improvement was due to the change of political policy on which Bartholomew and King had resolved. Despite the advertised declaration of independence of party political commitment, the public still associated the two papers with the Rothermere outlook. As Cudlipp has written, "The Mirror-Pictorial group had not yet reached the point of declared radicalism which became its hall-mark during the war years and after." He attributed the early improvement in sales of the *Pictorial* to a combination of glamour and sensation, as well as "earnest crusading and sense of social purpose."

The opportunity the *Mirror* needed for a prudent change of policy dawned in the winter of 1938/39, when the more perceptive members of the public were increasingly convinced by German actions that the Munich pledge, signed jointly by Hitler and Chamberlain, avowing that their two countries would never "go to war again against each other," was likely to prove worthless. The broad mass of the people, however, were under the influence of the memorable September day when Chamberlain flew back from Munich with that scrap of paper and was received with such acclaim that the *Times* was moved to declaim "No conqueror returning from a victory on the battlefield has come home with nobler laurels."

So high was Prime Minister Chamberlain's popularity at this juncture, and so profound the sense of relief created by the outcome of his mission, that the parliamentary Opposition were scared by the possibility that Chamberlain might exploit his success by instigating an immediate general election. Such were their fears that Chamberlain felt constrained to tell the Commons at the earliest opportunity that he had no such intention, except in unlikely contingencies. One reason why he declined to "snatch party advantage" from a situation so favorable was that "we may want great efforts from the nation in the months to come, and if that be so, the smaller our differences the better."

All the same, differences grew as Hitler's behavior destroyed confidence in the pledge he had given. In this reaction, the *Mirror* and its associate found an opportunity to voice the increasing dissatisfaction with the prime minister's refusal to safeguard the country against the consequences of the failure of appeasement, by taking Churchill into the government. Churchill's presence would ensure the maximum progress of rearmament that Chamberlain admitted was necessary if diplomacy was to be effective.

When, in fact, Chamberlain's policy failed, and war was declared, the disillusioned prime minister said, in a moving sentence, that everything he had worked for and believed in during his public life had crashed in ruins. There was widespread sympathy with him, but he did not accept the logic of his confession. Chamberlain, in his seventy-first year, frustrated and tired, was plainly not the person to lead the nation in war, especially a war for which his country was so ill-prepared that the utmost energy would have to be brought to the task of rearmament.

Though now he took Churchill into the Cabinet, Chamberlain could not unify the nation by setting up that coalition government which the First World War had shown to be an indispensable requirement of success. The Labour party refused to serve under Chamberlain's leadership, though they promised general support for the war effort.

Thus there was introduced into the situation much that was controversial but had no reference to party doctrine. Here was just the opportunity in which the *Mirror*—hitherto handicapped by long, proprietorial attachment to the Right and with no desire to affiliate formally with the Left—to acquire the political power which Cecil King had seen as essential to a commercial newspaper with a mission. The *Mirror* could make itself the mouthpiece of the broad mass of people in those conflicts that would arise from the immense task of organizing the nation for total war, and from the changed ways of life that war would impose.

Despite the façade of unity of purpose in Parliament and the general acknowledgment throughout the country that war had become absolutely unavoidable, there was much public bewilderment. King and Bartholomew foresaw that, in these circumstances, there would be a massive response to an attitude of firmness. "Bartholomew," says Maurice Edelman, in his history of the *Mirror*, "discovered that the use of the imperative mood was a stimulant to the broad mass of the people." The vocabulary adopted by the *Mirror* struck the recognized note of leadership. " 'Do this' and 'Do that,' " continues Edelman, "was the injunction which a public eager to be led and already conditioned by the disciplines of war-time Britain, welcomed." Bartholomew, seeing events instinctively in visual terms, ensured that the boldest black type was used to express the operative words of command.

As the *Mirror* had demanded the inclusion of Churchill in the government before the storm broke, so now it demanded the retirement of the septuagenarian Prime Minister Chamberlain. Politicians with memories of World War I wished him to resign before the country faced those military disasters that Britain's unpreparedness made almost inevitable. One of the earliest reverses, the failure of an inadequate British force to frustrate Hitler's invasion of Norway, created a parliamentary situation that made Chamberlain's continuance impossible. The prime minister, exhausted and mortally sick, relinquished office to Churchill, who secured the Opposition's partnership in a coalition government just in time to face Hitler's lightning offensive in France. The man in the street could not forget that, all along, the *Mirror* had said, for nearly a year, that Chamberlain ought to quit. Bartholomew's insistence on the imperative mood, with black type to impart emphasis, did much to increase the authority which the paper acquired at a time of much public bewilderment: also it introduced a style that remains a charactistic of the *Mirror*.

Another and different factor that aided the paper's influence for long afterwards was its reputation as the mouthpiece of the armed forces. There was a fundamental difference between the citizen-soldiers of the two World Wars, which the *Mirror*'s editorship was quick to perceive. For nearly half the period of the First World War recruiting was voluntary. With more than five million men thus enrolled, a switch to compulsory military service in the latter half of hostilities could not produce a massive increase. Thus, even when that war ended, the majority of men in the field were, despite heavy casualties, men who had gone to war voluntarily.

Even before war began again in 1939, compulsory service had been introduced, and though the general attitude of the men was to accept this disciplined service to their country philosophically, the fact that they did not ask to become soldiers made them less tolerant of hardship for themselves or their dependants which they regarded as unnecessary or unreasonable. Likewise, they were sensitive to the experience of regulations being imposed by superiors who were either ignorant of military law or indifferent to what in civil courts is recognized as "natural justice."

By giving publicity in its own pungent language to the grievances of the servicemen, the *Mirror* was able increasingly to secure redress. To some extent the process of ventilation by the paper was helpful to the War Office where, naturally, there existed a desire to maintain good morale; but that circumstance did not mean that the intervention of the *Mirror* with its brash demands was welcomed, in preference to old-established requirement that if any soldier considered himself wronged, he might complain thereof to his captain, and if that officer did nothing about it, to his commanding officer, and so on, to a point at which he might request an interview with the commander in chief—a procedure designed for the small peacetime army of Victorian or earlier times.

The *Sunday Pictorial* followed the *Mirror*'s lead by appointing to its staff an officer who had seen active service in 1939–40 and who, being a member of Parliament, was able to disengage from military employment to devote himself to parliamentary duties. As a contemporary soldier he knew the points of friction that created discontent in the new citizen-army. Moreover, because he was a member of Parliament, the military authorities were obliged to treat his representations with respect, distasteful though the exercise might be.

All the same, the ministers responsible for the service departments had reason to look on this new form of newspaper activity with concern, as something that might get beyond the intentions of the editors who fostered it and lead to collective acts of protest or other trends subversive of discipline. Later events showed that the prime minister was aware of this vexatious development.

Churchill who, when he first stood for election to parliament, described his occupation on the nomination form as "journalist," and who, when he had no ministerial office, earned a living largely by journalism, had now, as leader of the nation in most anxious times, a different perspective on the press. Indeed, as his correspondence with President Roosevelt shows, both statesmen regarded themselves as comrades in adversity in having to cope with a free press that they could not control and had no wish to curb beyond the proper requirements of security.

Despite his wartime duties, endless and vital, Churchill contrived to keep an eye on the press, day by day. He knew all about the new-style *Mirror* and its growing influence. Also, he knew Cecil King who, in the earliest days of the war, had lunched at Churchill's domestic table and was accustomed to uninhibited discussion with the then minister for the navy. When, therefore, in 1941, Churchill as prime minister was angered by sustained criticism in the *Mirror* and *Pictorial*, which he felt was animated by malice and hatred toward the government, he said so plainly in a letter to King, and, *inter alia*, described himself as a "regular reader" of the two papers.

King was neither overawed by the great man's displeasure nor moved to repentance. The verbal skirmish continued until the prime minister invited King to Downing Street, where, though an air raid on London was in progress, two obstinate men argued for more than an hour. Churchill persisted in describing the *Mirror*'s criticism as "malignancy." Still, personal feelings remained friendly, and when the discussion ended (though the air

raid continued), Churchill insisted on his official car being summoned to take King back to his "vitriolic" newspaper. Further
correspondence followed but petered out inconclusively.

A year later, however, the *Mirror* was in more serious trouble
which was not concerned with direct criticism of the government.
At a time when the war was going badly for Britain, and when
losses of shipping by submarines were making wartime austerity
for the population particularly severe, the *Mirror* published a
grimly realistic cartoon depicting a merchant seaman clinging to
a raft in a turbulent sea. The caption (written, it transpired, by
"Cassandra") was "The price of petrol has been raised by a penny
(Official)."

Now, the Home Secretary was disturbed. He was Herbert
Morrison, one of the ministers contributed by the Labour party
to the Churchill coalition and who, before he took office, had
been an esteemed contributor to the *Mirror*. The Home Secretary's view, as stated later in his autobiography, was: "The *Daily
Mirror* was read by many members of the armed forces and by the
working population to a far greater extent than any other paper.
Their cartoon was one of a series which could be interpreted as
meaning that the Generals, the factory owners and the businessmen were not pulling their weight in the war effort, if they were
not actually sabotaging it." That was how it struck Morrison.
Moreover, the cartoons appeared at a time "when morale was very
important," and he regarded this particular picture as "wicked,"
suggesting that "sailors were dying in order that petrol companies
could make bigger profits."

The Home Secretary soon discovered that the War Office had
already complained to the Cabinet, and that Churchill and other
ministers shared the Morrison view. The advice of the government's highest legal authority was that the wartime powers possessed by the Home Secretary were sufficient to enable him to
suppress a paper publishing so cruel and deplorable a cartoon.
Nevertheless, when the Cabinet discussed the matter decisively,
Morrison and other ministers did not favor so drastic a step. The
agreement reached was that Morrison should call the chairman
and the editor of the *Mirror* to the Home Office and deliver a
friendly warning of what would happen unless they amended their
ways.

A telephoned invitation to the chairman (Cowley) and the editorial director (Bartholomew) to call next day, encountered a difficulty in that Cowley was not available; so Bartholomew was substituted for the chairman, and Cecil Thomas, editor of the *Mirror*, became the second representative. At the outset of the interview the Home Secretary made it plain to the visitors that his purpose in meeting them was to convey the decision of the Cabinet that the paper would be closed down if it continued to offend.

Bartholomew was concerned to deny that what had been done was due to any influence from the directors, as such. The papers, he explained, were conducted substantially by the editorial staff, who were free to choose their course and whose continual purpose was to support the war effort. Differing meanings could be and had been read into the cartoon. (Some readers, it seems, took it as a grim reminder of the duty to economize in petrol.)

The wisdom of the Cabinet in avoiding the extreme step was justified by the sequel. Concern for the freedom of the press had been aroused by reports of the trouble, and debates were instigated in both Houses of Parliament. The discussions were as frank as the government's explanation. In the end, however, the debate was not pressed to the decisive point of a vote in either House. From that occasion until the end of the war, the *Mirror* pursued its policy of candor toward the government and other people in high places, justifying its boast to its readers, "You'll never find the *Mirror* among the 'Don't knows,'" All the same, it did not offend again, and the only development after the Home Office interview was the growth of a friendship between Morrison and Bartholomew that proved useful to the minister at times.

The Morrison episode served also to show that John Cowley, whose age had now reached the seventies, was not reacting energetically to his responsibilities as chairman of the two companies; and soon after that critical meeting in Whitehall, Bartholomew succeeded to the dual office. Evidently, the change was one of form and not of substance, for Bartholomew and King were already making the decisions and the papers were responding to their policy.

Morrison's assessment of the readership of the *Mirror* was accurate. Apart from its popularity among the millions in the armed forces, the *Mirror* was indeed "read by the working population to a far greater extent than any other paper." Here was a reversal of fortune for which there was no parallel in the British press. With no break in its continuity of publication, the *Daily Mirror*, which was in peril of dying in infancy, and for whose direction Northcliffe renounced responsibility when disaster had been averted, was now overtaking his prodigious *Daily Mail*.

Owing to the rationing of newsprint, there existed a much wider gap between sales figures and readership than was ever known in normal times. There was much borrowing of papers, particularly among the servicemen. They might buy, beg, or borrow the *Mirror* for its entertainment value, and especially for its copious strip features, one of which "Jane," was a protracted exercise in striptease that lasted for the duration of the war; but the sailors, soldiers, and airmen were aware of the paper's concern for the well-being of themselves, their families, and dependents. Further, they followed the *Mirror*'s sustained agitation for political policies that would afford a better life after this war than the broad mass of the people had known between the wars, or earlier.

It was significant that when, on V-E day, Churchill ended his victory speech to rejoicing crowds with, "Advance Britannia," as the keynote for the future, the *Mirror*'s slogan was "Forward with the people." What that meant in terms of social progress had been repeatedly explained by the *Mirror* since 1939. Quite as much as Bartholomew and Cudlipp, King had seen the *Mirror* in terms of political influence as well as commercial success. He had seen the welfare state as the ideal for which the country should strive, as the redeeming sequel to a second devastating war.

Sure evidence of success in propagating a political idea is provided when the satirists adopt it as a subject for their wit, in cartoons and light verse. Proof that the *Mirror*'s advocacy of the welfare state was finding wide, popular acceptance was tendered by the rhymester who put into circulation a jingle beginning,

Oh, won't it be wonderful after the war!
There won't be no rich and there won't be no poor.
There'll be pensions for all at twenty-four,
And no-one need work if he finds it a bore.

Any claim that the *Daily Mirror* won the postwar election for the Labour party and, to the astonishment of the world at

large, caused the removal of Churchill from the office into which
the *Mirror* itself did its utmost to put him, is too large an addition to make to the many achievements of that remarkable newspaper. Historians are unlikely to concede it. They will note that
at the time of V-E Day (May 8, 1945) the Labour party had been
in existence for nearly half a century and had long been the
second largest party in the House of Commons. It had never enjoyed a majority over a combination of the opposing elements and
so had never had a chance to implement its own distinctive
socialist policies. In May 1945, its opportunities to legislate added
up to two brief experiences of minority government and five
years as a subordinate partner in the Churchill coalition. Those
Labour leaders most closely in touch with their followers knew
that they faced a now-or-never situation. They must win this
golden opportunity to dictate decisively the very necessary reconstruction of Great Britain after the confusion of the war, or
their massive following of industrial workers would disintegrate
from loss of faith in the party. So, when Churchill proposed that
the three parties represented in his coalition should face the electorate still united, seeking a mandate to finish the war in the East,
Labour declined the invitation. The *New Statesman* commented,
"The Prime Minister could hardly have expected Mr. Attlee
would agree to prolong the Coalition for a period so indefinite
as the duration of hostilities with Japan."

Ironically, five years' service under the unfaltering leadership
of Churchill, who in other times had said repeatedly that Labour
was "unfit to govern," had now equipped the Labour party with
a nucleus of ministers who had experience of governing, and governing in the most difficult of circumstances. Churchill had thus
relieved the party of what had been a serious deficiency when it
sought the confidence of the middle-class voters. Added to that
important change was the advantage that the Labour party, even
while the war continued, had taken the opportunity of formulat-
ing its own distictive postwar policy, while Churchill, on the
other hand, refused staunchly to countenance any similar move by
his own Conservative party until such time as the war had been
won in the Far East as well as in Europe, to which end he had
pledged his word to President Roosevelt. This was the situation
that led to his "dismissal" from office at the moment when, both

at home and throughout the greater part of the world, he was being acclaimed as the savior of his country.

Having long exhorted the servicemen to demand the welfare state as the just reward of their service and sacrifices, the *Mirror* in the closing phase of the election campaign employed its black type and imperative mood to exhort the servicemen's womenfolk and comrades in industry to "Vote for *Him*" and "Vote for *Them*," while the Labour party amplified its emphasis on the welfare state proposals which Morrison and others had simplified in a program with the much publicized title, "Let us Face the Future." Thus the Labour party, for the first time in its history, won the power to govern without any possibility of veto by any combination of opponents.

At the time of this victory the sales of the *Mirror* were 2,400,000, second only to the 3,300,000 of the *Daily Express* whose superior circulation was due to its advantage in being able to print and issue the paper in Glasgow and Manchester as well as London. The Labour party's official newspaper, the *Daily Herald*, was not far behind the *Mirror* which, despite its unqualified support of the Labour party in the election, continued always to describe itself as "Independent." Thus it retained freedom of political maneuver. When restrictions of newsprint were relaxed, the curve of the *Mirror's* sales line, having kept close to the *Daily Mail's* track, soon made a vertical takeoff and caught up with the *Daily Express* near the four million mark.

The government's economic regulator, however, was made to operate both ways. In 1947 a financial crisis caused the Attlee administration to impose all-around measures of austerity. Newspapers reverted to wartime proportions, one-fifth their pre-war size. This compulsory limitation was the harder to bear by reason of the return from war service of many excellent journalists eager to make their presence felt in the progress of their papers.

Geraldine House welcomed back Hugh Cudlipp (who at once resumed his editorship of the *Pictorial*) and William Connor who bridged a six years gap in his pugnacious *Mirror* articles with an opening phrase of nine words, "As I was saying when I was rudely interrupted ——" One significant change that had occurred during the absence of these two key figures was that, by John Cowley's retirement, Bartholomew had become chairman of the board of each paper, while still retaining his position as editorial director of the *Mirror*. Thus there came a day in 1948 when Cudlipp as editor of the *Pictorial*, was called to the chairman's office. An important news cable from Africa that had reached the *Pictorial* too late for publication had not been passed on to the *Mirror* for use next day. For that lapse, Bartholomew dismissed him summarily.

Cudlipp's account of the incident suggests that the reason for this drastic action was immaterial. "I knew it was coming, but I never knew when." The timing was for Bartholomew to decide, and he chose a moment when Cecil King was abroad and could not intervene. Cudlipp says, understandably, that he experienced "grief" in being torn from the editorship of a newspaper he had helped to build up "from a falling sale of 1,300,000 to a rising sale of over 5,000,000." Otherwise he was not worried. An approach to Lord Beaverbrook brought a warm welcome by telegram, and an early appointment to the *Sunday Express* where he began as personal assistant to the editor, the redoubtable John Gordon. Despite some difficulty in tolerating his new chief's idiosyncrasies, Cudlipp says, "Only fools could not learn from him."

Cudlipp, whose *Sunday Pictorial* had been ahead of the *Sunday Express* in circulation, learned sufficient about the deficiencies of the paper he was now serving that Beaverbrook noted him as the prospective editor of the *Sunday Express*, to take over whenever Gordon should cease active editorship and assume the title of editor in chief. In that prospect, however, Cudlipp was not interested, though for two years he served under Gordon as managing editor. His heart remained at Geraldine House. After a time, Bartholomew came to regret his hastiness and to make a diplomatic approach with a view to reconciliation, but Cudlipp did not respond.

The time was at hand, however, when the relationship of the three extraordinary men who had brought about the phenomenal success of the *Mirror* was to be readjusted to the realities of the time. Bartholomew was changing, getting old and irritable, more unpredictable than ever, and Cudlipp was much more than the 'bright young man" caught by Bartholomew's chance advertisement, and who, developing greater confidence in Cecil King,

had been dismissed for exercising his own judgment when a conflict of loyalties arose. As for King, he had never been the man of
Bartholomew's imagining—merely a relative of the original proprietors, planted on the board to perpetuate the family's connection with the paper and to provide him with a livelihood. That
was an "image" born of the prejudice inherent in Bartholomew's
proletarian outlook and never corrected despite long and close
association. Though Cudlipp's antecedents did not differ widely
from Bartholomew's, he belonged to a later generation and, anyhow, he was given to judging men by character as revealed in
events.

King's background had nothing in common with that of the
other two members of the *Mirror* trinity. His father, Sir Lucas
King, educated at an Irish boarding school and Dublin University, had joined the Indian Civil Service and after holding a variety of posts, mostly on the political side, abandoned that career
to become Professor Oriental Languages at his former university,
where his distinction was eventually recognized by the award of
a knighthood.

To some extent the aptitudes of this learned man are reflected in the son's record. Cecil King was schooled at Winchester
College, founded in the fourteenth century by William of Wyke-
ham, a bishop who also completed the building of Winchester
Cathedral. As the capital city of England for some two centuries
before London superseded it, Winchester exudes history and
scholarship. From that environment, King went up to Oxford
University where he took honors in history. Though he is a
voracious reader of significant books in English and French,
travel is admittedly his chief recreation, and he knew something
of the world at large before joining the staff of a Harmsworth
daily paper in Glasgow.

The Glasgow posting seems to have been intended to give
him an insight into one of the primary operations of a newspaper. He has never displayed the aptitudes of a born reporter.
It is difficult to discern in him those gifts of objectivity, of patience to suffer fools gladly if the development of a story demands
it, or of readiness to mix and mingle amiably with all manner of
men, which are among the qualities of the ideal news-gatherer.
His commanding height (six feet, four inches), plus the prom-

inent chin and stern eye of the Northcliffian presence, could be intimidating on first contact, but their effects are mitigated by an unexpected quietness of speech that has a pleasing intimacy, so long as no controversial questions are raised. Argument, however, can lead to the disconcerting discovery that he is capable of making remarks of nuclear explosive power in dulcet tones, and that he can be very dogmatic.

Yet withal, Cecil King has an engaging personality. It became obvious in that spirited dialogue at 10 Downing Street in 1941, when Churchill implied that there were, behind the *Mirror*, sinister figures sustaining the criticism of the government and himself. King, repudiating the insinuation, explained that the paper had five directors and, "I'm more interested in politics than the others, so they leave politics to me." At that, Churchill, scanned his visitor up and down and remarked, "Well, *you* look innocent enough." No doubt other ministers and persons of importance with whom he maintained a kind of liaison service, received the same impression of King.

Such was the man who in 1951 felt that, although he was not yet the director endowed with the last word in *Mirror* decisions, his duty to the papers required that he should take a strong initiative in their domestic affairs.

Cecil King had been much abroad during the previous four years, and not merely to indulge his love of travel. In 1947 the *Mirror* and *Pictorial* companies had acquired in West Africa the *Daily Times* of Nigeria; and in the following year, on the Gold Coast, they had launched a *Daily Graphic*. These were the first expressions of a policy of overseas investment that was to become a large and valuable reinforcement of the companies' activities. In 1949 there was another new development in the acquisition of an interest in the *Argus* of Melbourne, Australia, and its weekly associate, the *Post*. Radio interests in Australia represented a further extension of policy.

During this period, the *Mirror*, outstripping its competitors by adventurous tactics in news gathering, had gone far beyond the limits set by the law for the proper administration of justice and had committed contempt of court.

In 1949 a man named Haigh, arrested on a charge of murder, was awaiting the initial, magisterial hearing of the case against him, when the *Mirror* (to quote a judicial description of its action) "published articles and photographs, and headings of the largest type," attributing to Haigh, not only the specific crime with which he had been charged, but other murders. In the long run, that larger measure of guilt which gave him distinction in the annals of crime as the "acid bath murderer," was established beyond doubt; but for the time being the law ordained that a person so situated must be treated as innocent. Thus it was that Sylvester Bolam (who had succeeded Cecil Thomas the previous year as editor of the *Mirror*) and the proprietors of the paper, were arraigned before the Lord Chief Justice and two other judges of the High Court, for contempt. As reported in the story of the trial published in the *Mirror*, what had happened was a blunder so crude as to admit of no palliation. The best that an eminent advocate could say on behalf of the *Mirror* was that in the forty-six years of the paper's existence, this was the first charge of contempt brought against it, save one so doubtfully valid that no penalty was imposed.

Giving the decision of the court, the Lord Chief Justice saw nothing to mitigate the offense. The editor (and it is the person so designated whom the law regards as chiefly responsible) was sentenced to detention in a prison for three months, and the proprietors were fined ten thousand pounds with the added warning for the future, "Let the directors beware. . . . They may find that the arm of this court is long enough to reach them, and to deal with them." Nearly ten years later Kingsley Martin was to write that the outcome of this case was to frighten everyone in journalism into a state in which "it would be daring to the point of indecency to report that a judge had a cold." Certainly it seems in retrospect that the campaigning, crusading *Mirror* kept clear of prosecution in the future.

At the time of the *Mirror*'s blunder there was much sympathy in Fleet Street with the unfortunate editor, who was known as an intelligent, perspicacious man who had entered journalism in Newcastle-on-Tyne from Durham University and had excelled as a subeditor. For such a man, the risks that infest a crime story once an arrest has been made should have been elementary knowledge. It was significant that the *Mirror* did not add dismissal to the penalty imposed by the court. Two years after his release from detention he was still the paper's editor, and had become a member of the board.

Bolam's directorship became particularly important when, in 1951, King had resolved that Bartholomew, now about seventy years of age, must quit. Office opinion intimated that he was slipping; that his instructions to the staff were vague and his judgment was untrustworthy. A gentle approach suggesting retirement, was sharply repelled. Whether he could be retired compulsorily depended upon how individual directors might vote on that issue. Seemingly, Bartholomew calculated that he would have a majority of one. On the day of decision the one director on whom he had counted most confidently was no longer attached to him—Sylvester Bolam. So it was that the man who had played an influential part in the remarkable development of the *Mirror* since the days of Northcliffe's ownership went into retirement sullenly, despite a golden handshake.

One of King's earliest actions as chairman was to bring back Hugh Cudlipp to resume at once his editorship of the *Sunday Pictorial* and to restore that paper to the position it had reached when he left it. That done, Cudlipp was to go to Australia for a while to apply his special gifts to the Melbourne *Argus*. As that overseas mission was ending, King recalled him by cable. A situation had arisen in which it was possible to drop Sylvester Bolam, who had never conformed to King's concept of an ideal editor of the *Mirror*. In the new chairman's opinion, he had always a tendency to instruct rather pedantically, whereas readers preferred an arresting presentation of facts accompanied by conclusions delivered in the imperative mood. When they wanted to be entertained, Bolam had tended to bore them. So Jack Nemer took over the *Mirror*, its eighth editor in forty-nine years. The periods of editorship of these men had varied from three years to fourteen. The longest innings was achieved by Cecil Thomas whose term included the whole of the duration of the Second World War. If any deduction can be drawn from this aspect of the *Mirror* story, it is that, once the paper's appeal was turned from a middle-class readership to the broad mass of the population, the peculiar needs of a lively, restless, tabloid newspaper required a constant freshness of touch that could not be expected of any single individual for long.

In the reorganization consequent upon Bolam's departure, Hugh Cudlipp, back from Australia, became editorial director of both the *Daily Mirror* and the *Sunday Pictorial*. That status, however did not reflect adequately the influence now exercised by the man whom Bartholomew engaged and sacked. The measure of King's confidence in Cudlipp was revealed several years later, when King was giving evidence before the second Royal Commission on the press.

The chairman of that inquiry, Lord Shawcross, having quoted the *Mirror*'s written evidence on the method of policy coordination in the group, asked about an allusion to a "committee to discuss strategy." King replied decisively, "There is no committee; there are only two of us—Cudlipp and myself."

Later in the dialogue, King explained, "On editorial policy, Hugh Cudlipp and I, who have been directors together for many years, work closely. . . . I suppose I see him very nearly every day, and if anything crops up we decide what we are going to do; but I very rarely see the editors. He sees the editors and the editors are responsible to him." Cudlipp, also a witness, corroborated.

This evidence related only to the *Daily Mirror* and the *Sunday Pictorial*. The answers, however, were broadly applicable to a partnership whose interests extended over a much larger area. Before that meeting with the Commission took place, the *Mirror* group had negotiated what Hugh Cudlipp, who participated, described as "a series of take-overs which had the effect of revolutionizing the business of magazine publishing within the space of a few months."

In the first of these bids, the financial attraction was supplemented, for Cecil Harmsworth King, by an interesting family association. The prize, known as the Amalgamated Press, was the first limited liability company to be formed by his Uncle Alfred (Harmsworth) nearly seventy years earlier, with the title of Answers Limited. It published the periodical *Answers*, firstborn of all the publications launched by Northcliffe. Following *Answers*, there came into being a variegated array of prosperous periodicals that enabled him to enter the newspaper field.

After Northcliffe's death, the Amalgamated Press was sold to the proprietors of the *Daily Telegraph* for whom popular periodicals were an unfamiliar sphere; and for some thirty years thereafter some growth but little pruning of the collection took place. When King and his colleagues overhauled what they had bought it was found to consist of forty-two weekly publications, twenty-three monthlies, and twenty annuals. They ranged from the venerable *Sunday Companion*, inaugurated in 1894 for Victorians who were averse from reading secular papers on the Sabbath, to *Marilyn* for modern teenagers. Had the deal occurred sooner, it might have included *Vogue*, but owing to an earlier option that arbiter of elegance was spared the indignity of inclusion in a package deal.

Hardly had this very considerable group, now renamed the Fleetway Press, been integrated with the *Mirror* organization, than King was renewing an old friendship with the chairman of Odhams, proprietors of the only other considerable group of popular periodicals and also of two newspapers, namely, the proletarian *Daily Herald* and the Sunday crusader, the *People*. Here was a merger problem more complex than the previous deal, inasmuch as the *Daily Herald* was virtually the official organ of the Labour party. Its political policy was controlled by the Trades Union Congress, but in all commercial respects its production was the responsibility of Odhams. Apart from the disadvantage that the *Herald* was no money spinner, there would be something incongruous in the idea of its being produced by the same publishing company as the *Daily Mirror*. While the *Herald* loyally proclaimed only the virtues of the Labour party, the *Mirror* was merely Leftist, and in so far as it was a friend of the Labour party, it was a very candid friend, reinforcing its candor by its long addiction to the imperative mood. Here, indeed, was something to test the considerable resourcefulness of both King and Cudlipp.

That apart, there was an immense advantage in gaining control of the only periodical house that competed seriously with the newly acquired Fleetway publications. Adhering to Odhams was the older enterprise of George Newnes Limited whose founder preceded Alfred Harmsworth as a pioneer of penny weeklies, and whose popular *Tit-Bits* inspired Harmsworth to respond by starting *Answers to Correspondents*. Nor was that the only occasion on which the young Harmsworth took a cue from Newnes.

Over the years, the Newnes enterprise had added many valuable properties to its assets by purchase. Several successful magazines came by a merger with the firm established by Arthur Pearson, a rival of Northcliffe in both the periodical and newspaper fields. Newnes would bring to the *Mirror* organization the unique weekly *Country Life* whose success so tantalized Northcliffe that, even after periodicals had ceased to be his major interest, he bought a quality weekly called *The World* with the intention of converting it into a rival to *Country Life*, a hope it never fulfilled.

The negotiations, however, did not maintain the smooth progress with which they began. News leaked that Mr. Roy Thomson was interested and disposed to bid. Indeed, according to rumors current in Fleet Street at one stage, the staffs of Odhams publications, discussing the reputations of the two potential buyers, were uncertain whether to cry, "Vive le Roi, or Vive le Roy!" Early in 1961, following a year that has been described as the worst in terms of newspaper closures in the history of Fleet Street, uncertainty ended. The *Mirror* directors won, and their company became the largest newspaper, periodical, and printing group in the United Kingdom.

In the report for the year 1966, when this process of expansion paused, the Press Council, whose constitutional responsibilities include the duty of reviewing developments in the press, published without comment the terms of an "independent examination" of the International Publishing Corporation, the name which, after the Odhams take-over, was given to the comprehensive structure headed by Cecil King. This survey stated explicitly, "The International Publishing Corporation is the largest and most comprehensive communications empire in the world. . . . In this country alone it publishes two major national dailies, and two of the three largest circulation Sunday newspapers, as well as a number of other dailies. It publishes 90 weekly periodicals in Britain and 123 magazines appearing less frequently, from fortnightly to quarterly. Even these figures (from the latest report) may fall short of the current facts as the group changes rapidly."

The survey noted that, apart from the firms producing newspapers and periodicals, I.P.C. embraced television and radio companies, a group of paper manufacturers, several book publishing houses, printing establishments, an interest in one of the largest English chains of newsagents and a half-share in Music for Pleasure, a disc-distributing enterprise.

To conclude this presentation of facts and financial information the independent examiners of the organization added their finding that the history of the *Mirror* enterprise "has been one of continuous expansion since Mr. Cecil Harmsworth King became chairman in 1952. Unlike other more personal empires, this one is firmly set in modern managerial ways. The management inherited with the constituent parts of the group, has been reinforced, as we have seen, with outsiders of proved success in their own fields. At the same time the group has not been afraid to slim, either by disposing of interests not in the mainstream of its activities, or by judicious pruning of duplicated managements within the group."

Somewhere in his copious reminiscences, Hannen Swaffer has told of a time when, as an editor, access to his proprietor became meaningless because whenever he opened the door of the chairman's room, he found his chief surrounded by bank men and accountants, studying balance sheets and doing sums. The typical British journalist, confronted by such a report as that published by the Press Council concerning I.P.C., would wonder whether he had been wrong in his belief hitherto that the success of a newspaper or periodical depended upon the wits and labors, and sense of professional dedication, of the journalists serving it; and that it is for the end product of those qualities that the public pays its pence.

In the context of the 1960's, however, the viability of the industry within which the profession of journalism is contained was never more important, for it had become possible, as Robert Donald had predicted half a century ago, to disseminate news and to interpret it without the aid of the printing industry. And no longer did the public at large insist upon "seeing it in black and white," before believing what they heard, as was the habit of their sceptical forefathers.

Hugh Cudlipp, whom King had extolled as "Unquestionably, the best journalist in the country" was with other directors, a party to the negotiations that had so greatly enlarged the interests of the *Mirror* companies and had buttressed them by association with other publishing enterprises in the I.P.C. In the evidence, written and oral, tendered by the companies to the second Royal Commission on the Press, 1961–62, he and the other *Mirror* men testified that "No newspaper can survive without charity unless it can balance its books." Cudlipp had indeed expressed his views more explicitly in his book, *At Your Peril*, published about the same time. There, he declared, "Roy Thomson is only partially right when he reiterates his favourite theme that newspapers are a business, like any other business. . . . But newspapers are not like any other business except in the sense that they make a profit to survive. . . . Their death is the death of an idea, of an attitude to life, a service to the public and . . . when that doesn't matter, democracy doesn't matter."

During his years as editorial director of the two *Mirrors*, Cudlipp had to combine large scale book-balancing conferences with his function as the mainspring of editorial enterprise; and there is no evidence of relaxed interest in either duty. Indeed, on the editorial side, the electoral defeat of the first postwar Labour government meant that the somewhat individual political policies of the *Mirrors* demanded a more sophisticated interpretation than hitherto. In retreating from government to opposition, a party always loses morale, due to the disappointment created by defeat and the inevitable critcism, and also to the fact that its relationship to the journalism of the day is seriously affected. What a government does, or intends to do, becomes news, and news hard enough to be reckoned among the facts of life in the editorial assessment of news values. What the opposition has to say commands less attention. It is mere declamation, rarely constructive and therefore at best no more than an expression of hope for the future, if and when the defeated party regains power.

In any electoral upheaval of parties, this situation recurs, but the change of 1951 was rendered the more acute by the return of Churchill to the premiership at the age of seventy-six. This restoration invested him with unique authority deriving from the widespread public desire to take what must be the final opportunity to express gratitude for his wartime leadership, to soften the memory of his rejection in 1945, and to honor him for the distinction in many aspects of life other than politics that had accorded him the title of "the greatest living Englishman." Soon after his return to office his impressive eloquence was turned to the melancholy duty of voicing the nation's tribute on the death of King George VI.

If the reader's choice of a daily paper were determined by political considerations, the *Daily Mirror* would have been on a falling market during most of the fourteen years that followed the general election of 1950, because the electorate, no longer enamored of Labour policies, showed increasingly by their votes, a preference for Conservative government. But it did not require any deep study of mass readership to show that political affiliations do not dictate choice of newspapers to any significant extent. As a new prime minister, Mr. Harold Wilson recognized when, replying to an afterdinner eulogy by Cecil King, he said, "Newspapers are not always bought for their political views but for their readability, their wider news value and their sport."

King needed no reminder of that truth, for one of his earliest decisions, after his election to the chairmanship of the *Mirror* companies, was to bring back to their service the man whom he regarded as "Unquestionably, the finest journalist in the country," to be the editorial director of both the *Mirror*s. With King's predominant interest in politics and Cudlipp's ability to evaluate every instrument in the journalistic orchestra, there existed a partnership that contrived to sustain a high level of interest in every issue of their papers, regardless of the fortunes of the Labour party to which they accorded support of a kind that was never slavish or uncritical.

From 1950, when the first postwar Labour government was nearly defeated at the polls, the political policy of the *Mirror* demanded a more sophisticated interpretation than formerly. When, as disappointed parties tend to do, Labour looked critically at its leader, the *Daily Mirror*, throughout a conflict over Attlee's successor, was particularly adroit. Where Churchill was concerned, the paper's continuous appeal to youth required frequent, disparaging references to the age of the Conservative leader, to inoculate the oncoming generation against undue admiration of his leadership.

Here was a love-hate relationship. The *Mirror*, with its aptitude for sensing the feelings of its readers, tended to pay tribute to Churchill's wartime leadership, but to deplore his continuance in politics at the age of seventy-six.

When in 1951 Attlee found it practically impossible to govern with a majority of seventeen seats in a House of six hundred and twenty-five members, and sought a fresh mandate and stronger support by bringing about a general election, the *Mirror* saw a need to be more aggressive. To quote Maurice Edelman, it "plunged to the aid of the Labour party" and "its impetus went ahead of prudence."

On polling day in 1951, its front page, carrying only thirty-nine words was virtually a poster. It was dominated by a hand clasping a heavy military revolver, finger on trigger, hammer cocked, requiring only that slight, second pressure to dispatch the bullet. The message displayed around the pistol and further illustrated by portraits of Attlee and Churchill, told the reader, "Today your finger is on the trigger" and exhorted him or her to defend the peace by voting "for the party you can trust." The words, obviously had been meticulously chosen with a lively awareness of the law of defamation. Unfortunately for its verbal ingenuity, the *Mirror* had made use of this pistol theme (derived from Pravda's retort of "Warmonger!" to Churchill's "iron curtain" disclosures at Fulton, Missouri, in 1947) in an article only a short time before polling day. Therein, the *Mirror* had said: "We do not of course imagine that anyone would want to pull the trigger, but in spite of our esteem for Mr. Churchill, we must point out that there are forces at work in the world which he dangerously misunderstands." Although the voting would have been completed before derisive action could be taken, Churchill caused a writ for libel to be issued against the *Mirror* on polling day. The defendants thought the question of whose finger was on the trigger was, in its terms, too general to be libelous, but that point was not one for hairsplitting argument by lawyers. It would be for a jury to decide, and in such suits British juries are notoriously unpredictable. Eventually, wise counsels prevailed and the *Mirror* sought a settlement, in which Churchill stipulated for a contribution of fifteen hundred pounds to a charity and the payment of his costs. Appropriately, the charity nominated by Churchill, whose advanced age was so frequently a subject of attention by the *Mirror*, was the Church Army Charitable Homes for

Elderly People. Summing up this episode, Maurice Edelman says: "Churchill had reason to be pleased. He had won the election, rebutted an attack, and opened up a new vista which was to lead to thirteen years of Conservative rule endorsed by the elections of 1955 and 1959."

The love-hate relationship between the *Mirror* and its most distinguished reader continued until his retirement. Other considerations apart, Churchill was news, whatever he was doing. Indeed, when he appeared to be doing nothing, the *Mirror* tended to become agitated about his health; and when he was officially admitted to be unwell, it viewed the announcement with scepticism, demanding medical precision. Of these occasions his personal physician, has told in his memoirs. Showing the doctor a magazine, *History Today,* Churchill remarked, "It is written by young historians for serious people. . . . I find all this very encouraging. . . . It would appear that not everyone in England reads the *Daily Mirror.*" A year before his eightieth birthday, the patient denounced the *Mirror* as "a rag" that was doing much harm; but when the crucial anniversary arrived, he noticed with pleasure that the *Mirror* had declared a truce and had commemorated the birthday with a souvenir issue. More also, the directors had subscribed one thousand pounds to the nation's birthday tribute, which stood at one hundred forty thousand pounds. To Lord Moran he remarked, "All this leaves me very humble; it is more than I deserve."

In its ambiguous attitude to Churchill the *Mirror* reflected with considerable accuracy the emotional inconsistency of its readers, exhibited directly when, in the election campaign of 1945 they cheered him vociferously as he toured the country, but dismissed him by their votes when they went to the poll.

In 1955, the directors of the *Daily Mirror* had cause to appreciate the advantage of its political classification as "an independent newspaper of the left." Since the defeat of the Labour government in 1951, its sales had continued to rise steadily, whereas those of Labour's official organ, the *Daily Herald* continued just as steadily to decline. The *Mirror* had tended to pipe down on politics, and to maintain its attractiveness for the public by playing fortissimo other themes of current interest, while the official organ was obliged to expatiate on the internal party con-

flicts that multiply the bleak winds of political misfortunes, dis-
turb confidence in leaders and in policies.

Between 1955 and 1959, a complete change occurred in
Britain's political leadership. Following Winston Churchill's
resignation as prime minister and leader of the Conservatives
(with Sir Anthony Eden succeeding smoothly to both places),
Clement Attlee, at the age of seventy-two, decided to retire from
political life. With three candidates in the field, this change was
accompanied by considerable controversy. A ballot of parliamentary representatives of the Labour party was inescapable, and
Hugh Gaitskell, who like Cecil King had been educated at Winchester and Oxford, was elected by a comfortable majority.
Another major change was to occur, sensationally. In less than
two years after his appointment, Eden who was never robust,
suffered a breakdown of health partly as a consequence of the
strain imposed by the attempt to resolve the Suez deadlock by
military intervention, to the detriment of Anglo-American relationship.

This brought to the premiership at the age of sixty-one,
Harold Macmillan who rallied his troubled party and, barely
three years later, through a general election with an overall
majority, increased it from sixty to one hundred seats, a feat of
political leadership for which it was difficult to find a parallel.
The caprice of political fortune was later to be illustrated by the
fate of Hugh Gaitskell who, though he was elected to leadership
of the Labour party at the comparatively early age of forty-nine,
did not live long enough to lead his party to electoral success and
to install himself as prime minister. He died in 1963.

Nevertheless Hugh Gaitskell figures conspicuously in the
history of the *Mirror* and the International Publishing Company.
In the competitive negotiations for the acquisition of Odhams
group in 1961, there was a stage at which success turned upon the
future which the rival bidders could offer to the *Daily Herald*.
Although the paper was controlled commercially by Odhams, the
Trades Union Congress held 49 percent of the shares of the
Herald company, and it was by reason of the T.U.C's support of
the Labor party that the *Herald* ranked as the official organ of
the Labour party. It followed from the probability that Odhams
would be taken over by either the Thomson organization or by

King's I.P.C. that the future of the *Herald* as a loss-making paper was precarious. Hugh Gaitskell, as leader of a party in adversity faced a dilemma. He needed the support of the only daily newspaper that would advocate whatever policy his party adopted, and as his personal ties with trade unionism were negligible, he valued highly the guidance of the leaders of the T.U.C. whose financial support of the paper had been hitherto a factor in maintaining it.

Though Roy Thomson allowed his editors to determine political policy, he was personally a Conservative. On the other hand King, though uncommitted personally had long demonstrated radical sympathies, and Cudlipp was so manifestly a believer in Labour's objectives that formal membership of the party had no significance. Moreover, the *Mirror* of King and Cudlipp was supported by more Labour party members than the *Herald* had ever been able to attract. If that were all, Gaitskell's choice would have been easy.

The crucial question, however, was—How long would either of these rivals permit the *Herald* to survive if that heavy deficit on its production could not be removed? Under the control of King and Cudlipp the continuance of that loss would always be a strong commercial argument in favor of merging the *Herald* with the *Mirror*, whose right to take its own view of Labour policy was unlikely ever to be abandoned.

Roy Thomson was under no similar temptation. He owned no paper to which the *Herald* could conveniently be married. Nevertheless, to carry on indefinitely a sickly publication that did not react profitably to the new money and new management that he could supply, would be inconsistent with his record. All the same, Gaitskell favored Thomson.

The *Mirror* men had cause for deep thinking. If the Thomson bid succeeded, all the Odhams periodicals would be lost to their empire, and the advantage of owning the Fleetway periodicals would be neutralized. Instead of a rationalization of the two largest groups of popular periodicals, there would be strenuous competition, a contest of giants. An awkward pause in the negotiations ensued, in which other bidders made their appearance. In all, the struggle continued for nearly three months during which offers from new bidders descended upon Odhams shareholders. Questions about a monopolistic merger were asked in Parliament, but the government's answers had to be founded upon inability to intervene by reason of lack of authority in law.

Eventually, the *Mirror* men won. They had not been opposed to the principle of guaranteeing the continuance of the *Herald*, and Cudlipp found the key to success in a proposal that they should undertake to continue the *Herald* as a separate publication, responsible to the Labour party for its political policy, for a period as long as seven years. With that concession, it became possible to complete the deal. In the sequel, however, considerable guarantee did not run its full term. On Gaitskell's death two years later and Harold Wilson's succession to the leadership of the party, a variation of the undertaking found acceptance. The *Mirror* men offered to launch an entirely new newspaper to replace the *Herald*, one with a wider appeal to people of radical views and one free of the disadvantages of an official alliance with the Labor party. In 1959 Gaitskell had detected "a breaking-up of old loyalties." In that process the disintegration of the Liberal party was discernible, and in 1961 the most widely read Liberal newspaper, the *News-Chronicle* died, mourned by 1,162,000 readers. Then there were always socialist intellectuals like Aneurin Bevan who, in the Commons debate on the 1942 ministerial threat to suspend publication of the *Daily Mirror*, spoke strongly against such repression, but added, "I do not like the *Daily Mirror*. I do not like that form of journalism. I do not like the striptease artists. If the *Daily Mirror* depended upon my purchasing it, it would never be sold."

So, on a day in September 1964, the *Daily Herald* made its last appearance after fifty-two years and, on the following morning, there appeared the widely advertised *Sun*, flying at its masthead a colored symbol of the sun in full glory accompanied by the description, "The Independent Newspaper." The change proved to have been well timed, for ten days later Parliament was dissolved and a general election took place in the following month; newspapers were being read more eagerly than ever.

From that appeal to the electorate, the Labor party, after thirteen years in Opposition, returned to power under Harold Wilson's leadership, but the "power" resided in a majority no greater of four seats in a House of 630 members. Still, the new government contrived to avoid a major defeat until the spring of 1966 brought a suitable tactical situation for another appeal to the country, from which Wilson returned with the majority augmented to the truly comfortable figure of 97 seats.

In the first of these two elections, which was much the more difficult for Labour, the *Daily Mirror* was a major factor in turning the tide. In the second appeal to the country, the energy that had been exhibited by the team of new ministers, and Wilson's call to them for "a Hundred dynamic days" contrasted sharply with the signs of exhaustion obvious in the Conservatives, due to their long spell of office and the loss since the last election of Macmillan's leadership through illness. This evidence of lost morale swung the confidence of floating voters who on the previous occasion had lacked faith in Labour's ability to govern.

During Labour's recent phase of recovery, Harold Wilson and Cecil King had maintained a process of consultation that was not always as harmonious as it was close. Wilson was constrained by party doctrine whereas King's political party consisted of one member— himself. The two men, differing considerably in their backgrounds had one experience in common, namely, their graduation at Oxford (of which university, ironically, the current chancellor was Harold Macmillan). A characteristic that the two possessed in common was less helpful. It was a degree of stubbornness which, in the earthy vocabulary of the *Mirror*, would most likely have been diagnosed as "pig-headedness." It derived from differing sources; in Wilson it came from his Yorkshire ancestry and in King from his Harmsworth descent.

Nevertheless at this period their consultation was of considerable value to the Labour party. The new prime minister was not ungrateful. He paid tribute to King's financial and organizing ability by nominating him for a directorship of the Bank of England and appointing him a part-time member of the Coal Board which administered the nationalized mining industry. But King, like his uncle, Northcliffe, believed himself to be no less endowed with political gifts; but it seems that Prime Minister Wilson (like his predecessor Lloyd George in assessing Northcliffe) was not disposed to rate that endowment very high. Moreover, prime ministers have always been shy, even in the exceptional requirements imposed by war, to admit active newspaper

men to the Cabinet. Such a situation was not a good omen for
their future relationship.

On the last day of 1965, after the new prime minister had
governed with his microscopic majority for some fourteen
months, the *Daily Mirror* submitted him to what it described as
"a searching appraisal." On the front page, in type nearly two
inches in depth, it proclaimed Harold Wilson MAN OF THE
YEAR, this typographical fanfare being accompanied by a photographic portrait by Karsh of Ottawa 8½ by 6½ inches. Almost
the whole of the double-page spread was devoted to the appraisal.
Of the character of the prime minister the article said, "In
strength of purpose . . . in brain power and energy . . . in breadth
of knowledge, he has erased his docile predecessor from public
memory with a puff of pipe-smoke." In the Commons he had
shown himself "more than capable of dealing with his critics" on
whose heads he heaped at a second's notice, "derision, invective
and innuendo."

With the addition of some roughage to make this eulogy
digestible by readers, Mr. Wilson was exhorted to remember that
"Europe, and only Europe, can apply the spur our industry
needs . . ." (an allusion to the European Common Market alliance, to which the *Mirror* was dedicated). "Here is Britain's and
Harold Wilson's great opportunity. And no politician is more
fitted by economic training, grasp of detail, and pertinacity to
lead this country away from its past and into its future."

Two years later, Cecil King was showing symptoms of unease
over the political situation. In a speech at a time when the devaluation of the pound and its consequences were having their
inevitable effect on the government's already declining popularity, King criticized the operation of the party system that
rendered impossible the formation of a coalition government
except in times of direst emergency, though there were other
times in history when the situation was less than disastrous and
when a coalition might form the most effective government.
Still, he concluded, if the government coped successfully with
the economic problem, and if they set in train the reform of
parliamentary procedure and overhauled the Civil Service,
"Harold Wilson might yet go down in the history books."

Obviously, King's faith in Wilson, now equipped with a

good parliamentary majority, was impaired, and his patience ebbing. That process continued for three months and then on a May morning in 1968, the *Daily Mirror* created a sensation with an article entitled sternly, "Enough is Enough!" in which Cecil King (with his by-line printed conspicuously) declared that Britain was threatened by "the greatest financial crisis in our history" and called for the resignation of the prime minister. In the furor that followed, the fact emerged that shortly before the article appeared, King had tendered his resignation from the Board of the Bank of England. In that step, it transpired, he only anticipated what the Chancellor of the Exchequer would have demanded of him as a sequel to King's alarmist prophecy. As it was, all the Chancellor could tell the Commons in reply to questions was that the resignation had been accepted promptly and without regret.

The more serious consequence of King's outburst did not come so swiftly as the Chancellor's acceptance of his resignation from the Bank of England. Nearly three weeks afterwards the secretary of I.P.C. made an early call at King's home ("Whilst I was shaving," says King) bearing a letter from the board requesting him formally to resign his chairmanship and directorship of the corporation. His reply was an emphatic refusal. So, a few hours later there arrived another hand-borne letter from the board intimating that he had been dismissed.

Toward evening, when Cecil King went to the multistoried headquarters of the *Mirror*s and the I.P.C., in the foyer of which a commemorative plaque proclaims that the building was opened by Cecil Harmsworth King in 1961, reporters and photographers from the press at large were waiting for him. The news of his removal was making the lead story in the afternoon papers, and the morning papers wanted more information for tomorrow's issues. The story had started by a special television flash. It quoted a statement issued by the board of I.P.C., bearing the signatures of all the directors announcing the dismissal of King and the succession of Hugh Cudlipp to the chairmanship. Then—possibly to forestall the kind of rumors to which such summary action might give rise—the directors added a tribute to "Mr. King's tremendous contribution to the expansion of I.P.C." and an avowal of the "great esteem and affection" in which he would always be held by his colleagues.

King lost no time in disseminating his own version of events by interviews on the television screen and in the press. He described the delivery of the letters at his home, without any prior confrontation with those who made the decision. Nevertheless he acquitted his protégé and successor, Hugh Cudlipp, of intriguing with the prime minister to bring about his removal; but he hazarded a guess that, under the new regime, the *Daily Mirror* would switch to the support of the Labour party "just in time to nail the flag to the mast of the ship as it goes down." Then, with King's philosophy rising superior to his resentment, and with an excessive awareness of his sixty-seven years, he remarked, "I've always been tough on older men who cling on, past the time when they were wanted. When you dish it out, you must be prepared to take it."

The personal aspect of this clash, its relevance to politics, to the stock market and to a current controversy about press monopolies, kept the subject rumbling in the news through the two months that elapsed before the annual meeting of I.P.C.'s shareholders. For that occasion, the directors' report, published in advance, took the form of a colorful brochure describing the corporation's highly diversified properties and its ramifications as an instructive background to the facts and figures of the year's trading. It served to remind shareholders that in little more than five years this massive undertaking had been constructed on what the directors described as the strong foundation of the *Daily Mirror* company. "Great progress," they said, had been made in combining the several groups of companies, formerly unconnected, into one efficient and cohesive organization, ranking as "the world's foremost publishing group." As now organized into autonomous "Divisions," their interests were newspapers, magazines, business publishing, books and printing, plus a division for staff training and one for new enterprises, this last having been devised to launch and develop commercial activities to supplement the traditional areas of the corporation's business, particularly in new communication technologies that "are revolutionizing publishing and printing methods . . . which will create vast expanding new markets."

An example of the kind of new communication technologies was, no doubt, a recent innovation that enabled the *Daily Mirror* and its Sunday associate to be printed on a new web offset plant in Belfast and distributed throughout Ireland. These editions were prepared in the *Mirror*'s Manchester office and, by means of facsimile transmission, using cable and radio links, were reproduced in Belfast 175 miles away.

On the more prosaic subject of the past year's business, the report recorded a recession whose total effect was to reduce the dividend for the year to 18 percent, against 21 percent for the previous year. Trading conditions had been "very difficult," advertising revenue was lower, and the general tendency for costs to increase had been "exacerbated by the devaluation of the pound." All the same, the corporation had gone ahead with its plans for development.

Viewed thus, there was no cause for turbulence at the shareholders' meeting, though some present descanted, as disgruntled investors could be expected to do in such circumstances. There were only a few who gave Hugh Cudlipp an opportunity to show that he was not entirely new to chairmanship and had the ability to handle irrelevant speakers and disorderly hecklers quite effectively.

Despite the paramount importance of dividends to investors, the major interest of this meeting of shareholders was provided by the two chairmen, the relegated King and the ascendant Cudlipp. Here was a public confrontation. In the body of the hall was Cecil King in his capacity as the holder of 48,206 ordinary and 51 preference shares. Although his holding had been calculated to represent less than one percent of the corporation's capital, he had been for many present, the personification of I.P.C. since its formation. No one doubted that he had something to say and that he would say it in unambiguous terms. On the platform was King's successor, thirteen years younger than King, and looking it. He was as tough in negotiation as he was in physique, but possessed of a ready sense of humor. In him, the born journalist's instinct for the telling phrase and the striking headline could show itself equal to the swift, witty retort, and where that would not serve the need of the situation, he could assume not less quickly a "You-be-damned" attitude, especially if the critics were asking for trouble.

King, when his opportunity came, though he spoke with his characteristic quietness and control, did not mince his words. He described the dismissal episode as "a conspiracy of a particularly squalid kind," nor did he play down his resentment of the effrontery implicit in the request for his resignation which, had he conformed to it, would have left the impression on the public that he had been "caught with his hand in the till." Despite such strictures on his former colleagues, he paid tribute to Cudlipp as "the best popular journalist in the world," and in conclusion expressed his good wishes not only for the future of the corporation but his former fellow directors. To the concilliatory mood of the man who had been his mentor for thirty years, Cudlipp responded in a similar spirit. He announced a payment of thirty-five thousand pounds to King for loss of office, in addition to the full retirement benefits he would normally receive. On the political aspect of the revolution (and it was on King's increasing involvement in politics to the detriment of the corporation's interests that action was based) Cudlipp went so far as to disclose that he shared King's censures of the government.

The shareholders' meeting was, officially, the end of the unhappy episode. Although in the course of the controversy King had referred to it as the fall of the curtain on his newspaper career of forty-three years, there were those who doubted its finality. They had recognized in him, despite occasional manifestations of impetuosity and didacticism, qualities of vision and boldness necessary for the maintenance of a free and viable press in a new era of communications which had saddled the printed word with some serious disadvantages. Consequently, there was speculation when the *Times*, soon after his departure from I.P.C., began to publish articles by Cecil King. The earliest were interpretations of the decisions and debates of the Conservative and Labour parties at their annual conferences; but succeeding pieces were essays rather than articles, one of which was concerned with his personal concept of prayer.

Although the publication of these contributions could be justified by their inherent merit, even so tenuous a link with his former rival, Lord Thomson, was a piquant novelty. Only a few months earlier, King had been reported as criticizing Thomson as being "interested only in money" whereas "I have to promote what I conceive to be the interests of my country." Later, in a broadcast interview, he said he regarded Lord Thompson's interest "in stuffing his pockets full of money as unworthy—sometimes amusing and sometimes contemptible." Thomson's early retort to that was to accuse King of being interested in power; but later the proprietor of the *Times* was to say, "I like Mr. King. He is a man of honour and integrity . . . and I think he feels much the same way about me."

Socially, politically, and journalistically, the evolution of the *Daily Mirror* is a most instructive event in the history of the British press since the advertiser emancipated newspapers from the rich individual who was prepared to maintain a newspaper or an influential periodical so long as he could dictate its political policy. Though that kind of service usually had its reward in the form of titles or of safe seats in Parliament from the political party benefitting by the newspaper's advocacy, the time came, soon after the First World War, when the costs of maintaining newspapers reached too high a level for that process to be attractive. Political parties themselves could not afford to subsidize newspapers. Even the official organs of the Labour party, the *Daily Citizen* and its successor, the *Daily Herald* were financed by trade unions.

Fortuitously, the *Daily Mirror*'s financial structure underwent a change that produced an example of a newspaper sustained by a body of shareholders, none of whom had a sufficient holding to dictate policy and appoint directors. The shareholders were interested in commercial success—in dividends; and the people who knew how to produce attractive newspapers that would enjoy mass sales and earn profits, were the journalists and those skilled in the administration of newspaper enterprises. A combination of journalists, technicians, and administrators, working in coordination as directors could be self-renewing, and shareholders would support boards thus composed of men who, manifestly, knew their business.

Still, somewhere in the combination there had to be a superlative editor, one who could be described also as a "born" journalist. Cecil King detected such a one in the young Cudlipp, about whose qualities he maintained his opinion even at the moment when anger and personal resentment might have impinged on integrity of judgment.

13

A. J. Cummings

The columnist with a spotlight on politics

Arthur John Cummings (1882–1957) won a wide reputation as the best British political columnist of his time. He had for me when I first saw him an instantly captivating personality. Slimly straight, lean-faced, with closely scrutinizing eyes, he looked like a born leader. Even before I heard him speak in a slightly authoritative voice there could be no doubt in my mind that this was the older brother of my school friend Harry Cummings. Harry and I had been in the same house, Sixes, at the Bluecoat School, the Religious, Royal and Ancient Foundation of Christ's Hospital, Newgate Street, London. He had played halfback to my wing three-quarter in a football cup-winning house team. Once, at school, I met Harry's younger brother, Bruce Frederick, who became a biologist and, when facing early death from disseminated sclerosis, wrote a brave and haunting book *The Journal of a Disappointed Man*, to which H. G. Wells wrote a generous introduction. All three brothers inherited literary skill from a journalist father. All had the same look of penetrating intelligence.

The year of my first meeting with Arthur was 1904, the scene, the press tent at the Great Yorkshire Show at Huddersfield. This annual show, now with a spacious permanent ground at Harrogate, used in those days to visit different towns. Arthur,

who was then about twenty-two (I was four years younger) had
come to report for the *Sheffield Telegraph*. I was on a paper that
must have had one of the feeblest circulations in Britain, the
four-page *Huddersfield Daily Chronicle*; its large weekly issue on
a Saturday kept it going precariously, but it died years ago. From
that famous wool textile town that sells so much excellent cloth
to American tailors I moved a little later to the *Sheffield Telegraph*, possibly with the help of a word in season by Arthur, and
so became a colleague of his till I broke away from staff reporting
and went to try my luck as a free lance in Paris.

The junior reporters' copy at Sheffield did not go to the subeditors as it would now, but was read and if necessary revised by
senior reporters or the chief reporter himself. In this way I
learned a great deal, especially from the encouraging and warmhearted Cummings and a more censorious senior, Harry Mince,
who excelled as a reporter of the old school.

I had no doubt Cummings would become one of the masters
of British journalism. He did. By the late thirties of the twentieth
century he had become as the chief columnist of the *News
Chronicle* probably the most influential political commentator in
Britain. His early years at home and in journalism gave excellent
training for this unforeseen role. To begin with, he learned much
about journalism, literature, and the practical arts of writing
from his father, John Cummings, Barnstaple and North Devon
representative of the *Devon and Exeter Gazette* and a columnist
of more distinction than most provincial reporters. His household
was one of strong religious faith and family loyalty.

Arthur went to Rock Park School, Barnstaple, probably then
the only independent school in the town. Its headmaster was
imbued with classical learning, and at Arthur's last speech-day as
a student, praised him as *facile princeps*. Before this, when on a
summer holiday, Arthur had impressed a young man, Philip
Ernest Richards, then at Oxford and later to enter the Unitarian
ministry. Richards wrote *Vagabonds in Kashmir*, a record of a
three months trip in 1912, published by the Orient Publishing
Company, Lahore. How much Richards did to influence his
young friend may be gathered from this tribute that Arthur
wrote in a foreword to the book:

Courtesy of Barnet Saidman

A. J. CUMMINGS

During my early years he was in a very real sense my guide and philosopher and friend, moulding my judgment of men and books and life, stimulating my ambitions, directing my impulses, generously tolerant of boyish crudenesses and conceits, until in time he became for me and long remained the standard and very type of behaviour, of culture, of all moral and intellectual excellence. In his presence, I felt, as others have confessed to feeling, the irresistable influence of a fine thinker, an acute observer, a fastidious critic, a man exquisitely sensitive to all forms of beauty, a noble spirit, far emoved from the squalid meannesses of life, cherishing lofty ideals, expressing a wise benevolence that could embrace the whole world.

This appreciation may well be accepted as a mirror of its author's own awareness and sensibilities. Probably under the combined influence of his headmaster and Richards, Cummings hoped to study law at Oxford. This ambition, as happened so often with middle-class aspirants before the First World War, failed. His father's health broke down. Arthur's dream of a forensic career faded. He needed a calling that did not demand an outlay of capital, could use his special abilities, and would yield an income, if at first small. To be a journalist offered an obvious solution of the problem. The *Devon and Exeter Gazette* engaged the youth. Usually a beginner had to perform only the most humdrum tasks, such as reporting what were flippantly known as chapel bun-fights. Not so Cummings. He played the violin. So he wrote concert critiques. He knew something of economics. So he even wrote stock market notes. He kept himself up to date in current events and studied the how and why of them. Soon he was writing editorials. The *Devon and Exeter Gazette* must have thought it had found a prodigy.

Cummings, as was the way of young journalists at that time, wanted to broaden his experience, and an offer from the famous *Rochdale Observer* drew him to Lancashire. He may have been sorry to separate himself from the scenic beauty of glorious Devon, but he found consolation in the political and economic importance of a town that was not only the home of John Bright but also the birthplace of the Cooperative movement in its modern form. Thence he moved to the reporting staff of the

Sheffield Telegraph under the chief reportership of Charles H. Chandler, a fellow Devonian who had been a schoolmaster.

It was on my joining the paper in 1905 that I came to know Cummings well. He became very much to me what Philip Ernest Richards had been to him, an encourager, guide, and friend. Not that I always accepted his criticisms without an effort at self-defense. He once made fun of my reading *Troilus and Cressida* one day and *The Blue Lagoon* the next. I maintained in reply that for a young journalist a catholic taste in reading would do more good than a pernickety, premature specialism and that a newspaperman's mind should burn brightly on all kinds of fuel. But my friend thought concentration on his own hero, William Hazlitt, who had been described as "the common sensible man raised to a high degree," would improve a newspaper writer much more than reading light popular romances of the moment, even if I did intersperse them with Shakespeare. I warmly admired Hazlitt's essays, especially those on books, plays and people, but saw nothing wrong in reading what so many friends were reading. Finally, I argued against my unyielding mentor that a really popular novel, however soon its vogue would vanish, was news and so a proper subject for a reporter to know about.

One day Cummings censured me for referring to a motorcar as a vehicle, on the ground that the word vehicle derived from the Latin word *veho*, to draw, and that it should not be applied to a motorcar, which was not drawn but moved under the power of its engine. I rejected the censure with the confidence of one who had spent years on Latin and Greek at the great classical school of Christ's Hospital. Surely *veho* often meant to carry or convey and not necessarily to draw. But Cummings was a hard man to convince that he had slipped, and this no doubt added to his strength as a controversialist. Certainly his own reading gave him a scholarly and attractive use of words, especially in descriptive or essayistic work. In the ample reports of those days, a regional paper like the *Sheffield Telegraph* printed detailed descriptions of ceremonious events, such as royal visits, and no one challenged Cummings as our star man for such occasions. I, town bred, used to study such books as *Trees Shown to the Children* and *Flowers Shown to the Children* to enable me to write picturemaking phrases for events in the countryside. Cummings never seemed at a loss for naming trees, flowers, birds, or beasts.

On one occasion he was describing a visit of King Edward VII and Queen Alexandra to a great house in The Dukeries. Watching from a distance the King shoot, he saw the Queen motion to a courtier to put a wounded bird out of its misery. He mentioned in his report this example of a much-loved lady's compassion. For some unknown reason, perhaps because he had been twitted about it at his club, the chairman of the paper, Colonel Charles Clifford, assumed that Cummings had invented this incident, which no rival reporter mentioned. My colleague passionately resented this slur and demanded an apology. I had not the slightest doubt that Cummings, most observant of men, had seen what he said, and I believe Colonel Clifford, a sometimes hasty but in the main fair-minded man, soon regretted that he had not trusted his own faithful reporter.

The *Sheffield Telegraph* printed many essayistic special articles, unsigned, not rewarded with an extra fee, but labeled "Sheffield Telegraph Special," a term we regarded as a sufficient compliment to the writer. In these days of frequent by-lines, even in the *Times* of London that favored anonymity so long, it seems strange that Cummings was not allowed to sign his work. But perhaps his Hazlitt-like style was enough signature. A Devon master of a workhouse in South Yorkshire used to offer him cider and tell him of strange characters who sought the shelter of the casual ward. Cummings excelled in writing sketches of these humble adventurers and thoughtful articles on Poor Law hardships. He told me one ambition of his was to have a book of essays published, this no doubt because of his hero worship of Hazlitt, but this hope was never fulfilled in the form he then had in mind. It was in political journalism rather than in belles-lettres that he was to make his mark.

The only indication of this that I remember from his Sheffield days was in the trenchancy of his reports on parliamentary by-elections. To describe a varied constituency, perhaps far from Sheffield, to watch day after day the fluctuations of political feeling in a contest, to weigh the effect of the arguments used, to estimate what the outcome would be, and to produce a lively column each day, above all, to stay in a comfortable hotel with election officials and local opinion formers all at hand—this we reporters regarded as a most enviable engagement. If at the end we predicted the result with fair accuracy, we plumed ourselves on our temporary prestige. Cummings reported by-elections with the shrew discernment and vivid phrasemaking which were to make his "Spotlight on Politics" in the *News Chronicle* years later probably the most influential personal commentary in Britain in its own sphere.

In 1908, with every assurance of happiness, he married someone in Sheffield I knew well, the beautiful and gentle Lilian Boreham. Seven months later, after an operation for appendicitis, she died of peritonitis. It was a most cruel blow to Arthur's sensitive nature.

A few years before the First World War, and after I had left England to free-lance in Paris, Cummings moved to the *Yorkshire Post* at its head office in Leeds. Early in the war he joined the 4th West Riding (Howitzer) Brigade, Royal Field Artillery, Territorial Force, served in many actions and became a captain. In 1915 he married an artist, Miss Nora Suddards, a daughter of Mr. and Mrs. Arthur Suddards, of Leeds. After the coming of peace he rejoined the *Yorkshire Post*. Arthur H. Mann, an editor exceptional in recognizing talent, made him an assistant editor with considerable duties as an editorial writer. Mann was not a writing editor, but had close contacts with leading politicians, especially Winston Churchill, Anthony Eden, and other fervent Conservatives, and often wrote out a long brief for an editorial writer. Like Delane, of the *Times*, he could greatly improve his men's work, using his knowledge to turn some surmises into definite statements, toning down some bold statements into speculative questions, cutting out pretentious phrases, and often ending an editorial with what we should now term a punch line. But he had such warm admiration for Cummings's work that he would not change a word. When the paper was short staffed, as often happened, Cummings would write more than twenty-five hundred words of editorials, an editorial on a timely political issue and one on a social or literary theme. I have no doubt which gave him greater pleasure to write. The *Yorkshire Post* was by no means a Tory hack: it interpreted the Conservative philosophy in its own way, and this was by no means always in accordance with Conservative central office doctrine. Even so, saddened by what he saw of some aspects of North Country industrial life, Cummings did not always admire the paper's politics.

So when, in 1920, the *Daily News* (which became the *News Chronicle* in 1930 and is now merged in the *Daily Mail*) offered him an assistant editorship, he eagerly accepted. This proved to be the start of thirty-five years' service for a paper that welcomed the kind of reforming zeal and stalwart radicalism he had come to believe in. After being deputy editor he became political editor. Hoping to become editor, he felt disappointed when this honorable if onerous prize went to Tom Clarke, who had made his reputation as Lord Northcliffe's trusted news editor of the *Daily Mail*, and was an adept in popular journalism. Tom was also a most likeable colleague, as I found when I, too, was on the *Mail*. No doubt the directors of the *News Chronicle* believed that a man credited with the circulation-raising Northcliffe touch would do them more good than a man steeped in politics, however much of an expert in that department of journalism. Cummings was not a man to take umbrage. He had much to give him satisfaction. His regular feature, "Spotlight on Politics," was achieving a steady moral success like that of the most thoughtful of American columnists. Their work, favored by syndication, appears in many newspapers. Cummings's, though much quoted abroad, appeared in one. That one did not command a top place among mass circulation papers. But it was then the sole Liberal morning paper in London. Also it had a literary reputation; it never forgot that the first editor of the *Daily News* was Charles Dickens. It enabled Cummings to gain an international name. Many statesmen read his dispatches.

He went to the Ottawa economic conference of the British Commonwealth of Nations in 1932 and wrote lucid, attention-compelling accounts of the efforts to integrate the new protectionist policy of the mother country with the Dominions' tenacious old protectionism. This deeply disturbed Liberal Free Traders. The reciprocal trade agreements seemed to them to violate Britain's international obligations and to be grossly unfair to neighbors with whom we had long traded satisfactorily and whose livelihood would now be threatened. The treaties indeed had soon to be modified, partly under the retaliatory pressure of foreign nations.

In 1933 Cummings attended the Reichstag fire trial at Leipzig and sent home dispatches imbued with a hatred of injustice. The fire became recognized as one of the most contemptible hoaxes in history. The Communists, by fighting the Nazis in the streets and fomenting strikes, were obstructing Hitler's long-meditated plan to seize complete power. He had not been chancellor of Germany for a month when the Reichstag building went ablaze. Instantly word spread that the Communists had set it on fire. Hitler's forces swept into action with orders to put down a Communist rising. A dim-wittted creature was accused of arson. Goering authorized four thousand arrests. But was there to be a Communist rising? Was the dimwit guilty? It was all planned by the Nazis to put the blame on the Communists and make the world believe that Hitler was the bulwark against their plots. Cummings's accounts of the trial gripped the reader's attention like the unfolding of a detective novel. It did not take long to guess the conclusion, little as we then expected the later infamies that stained the Nazi record.

The Moscow trial of British engineers and a number of their Russian associates, on charges of anti-Soviet sabotage at power stations, bribery, and collection of secret information, gave Cummings another chance in 1933 to show his skill in disentangling a mystery complicated by suspicion and distrust, a mystery that led, in his judgment to, the "astonishing sight of an emotional brainstorm such as our sober little island had not indulged in since 1914." News of the arrests of Metropolitan-Vickers engineers caused the wildest indignation. Mr. Baldwin, who had been prime minister and was to hold that office again, said in the House of Commons, "There can be no justification for the charge on which the arrest was made." Sir Robert Vansittart, on the instructions of the government, said to the Soviet ambassador, Mr. Maisky, that the arrests were "a stage performance, and a very bad one at that, mounted simply to disguise, by serving up scapegoats, the ill success of certain industrial undertakings in Russia." Most of the British press flamed with anger at what it considered a barbarous act or, as the *Times* put it, "a tragic farce." The Russian press hit back hard, denouncing "damagers caught red-handed preparing to smash our electric stations."

In this superheated atmosphere of Anglo-Soviet recriminations Tom Clarke darted abruptly into Cummings's room at the

News Chronicle office one morning and asked, "Will you go to Moscow at once and report the State Trial?" He could not have chosen a better man to armor himself against the kind of patriotism that flouts justice and condemns a foreigner because he is a foreigner. Cummings regarded the Bolsheviks neither as an imminent deadly menace to the peace of the world nor as heaven-sent pioneers of a purer civilization that we had ever known before. He prepared eagerly to attend the trial, see all he could of Moscow, and judge for himself the efforts of the so-called dictatorship of the proletariat to rescue Russia from her continuing shortage of food, houses, schools, universities, and much else that the West enjoyed.

Arrived in Moscow he soon had an illustration of the quality of British diplomacy at a highly critical moment. He cabled that the accused Britons were well and cheerful and that there appeared to be good hope of their receiving a fair trial. Between two and three in the morning a man from the British embassy woke him up, and behaving like a small British lion rampant demanded to know whether he thought it was playing the game to send such statements to England. If the embassy man thought he or the ambassador could make Cummings color his news messages with their own bitter prejudice and damn the trial as a tragic farce before it had started he was soon undeceived. Cummings was capable of blistering scorn at any time of the day. With this insolent creature invading his bedroom after 2 A.M. my old friend reached a towering height of indignation.

The first important feature when the trial opened was the reading of the indictment of six Britons and twelve Russians, one of them a woman. This was a detailed document running to twenty thousand words and took three hours to read. No doubt Embassy officials listening to it suspected the O.G.P.U., the state security police or secret service, of a vicious frame-up. Then followed an event that made the foreign press in court gasp. As expected, all the Russian prisoners pleaded guilty. All the British pleaded not guilty with one startling exception—Macdonald. Had he been tortured? Or was there some truth in the accusations?

Cummings, with the help of an intelligent woman interpreter, sent vivid and fair-minded reports of the proceedings. He soon foresaw that, in accordance with the Soviet system of justice and psychology, some of the British prisoners must be found guilty. He thought the frame-up theory looked more and more like hypocritical nonsense. He was not happy about the tactics of the counsel for the defense, who were not the equals in skill of the redoubtable public prosecutor, Vishinsky. They might have done more to test the evidence of the Russian prisoners who incriminated the British. Indeed he declared himself often angered and humiliated by the poor show made for the defense. He could not see any sign that the British government, through its law officers, had taken the slightest trouble to coordinate the case, marshal the facts, or do anything positively and creatively to justify with effect the view it had so spectacularly presented to the world. It was easier to believe that Macdonald and his colleague Monkhouse might acquire state secrets of military value, or what the court considered state secrets of military value, than that they would organize the wrecking of machines at power stations. But some of the embittered anti-Bolshevik Russians did seem to be wreckers.

In the end there were no death sentences. Punishments for the British engineers were to be mild. Thornton was to be deprived of liberty for three years, Macdonald for two. Monkhouse, Nordwall, and Cushny were to be deported and prohibited from reentry for five years. Gregory was acquitted. Within ten hours of this surprising end to the trial, the British government—in Cummings's view stupid, obstinate, reckless, and more than a little ridiculous to the very end—put into operation an act prohibiting the entry into British ports of any Russian goods except under license. Negotiations for a new trade treaty were broken off. The Russians imposed an embargo on our goods. Many British industrialists were shocked. But presently Sir John Simon, Britain's Foreign Secretary, and Mr. Litvinov came to an agreement. Thornton and Macdonald were released. Embargo and counterembargo were taken off. Trade treaty negotiations were resumed.

Cummings was pursued from one end of the country to the other with requests to speak and write on the trial and Russia. An outcome was a book, *The Moscow Trial*, published by Gollancz and hailed as a classic in the literature of great trials. It combined graphic description, an unforgettable narrative tension, close analysis, and a denunciation of diplomatic blunders. The book should remain a lasting reminder of the errors that well-meaning, patriotic governments can commit. Cummings wrote that when Britain declared economic war to the knife upon one of its greatest potential customers because "a few Englishmen were judged to be spies and 'wreckers' in a properly constituted court of justice and mildly punished" this action was "a masterpiece of imbecility unparalleled in the political annals of our time."

Some critics thought Cummings was too pro-Russian. But again and again, surveying as carefully as he could from limited experience a land of nearly 180 millions of people under the inadequate control of a then poorly trained official class, he pointed to Russia's pitiful sufferings and clamant needs. He described it as a land of hunger, strain, and conflict. But he did not believe the revolution was doomed to destruction. The revolution impressed him as the most stable force in Europe and the Soviet government as the most secure. Even if millions more of the citizens died of starvation, he believed the regime would go on. There was no alternative. The people did not want one. Who now would say that this was a false prophecy?

I once reminded Arthur of his desire in our Sheffield days to write a book of essays. Was he not much happier with his authorship of a book that could influence the history of East and West? He smiled—"I'm deeply grateful to the *News Chronicle*," he said, "for giving me this wonderful chance of seeing something of Russia and of its control system in action. You noticed the dedication of my book?" I had noticed it, with warm appreciation. The dedication was "To Tom Clarke, best of editors and best of friends." It is one of the ironies of journalism that in the very year of this tribute, the best of editors resigned from the *News Chronicle* because of a difference with colleagues on the board, whose divergent sections of liberalism were at times hard to please.

Cummings might well have exploited his increasing fame by joining a richer paper than the *News Chronicle*. Lord Beaverbrook had a warm and friendly admiration for him, but never persuaded him to make the short transit from Bouverie Street to Fleet Street, the wide leap from his own individualism to that of the man of unquenchable optimism and persistent imperialism who had made such a success of the *Daily Express* and the *Sunday Express*.

Pressed to write more books, the now widely accepted commentator agreed in 1936 to contribute to a service known as the Twentieth Century Library, published by the Bodley Head. His theme, "The Press and a Changing Civilization," attracted him because he wanted to call attention to what he believed to be "the most formidable and at the same time the most suitable menace to human liberty since newspapers began. . . . Kill or swamp the Press in any country, and at once for millions life ceases to be worth living. And soon or late, whether they want it or not, they will be inveigled into war. If you cannot write or talk against war you cannot write or talk against war-mongers; and war-mongering is one of the special prerogatives of unlicensed censors of public opinion who thereby make themselves the arbiters of a nation's destiny and the controllers-in-chief of a nation's cannon-fodder."

The author admitted grave defects of the press in wartime. He thought war must of necessity demoralize, depress, and render the press conscienceless. This demoralization did not cease with the cease-fire. Yet he emphasized that no private weaknesses or irresponsibilities were nearly as bad for journalism as government control. He drove home this moral by a devastating exposure of Nazi censorship.

In 1944 he wrote *This England,* a book with full-page illustrations, in which his love of the countryside found expression in many terse, happy phrases. As his old age approached, the newspaper profession, thinking of all he had done in defense of the freedom of the press, honored him as an elder statesman. The Institute of Journalists elected him as its president in 1953. In his presidential address, to my delight he gave strong support to the Press Council I had helped to start that year. "The Press," he said, "has now an authoritative voice which cannot with impunity be disregarded." He deplored the increasing parliamentary tendency to raise questions of privilege and foresaw growing difficulties for legitimate press criticism.

He retired from the *News Chronicle* in August 1955. His family life could not have been happier. He enjoyed as much as his own success that of his son Michael, who became a political cartoonist of the *Daily Express*, and his daughter Jean, a journalist. Living at Finchley in the north of London, he took much pleasure in the big, wide magnolia trees that blossomed beneath his study window in the sunshine.

The last time I saw him was at a Whitefriars' gathering at the Cock Tavern in Fleet Street. He looked frail and tired, but we both talked of Leeds and Sheffield with the eagerness of men to whom those towns meant much. He was to have debated with Aneurin Bevan the virtues and shortcomings of the press. Since his doctor had warned him against exertions he asked me to take his place. I could not refuse my friend, even though Bevan was a redoubtable opponent to take on. It proved a vigorous encounter, but I do not suppose either of us changed a single listener's attitude to the newspapers. Cummings died on July 5, 1957, in a London nursing home.

The columnist became a popular institution of the American press long before British newspapers welcomed his advent. Arthur Cummings set a sustainedly brilliant example in England. If it was not at once widely copied the reason may be found in those gifts of his that were hard to equal. Even now we have, to my mind, no one to match him.

14

George Murray

The champion of the editorial

George Murray has shown his mastery of creative journalism in an unusual way. He has become the most admired and the best-known editorial writer in Britain. Though he is not now working a full week, his editorials appeared on the front page of the *Daily Mail* five days a week for twenty years. Before that they were appearing for eight years on an inside editorial page. This is a unique record in morning paper journalism.

But there has been an invisible screen between George Murray the man and his multitudinous readers—a screen of anonymity. Had his editorials been signed with his name he would have been famous long ago—famous like the American Arthur Brisbane in his heyday, famous like the British Cassandra (William Connor) in the *Daily Mirror*. It is his style, the carefully researched facts, the persuasive progress of argument, the brightly-minted phrases, that have pierced the screen of anonymity and revealed the kind of thinker and craftsman George Murray is.

Oliver Edwards (the pen name of Sir William Haley when writing a bookman's essays in the *Times*) classed Murray and Cassandra as writers of two of the most successful features in British journalism. He said they called upon no bizarre or striking devices to put themselves across. "One of their attractions," he explained, "is that their appearance is stereotyped. Every column depends entirely on what it has to say—and says it in language as effective for our day as Cobbett's was for his." Both Murray and Connor richly deserve to be praised for the kind of racy vigor and copiousness that Cobbett possessed. But neither has been tainted with the reckless overconfidence that threw Cobbett into jail and prompted him to choose for a time his exile as a farmer on Long Island, New York.

The powers and the limitations of editorial writers should be understood before we can do justice to George Murray. Masked by editorial anonymity, he had a harder task than Connor to win recognition. A columnist with a by-line starts with an immeasurable advantage over an editorial writer. The columnist appearing with his name and often his picture is assured of a welcome rather like a star's in a theater. He is clothed in importance. The more he writes like an oracular dictator and the harder he hits, the more devotedly his followers admire him. But when the editorial writer shows these qualities he does not get the full credit in the same way. What he writes may be highly important, but it takes its importance from its environment: its importance is largely conferred by the newspaper in which it appears. It is the paper that is speaking. It must not be vitriolic. That at least is the tradition.

Readers may believe that the opinions the editorial writer has expressed are not necessarily his own. It may be surmised they have been written to a brief. They are presumably the opinions of the editor, or of the editorial council if there is one, or perhaps of the proprietor. The personality of the newspaper, shaped by much experience and by devotion to a certain political philosophy, has a far tighter hold on the editorial writer than on a columnist whose views, in, say, the United States, may be appearing syndicated in fifty papers or more, not all of the same political allegiance, by any means.

The impression still prevails among many people that the editor writes the editorials. At one time he usually did. When Gladstone thought ill of an editorial in the *Standard* (the morning paper of which its evening companion survives) he used to remark, "Mr. Mudford [the editor] must have been having a night off." Much the same thing was said by many people when a

Courtesy of James Janché
Photograph by the *Daily Mail*

GEORGE MURRAY

thinnish editorial appeared in the *Westminster Gazette* (1896–1922) during the editorship of John Alfred Spender. His editorial used to appear in large type on the front page of "the sea-green incorruptible," the Carlylean quotation applied to the more or less pea-green evening paper. Spender's editorials in the great days of the Liberal party had a remarkable influence. He was a close friend of most of the Cabinet ministers in the party and was often consulted on what lines policy should take. Some admirers called him the minister without portfolio. All serious political leaders within reach of the London circulation area made a point of following Spender. His paper, though valuable politically, did not make a profit. It rarely had a sale of as many as twenty thousand copies. It had rivals not so authoritative in political views but far more abundant with news, and it was, and is, mainly news that sells papers.

As our papers became much bigger and more intricate.organizations, the writing editor became rarer. The mass circulation papers in particular flourished under editors who were supreme technicians in the gathering of remarkable news stories and giving them an arresting display.

The editorial writer may gain from this trend. He may not be beset like the editor himself by politicians armed with confidential news and ready to offer hints on the press support they would like. But a studious editorial writer can follow world news even more carefully than a much-sought-after harassed editor with a full engagement book. Such a colleague as George Murray, always replenishing his up-to-date and encyclopaedic knowledge, always mentally active, always cool in judgment in the most feverish crises, and with a wider range of subjects than the almost always political Spender, can be an invaluable support.

I do not think Murray, however rushed by the pace of changeful events, ever wrote a dull or weak editorial. Nearly all his editorials have been his own in conception and execution. Ever since World War II, he has been intermittently urging a wages policy—rejected for years, recently adopted. In 1950 he deprecated the Labour government's refusal to take part in the European Iron and Coal Community, which foreshadowed the European Community. Time and time again it has been stated that the first criticism of the Eden government was in a *Daily*

Telegraph editorial early in 1956, the year after Sir Anthony succeeded Sir Winston Churchill as prime minister and the year
before, broken in health, he resigned the premiership. The *Telegraph* was not the first great paper to criticize the Eden government. It did this after Murray wrote a strong editorial headed
"A Reel of Negatives." Another editorial of his that gave a new
warning to Britain foreshadowed about ten years ago the coming
menace of Red China.

Murray has written for the *Daily Mail* not only editorials
but also hundreds of signed articles, and these, too, contained
many firsts. I believe he was the first to suggest a medal for conspicuous civilian gallantry during the war, perhaps to be named
after the sovereign. Not long afterwards the George Medal was
created. After a wartime chancellor, Sir Kingsley Wood, had said
it was impracticable to introduce PAYE (the pay-as-you-earn taxation system) Murray wrote an article giving details of PAYE in
Canada, and saying it was absolutely feasible here. The next day
the *Times* had an editorial saying much the same thing. Not long
afterwards PAYE was introduced. In December 1956 Murray
wrote a major signed piece saying that Suez had shown that Britain was no longer a first-class Power. A few days later Henry
Fairlie had an article seeking to prove that he was wrong; and Mr.
Harold Macmillan said in a speech that it was nonsense to say
Britain was no longer a first-class power. But most Britons say it
now—and they cite Suez as the crisis which proved it.

Among Murray's wartime tasks was a weekly contribution
he made for the Transatlantic *Daily Mail*, sent to the United
States on microfilm, set up there, and distributed to influential
people throughout that vast country. For three years he wrote a
weekly column of political comment in the *Daily Sketch*, an associate of the *Daily Mail*, under the pseudonym Colin Shaw. In the
last of these columns before he went into the hospital with heart
trouble in 1966, he suggested a wages-and-prices freeze for a year
or two years in order to get Britain out of her economic trouble.
In the next issue of the *Sunday Times*, William Rees-Mogg (now
editor of the *Times*) proposed the same thing. Soon afterwards it
became government policy.

Today George Murray has become one of the best-known
figures in the little world of Fleet Street, always welcome at the

Press Club or the Garrick, but spending far more time at his desk in Northcliffe House. Some writers have suggested that he looks like a William Makepeace Thackeray. He has a slight resemblance to the best-known portraits of that great man, but has a friendlier look, a very alert face, wavy gray hair, and a ready smile. I saw him at meetings of the Press Council before he succeeded me there as chairman. Calm deliberation showed in his bespectacled, blue–gray eyes. He never rushed in with breathless opinions on the issue before us, but spoke from broad experience with solid common sense. He would correct any misstatement by excited colleagues, but always with good-natured courtesy.

In spite of his name, George McIntosh Murray, he is a Londoner born and bred, the son of Dulwich people, and an old boy of Archbishop Tenison's School. Born on December 16, 1900, he was twenty-three before he joined a newspaper staff and went on its payroll. Yet he says he always wanted to be a journalist, and longed to know how to become one. His first recorded piece (which his mother kept for years) was written at the age of seven. At eleven he was writing verse (which he still has in an old exercise book), and at sixteen onwards was sending articles to various papers, without success.

During two years in the merchant service he subscribed to a correspondence school of journalism, but it did him no good at all. He left the sea in 1921 and became an insurance agent. His father was acquainted with the editor of a local paper in South London, and it was arranged that the young aspirant should do reporting for it in his spare time. This he did for two years, for no payment or expenses, and without ever going to the office. His object was to collect a number of cuttings which he could send to other papers as specimens of his work. During those two years, like many other young men, he was constantly writing for reporters' jobs advertised in the *Daily News*.

At last he was rewarded with a call to see Sir Charles Igglesden, of the *Kentish Express*. This leading journalist was interviewing candidates for a reporter's job on his paper. He had evidently taken an office in London for the day for that purpose. When he saw Murray he seemed to be suitably impressed and, at the end of the interview, informed him that he would probably get the post. "I will telephone you," he said. "What is your office number?" Murray did not know it, never having been to the office; so he did not get the job.

But that very weekend he received a call from the *Farnham Herald,* in Surrey. The editor and the owner interviewed him. They asked him if he had done police-court work. George said; "Yes." They then said; "What police court?" He had never been in a police court in his life, but he remembered to have seen the name "Camberwell County Court" over a building in South London, so he answered; "Camberwell County Court." They said; "Oh you've done county court work as well, have you?" He assured them he had—though up to that moment he had no idea that there was any difference. Nor did he know what reporters were paid. When asked how much he would expect he said, at a venture; "three pounds a week"—and that happened to be about right. They hired him—and his foot was on the road. He now tells the story with zest and says it was the only way he knew of getting into a paid newspaper job.

Journalism did not then, and does not now, offer an easy path to the British aspirant, though the way is much less difficult than it was forty years ago. For seven years Murray worked on various provincial newspapers. The next problem was how to get to Fleet Street. He began writing to a few national newspapers, only to receive stereotyped, noncommittal replies. He wrote an article for the *Newspaper World* headed, "A Footing in Fleet Street; How Is It Obtained?" hoping some alert editor would see it and drop a line to the writer. None did. He got introductions to a couple of London news editors and lunched with them. He badgered various people. All to no purpose.

Finally he threw up his job on a provincial evening paper, the *Southern Daily Echo,* Southampton, to become an assistant in the editorial publicity department of a big advertising firm. His purpose was to get near Fleet Street. Within a few weeks he became a Saturday reporter on a national Sunday newspaper. He left the advertising office at one o'clock on Saturday afternoon and went straight to the *Sunday Dispatch,* where he did a twelve-hour stint, finishing at one o'clock on Sunday morning, and sometimes much later. A sturdy young man, he stood the pace.

After about eighteen months he became a full-time reporter and feature writer on the paper—though still on a contributory basis—and finally began to write the editorials. It happened one week that the editorial writer on the *Daily Mail*, the prestige paper of the group owning the *Sunday Dispatch*, was to be absent for a few days. This was a Yorkshireman, Herbert Wrigley Wilson, a Northcliffe veteran, who later spoke of the early days of the paper as "days of youth, full of romance, which will live in the memory of all who shared those early triumphs." His pounding vigor, knowledge of defense problems, command of simple English, and loyalty to the paper won him Lord Northcliffe's affection. Murray was asked to stand in for him for a week. This stretched into well over thirty years. He took over as chief editorial writer in 1939 when his predecessor retired.

George Murray has often been pressed to republish his best editorials in book form. He does not think it a good idea since, as he says, editorials are by their nature ephemeral. Yes, as a rule. Some of us have reprinted the best editorials from our newspapers, but with little success. For years I had a book reprinting some of Arthur Brisbane's columns, but these were essayistic on subjects of permanent interest rather than editorial and evanescent. Re-reading notable editorials in my own papers after many years, I have been astonished how anaemic were some that might be termed historic, such as those leading to King Edward VIII's abdication. Editors had to be tactful with disclosures that were then startling and conclusions that many readers would bitterly resent and reject. Some arguments then put forward with an air of experiment read now like dithering clichés

Whatever the fate of most editorials there are many still treasured that Murray wrote years ago. There is "The Old Cricketer," written when George Hirst, of Yorkshire and England, died. I was of a generation to whom, as Murray puts it, Hirst was captain, king, and hero. I knew him when he was young enough to be at the height of his powers and friendly to a young local reporter; I knew him when he was old and blind. Murray wrote:

> Others may writhe with impatience at the unhurried placidity of cricket. But to the English the game is all mixed up with May and June and elm-trees and the years when every day was a summer's day because the heart was young. George Hirst was a superb cricketer and, by the same token, he was English of the English. He was good-humoured and obstinate, cheerful and stubborn, a tradi-

tionalist and an innovator. He loved cricket—and Cricket loved
him. His name evokes recollections of endless, idealised hours in
the matches of 40 years. But it also evokes memories of the long,
late afternoon of England herself before the dams burst in 1914
and overwhelmed a world. It was an uneven world. . . . The
landed gentry hunted during the winter and played cricket all
the summer; while professional cricketers, lacking shop stewards,
were doubtless engaged in a "sweated industry."

But they appeared to like it. Somehow they managed to lead
a good life—and somehow to pass on something of gentleness,
dignity, and fair play. It was a simpler and a sweeter world. It
had its dark blemishes, but it was precious enough to send the
flower of our young manhood out on the battlefields to defend it.
And it was sound enough to provide foundations upon which,
even today, our nation rests more stable than many others. We
seem to have come a long way from George Hirst. Yet he and
such as he are woven into the theme of our country.

Even those to whom cricket was a game they could not follow
must have understood, after reading that tribute, why Murray
and countless others thought George Hirst did as much, or more,
for England than some of the great ones whose footsteps shook
the earth.

In another editorial, starting with a little fairy tale of his
own, Murray roused compassion for a poor hunted white hart in
Epping Forest, near London. Verderers were after this creature
with guns. They did not want him keeping company with the
deer already there. "If he starts breeding he will spoil the only
herd of pure black fallow deer in the world," they said. This led
Murray to ask, "Is the white deer only to be found in a forest of
trees, or does he not run also in the jungle of the world? This
hart was the Odd Man Out. Is that not also the unforgivable sin
in human society? Was that not the 'crime' of the Jews in Germany? One can hear Verderer Hitler saying of them: 'If they start
breeding they will spoil the only pure herd of Aryan Herrenvolk
on earth.'" Then Murray went on to cite other examples of intolerance, the age-old feuds between Teuton and Gaul, Hindu
and Moslem, Greek and Turk, Jew and Arab. Hundreds and
thousands of newspaper editorials have been written on these
themes, but very rarely has there been comment so touching, so
thought-provoking.

Most editorials in British newspapers are fairly predictable in line and tone. They do not prompt the reader to explain, "I never thought of it in that way. How different this is from most editorials—so fresh, so—well imaginative! There was the day when 262 persons, the entire community of Tristan da Cunha, were due to be landed at Southampton, refugees from volcanic destruction. Coming from the loneliest of habitable islands, two thousand miles west of the Cape of Good Hope, they moved George Murray to more than conventional pathos. He thought of them as a people "violently plucked from the past and hurled, willy-nilly, into the undesired present of the present 20th century. . . . They arrive in this era straight from the Age of Innocence, like some patriarchal tribe of Israel or some medieval religious sect who have lost their way. A pastoral existence, with no anxieties beyond those that God could send and Nature bring, is behind them. In front lies the roaring, raging, raving world in which they are soon to be plunged. What will they make of it?"

What indeed! Murray imagined questions the leader of the Tristans would ask seeing a people with one of the highest living standards of the world, with amenities the newcomers had never known—television, motorcars, piped water, central heating, washing machines. The leader would ask: "You are, of course, contented with all this?" Murray said the truthful answer must be: "No. We strive always for more and more, and cry havoc if we do not get it. We shall double our standards within a decade and then . . . well, then we have no recourse but to double them again."

Then the Tristans would say: "With all these excellent things at your command, no one need steal, or defraud, or kill for gain?" Murray said the reply must be: "Crime increases with increasing prosperity." And if asked, "you are grateful to Providence for its bounties," we must confess: "It is hardly like that. Our churches are half-empty and our pastors preach largely in vain."

The Tristans' leader wanted his people to remain the self-contained, close-knit society they had always been. Murray thought it would be a miracle if this could be achieved, but "everything must be done to help him cherish and protect his flock. The sketchy arrangements made for them to live in a hutted camp are not enough. If they wish it, an island should be offered them so that they may cling together." But it was their own island they wanted, the simplicities of life on Tristan da Cunha, the freedom from strikes, riots, the slaughter of the roads—yes, their own beloved island in spite of its volcanic danger. And some of them went back the moment it seemed safe to go. Probably the prophetic conclusion of Murray's editorial then came true. He imagined the returning exiles' leader watching the lights of civilization fade astern of the ship and murmuring, "For what shall it profit a man if he shall gain the whole world and lose his own soul?" It is editorials of a reflective and philosophical type that have given Murray himself the most satisfaction.

Nevertheless, it is editorials of a more conventional kind that brought him the compliment he values most. In 1949 he was attacking the Labour party hip and thigh, day after day. A man wrote to Labour party headquarters asking whether some statements Murray had made were true. The reply said: "We have been unable to check the exact statements given in the *Daily Mail*, but I am pretty sure they must be correct. The *Daily Mail* is very careful in quoting any figures it gives in its editorials, and no correction or criticism has appeared in the paper." Murray has always done his own research. He has good reason to treasure that letter on Labour party notepaper, just as he appreciates that the English classes of many schools, including Eton, have been told to study his editorials as examples of how to write good English. His literary heroes are Thomas Hardy, Charles Dickens, and Winston Churchill.

Like many people whose business is words, he enjoys the discipline and the rewards of ingenuity in writing verse. Nearly every Christmas for fifteen years, between 1947 and 1962, he wrote for the *Daily Mail* a fairy tale in rhyme, set like prose, around the events of the year.

How does he see the editorial writer's duty? I have discussed this with him at times and heard him lecture on it to American editors. (He has lectured in Britain, the United States, and in West Germany). He has also written on "Writing the Leader" for *Fleet Street: The Inside Story of Journalism*, a book published by Macdonald in 1966, with a contribution by the Duke of Edinburgh, for the benefit of the London Press Club's restoration fund.

He objects to the likening of the editorial writer to a counselor paid to argue a case, no matter what it be and what he privately thinks of it. The counselor, says Murray, is a "professional pleader for an abstraction called a client in whom he need not have the slightest interest apart from the one episode which has brought him into contact with the law. The cause is everything; the person nothing. The leader-writer is also a professional pleader, but his own feelings are, and must be, engaged. He is identified with the cause for which he speaks. He is not out merely to win a case but to convince so many others that it is just and righteous that they *will* appoint its principals to govern the country. To imagine that leader-writers are compelled to perjure themselves under the lash of some tyrannical proprietor is a gross distortion, sometimes propagated by those who know better but more often believed through complete ignorance of newspaper practice." Murray has always sought to write simply, to reduce a complex situation to understandable terms, and not to hedge with the conclusion but to say something in forthright terms. Ruskin said it is far more difficult to be simple than to be complicated. Murray achieves his aim so well that his writing seems the most natural of all.

A necessary lesson he teaches the would-be editorial writer is this: "To do the job properly and to keep at it over the years requires constant unremitting devotion to the task. As one editor used to say: 'You cannot keep emptying a pint pot unless you also keep filling it up.'" An editorial writer, says Murray, may be able to keep going for a month or two without running dry, but if he hopes to continue he must fill himself up and keep doing so. He must read everything that comes to hand—newspapers, books, reviews, periodicals, British and foreign, and keep in touch with the news wherever he may be. He must know what important people are saying, doing, and thinking. And he must achieve the utmost accuracy. All this is what Murray himself has done. This is recognized by exacting critics. Not long ago the *Daily Mail* published a series of tributes to itself from leaders in public affairs and the arts. The editorials received more praise than any other feature. A typical comment was from Lord Elton, historian, essayist, biographer, and broadcaster: "The quality of the *Mail's* leading articles seems to me remarkable. Few indeed since William Cobbett have been the writers able to convey common sense on political and economic subjects both lucidly and entertainingly to the man in the street, but the *Daily Mail* certainly seems to have acquired the art." The fruits of Murray's hard, unending yet congenial work are to be seen not only in his editorials. They showed in his ten-year spell on the Press Council, as a founder member and in time as chairman. When he resigned to facilitate the reconstruction of the council with a lay chairman (Lord Devlin) and a proportion of other lay members Henry Bate, the vice-chairman, wrote sincerely, "His was the opinion most sought for in discussions on the most difficult ethical and other questions before the council."

Such is the story of one of Fleet Street's hardest workers. It should encourage young aspirants. George Murray had many harassing obstacles to surmount. He forced his way into journalism. He forced his way to Fleet Street. He became one of its most conspicuous and superb craftsmen, and this in a branch of journalism without the help of the writer's boldly proclaimed name. He did it by sheer devotion to the job in hand. He believes in the importance of the editorial. I hail him as a champion in a double sense. He has never ceased to train himself well and to equip himself well with the skill and knowledge to sway the hearts and minds of men and women. He offers an example of continuous self-criticism and self-training. These are the qualities that have made him rich in public spirit, technical skill, and grasp of public affairs.

Many critics have disparaged the editorial. Some have suggested that it could be dropped from the popular press without detriment to anyone. George Murray has shown how persuasive, attractive, and important it can be. In the evolution of the modern British press he has done more than any competitor to prove the power of good editorials.

Courtesy of Thomson Newspapers, Ltd.

LORD THOMSON OF FLEET

15

Lord Thomson of Fleet

The newspaper group creator extraordinary

My acquaintance with Roy Thomson, afterwards Lord Thomson of Fleet, began with my giving him advice in his Canadian days about buying a British newspaper. He drank it in like a school-boy getting examination tips from an experienced schoolmaster. It was good advice, though I say so myself. It must have made an impression, for a bit of it was recalled seventeen years later in a book for which Roy provided much information, *The Glorious Privilege: the History of the Scotsman.*

We had met at the Chateau Laurier Hotel in Ottawa in June 1950 during the tour of delegates to the Seventh Imperial Press Conference. I was one of the United Kingdom delegates. Roy, then at the age of fifty-six owner of twenty-three newspapers and president of the Canadian Daily Newspaper Association, was honorary treasurer of the arrangements committee. He had been described not many years before by Lord Beaverbrook as "A little guy, owning a lot of little newspapers."

Cheerful, ebullient, constantly observant through his powerful round spectacles, quick to act, he helped us to make the most of our tour. "My name's Thomson. Call me Roy," he said when we met first. "My name's Andrews. Call me Linton," I replied.

Roy asked whether I played golf. "Very badly," I admitted. "My son Ken will give you a game," Roy promised. Kenneth

Thomson did so and won almost every hole. The waterlogged battlefields of Flanders and the mud of Passchendale had shortened, stiffened, and distorted my swing, just as they had ruined my speed as a Rugger three-quarter back. But I enjoyed the game in the beautiful surroundings of a country club. Kenneth was most polite about it. "Thank you very much for a grand game, William," he said, having at some time looked up the conference handbook for my first Christian name. I came from Christ's Hospital, Horsham, Sussex, where it would have been considered the act of a sissy even to ask a boy what his Christian name was. But I liked the friendly habits of Canadians, just as I relished their quick-as-a-wink wisecracks.

All the same Roy startled me when he said, "Linton, what would you sell the *Yorkshire Post* for?"

I replied, "Roy, don't imagine I own the *Yorkshire Post*. The *Yorkshire Post* owns me."

At that time I was the editor in chief of our newspaper, and as journalists go a fairly large shareholder; but the notion that we might sell the concern was breathtakingly unreal.

Roy pressed for my opinion and I assured him we had no intention whatever of selling. "Probably five or six million pounds would not buy the paper," I added as an afterthought. "It's an awful price for a small return", said Roy.

Then I gave advice. "If you want to make quick profits," I said, "don't buy a British provincial morning paper. Buy or start an evening paper in an expanding industrial city where it has no rivals. No provincial morning paper in England has a monopoly. The London morning papers go everywhere and fight the locals hard."

"Which is the biggest town without an afternoon paper?"

"In the North of England probably Salford, with almost one hundred fifty thousand people, but the Manchester papers cover it as thoroughly as they do Manchester. In the South of England possibly Southend on the Essex coast, with even more people than Salford and many more in the summer holiday season, but for evening papers almost a suburb of London. Don't start an evening paper close to a big town, or it will be swamped by competition." The only exception I could think of was Wolverhampton, with a fine evening paper only thirteen miles from Birmingham.

At his request I promised to let Roy know of any British evening papers which might welcome a deal. I thought I had warned him off buying provincial morning papers. It gave me a shock when word came that he had bought the *Scotsman* and its companions the *Evening Dispatch* and the *Weekly Scotsman*. Not that the morning paper he had bought was a provincial. Edinburgh is a capital and the *Scotsman* proudly calls itself Scotland's national newspaper. But almost every senior journalist knew that the *Scotsman* was losing ground and its evening paper, after a career marked by exceptional pioneer enterprise, had a doughty rival in the Edinburgh *Evening News*. I thought disaster lay ahead of the self-confident, cheerful Canadian unless he showed an unlikely grasp of the journalistic needs of Scotland. I was wrong. Not disaster but almost unparalleled success lay ahead. This was a cardinal turning point in Roy's life. Behind him stretched out a long, desperate, often frustrating struggle. Now he was to taste the fruits of the good fortune he had longed for and worked for. His Edinburgh purchase was to lead the way to a vast newspaper empire, to immense television profits, to the control of world-famous newspapers, the *Times* and the *Sunday Times*, and to a peerage. How he managed all this makes one of the most surprising romances of journalistic history.

Many a Scotsman, emigrating to Canada from his unrewarding little croft has done remarkably well in the wide, fertile spaces of the prairie provinces. Roy Thomson reversed the process by winning a fortune when he left the Dominion and returned to the land of his ancestors.

His start in life was unpropitious. His father, a barber who smoked too much and liked reading but was not a man of stern ambition, had married a hotel maid who faced poverty with unceasing hard work and unfailing courage. To help financially she usually had five women boarders. Roy was her first son. Two years later came Carl. The brothers were not much alike. Roy, suffering from myopia, could not join in vigorous games. He read detective fiction and the novels of Horatio Alger, with their underlying doctrine worthy of Samuel Smiles—poor boys who worked hard always got to the materialistic top. Though he loved watching baseball with his father, he kept his thoughts mostly to himself. Carl was not introspective. He cheerfully ganged up with other small boys in their escapades.

The resolute, economical mother taught Roy a lesson of untold value. It was not the Victorian lesson, dinned into me as a child, that thrift led the way to personal independence. Poor Mrs. Thomson could not look so far ahead as a life of moneyed ease for her family. A feckless husband, who sometimes drank more than was good for him, had to be reckoned with. The lesson Mrs. Alice Thomson learned and taught was that every possible cent was to be made and never wasted, not in the hope of making a million dollars, but simply to keep going.

At the age of thirteen Roy entered a business college, fees being waived in return for his services as a cleaner or caretaker. Thus he learned shorthand, typewriting, and bookkeeping. At fourteen he became a coalyard clerk. He loved figures and arithmetical accuracy. He was an excellent clerk and grew self-confident. At seventeen we find him predicting that he would be a millionaire at thirty. But to achieve that glittering goal needed more than his youthful business abilities and his nonsmoking, nondrinking, thrifty virtues. Still, he made progress. He became a salesman for a young dealer in rope, twine, cotton, cotton waste, and fishing tackles. This was good for his shyness. In future it rarely hampered his business deals. He acquired shares in his employer's business.

The reader may be surprised that we know so much of Roy Thomson's early life and business career. We owe it partly to his unfailing candor, partly to his cooperation with his biographer, Russell Braddon, and partly to Braddon's searching zeal for detail. More than two hundred people furnished the author with information, but much of it must have come from Roy himself. The book is the most revealing and astonishing biography of a journalist that I have ever read.

Roy married a young redhead stenographer, Edna Irvine, who was quite sure he would "go places." He did. When he had saved fifteen thousand dollars he decided to act on Horace Greeley's famous advice across the border, "Go west, young man." The prospect of farming in Saskatchewan may have touched some ancestral element in his character, perhaps a country Scot's love of the soil. He bought a farm hopefully. But he knew nothing about farming. This proved to be a handicap even to a twenty-five-year-old illimitable optimist always eager to learn. Roy would never become a millionaire that way. He soon realized it. A significant pleasure of his at this time, as indeed afterwards, was to read newspapers. A born salesman, he was always looking for bargains.

He decided to go into business with his brother Carl, who was ready to supplement with his savings what was left of Roy's fifteen thousand dollars after losses on farming. The partners made what seemed a promising choice. They would sell spare parts for motorcars. Why not? Motorcars on the roads of Toronto were multiplying fast. No one thought of any limit to their future. Roy's optimistic salesmanship brought in plenty of business— too much in fact. As middlemen, the brothers found the manu- facturers insisted on quick payments, but the garages selling the parts were slow to get their money from customers and could not pay the distributors quickly. So Automotive Supply was burdened with debts, which could be paid off only slowly, though paid off they all were in a few years.

This insolvent situation proved to be a thoroughly disguised and long unapparent blessing. Seeking fresh scope for salesman- ship, Roy agreed to sell radio sets in eastern Ontario for the De Forest Crosley concern. Then the head of this business, short of a distributor in northern Ontario and thinking Ottawa customers could be handled profitably without a middleman, sent him to North Bay, a desolate, cruel place in winter, presently to be worsened by a great depression. Even if Roy persuaded a house- holder to give the radio a trial, the usual report on his next visit was that no program could be heard, only a howling cacophony. What could be done? Nothing tangible now encouraged the day- dreams of millionairedom. Some men would have given up all their bright hopes. Not so Roy. He saw a wonderful future for radio. The more lonely and desolate the area it penetrated the more of a blessing it would be. He decided to create a radio station at North Bay. He was still a shabby, shambling figure, too plump, and wearing a patch on his trousers, but with exceptional courage and friendliness. Amiability was not his only ability. He knew very little about radio, but he inspired confidence. He could persuade a bank to trust him.

First he had to get a license to broadcast. A company with a lumber camp had one it did not use; it found the telephone more suitable for keeping touch. Roy borrowed its radio license for one dollar on the understanding that it would be his at the end of a year unless the lenders wanted it back. Then he bought for five hundred dollars, with a promissory note for three months, a discarded, old-fashioned transmitter at Toronto. Who could make it work? Roy had the good luck to find a young technician, willing to give up a secure job to work with him. Jack Barnaby improvised ingeniously in predicaments that inevitably arose. Was it in those days Roy's warmhearted personality or a belief in his ultimate business success that gained him that kind of support? I do not know. Was it a mixture of both? Probably. But we have in journalism men whose character is even more persuasive than their arguments.

Roy opened his second radio station at Timmins, a gold-mining town, and his third at Kirkland Lake, also busy with the lure of gold. At Timmins he became a newspaper proprietor. Why? His own answer is that a newspaper occupied part of his radio building, so he bought it. More lies behind this non-sequitor. Roy had long been captivated by newspapers, and not only by their news thrills and editorial wisdom. He also liked to calculate how their advertising revenue worked out. He was good at selling time on his radios. Would he not be just as good at selling space in his paper? So he bought the *Timmins Press* in 1934 and, after a while, made it an eight-page daily. He still owns it with, at the time of writing, about forty other Canadian papers among his vast and varied press holdings. But its future must have seemed precarious when Roy was running it with almost broken-down machinery, a tiny staff, and precious little money.

The Second World War, though it brought sorrow to the Thomson family, the fiancés of Roy's two daughters being killed, and caused many business worries, ensured the prosperity of both radio and the press. At last, though well into his forties, it looked as if Roy's ambition to become a millionaire might be realized before long. He owned or had substantial interests in eight radio stations and he seized a chance to buy four newspapers. He could not start new ones because of the paper rationing regulations. But he had a glowing faith in the commercial potentiality of newspapers and began to ask almost every newspaper owner he met, "Will you sell me your paper?" The question became almost automatic.

I was with him when a woman who owned a rich group of papers asked him for advice on a worrying problem. Not listening carefully Roy answered, "Name a fair price and I'll buy your papers." The lady's expression of aristocratic horror is one I shall never forget. But that incident happened later. While Roy was collecting his little papers in Canada, he was looked down on by proprietors of great metropolitan sheets. One of the stories used against him was that he defined editorial matter as "The stuff you separate the adds with." He might have said it when demonstrating how eagerly people bought newspapers to study the advertisements. To think he despised editorial matter would underrate his grasp of newspaper essentials.

Collecting little papers had become an exceedingly shrewd enterprise. These papers, often family owned and subject from time to time to the exaction of death duties, might not serve large communities or reflect much technical skill. In wartime most of them prospered because advertising spilled over from the space-rationed metropolitan papers into the little community papers that had had hitherto to struggle fiercely for local advertisements. With the victories of peace assured in a land of a golden future, little communities were sure to expand. Weeklies would become dailies. Where competition was deadly, it would kill the press weaklings, but in every community one paper would become richly dominant. The more Roy Thomson gathered into his net the more profitable the network would be, thanks to group economies.

If a man had ten, twenty, or more papers he could get detailed accounts from each of what printing a column cost, what making a block cost, what every other part of production cost. Then the papers that spent more than others to produce something must learn from the champions of thrifty production. They must live up to or down to the detailed budgeting they were allowed. With a kind of control not subject to death duties one great handicap would be removed.

Now that this system of newspaper group supervision is practiced so widely, it seems simple, but Roy was one of its great pioneers. He began to boast that his credit rating had no limit. The Royal Bank of Canada was so impressed that it arranged a debenture issue that attracted from the public one million one hundred thousand dollars. No longer was Roy a shabby figure with a crumpled old suit and with a patch sewn on his trousers. He remained a personification of good nature as he peered through his pebble glasses at balance sheets and asked newspaper owners to sell him their weeklies or dailies.

He had disappointments. He did not get all the papers he wanted. As part owner of *New Liberty* he lost money. But his dream of millions was now much less a daydream than a probably attainable project. It was at this stage of his career that I came to know him, and heard the greeting, "My name's Thomson. Call me Roy." I did not know then that this was his invariable greeting to strangers with whom he would be associated for a time. Nor did I know then that his request to me to tell him of any promising afternoon paper in Britain that might be for sale was a request he made to many new friends from the United Kingdom. That he would become a British press lord within fourteen years would have seemed ludicrous if anyone had made such a prediction, but no one did, not even, to the best of my belief, the ever candid Roy himself. I think he did more than hint that he would like a knighthood. Later his expectations illustrated the soldier's maxim, "Lights up, sights up." That is to say, the more his prosperity brightened, the more he raised his social ambitions.

He came to Fleet Street by way of North Bridge, Edinburgh. One of our Commonwealth Press Union party visiting Canada in 1950 was Major Colin Neil MacKinnon, a thirty-eight-year-old and Australian-born director of the *Scotsman*. I remember him as one with a record of war service in India and Italy and a love of yachting, lawn tennis, riding, and golf. Roy asked him the inevitable question, "Would the directors consider selling me the *Scotsman*?" MacKinnon thought not. He promised to let Roy know whenever such a possibility arose. It arose in about two years, soon after Roy's wife died, and when he wished for some absorbing new interest to occupy his mind. His heart leaped up when he heard from MacKinnon that the majority shareholding might be negotiated for.

The *Scotsman*, though few of its readers ever guessed it, was in a bad way. It had immense prestige, as it deserved to have after a long record of pioneer enterprise and leadership of opinion. But now, like many provincial morning papers in England, it had begun to lose a good deal of money. Such papers had profitable evening papers to keep them going, but Edinburgh had two evening papers and the *Evening Dispatch* was not the more profitable one in a city too small for two. When the chairman, Sir Edmund Findlay, died, the concern would be affected by crushing death duties.

It was high time to sell. But to whom? Preferably, the directors thought, to a Scotsman; certainly not to an Englishman and not to someone who might then sell the business to an Englishman. A Canadian of Scottish descent? Maybe. But a Scot would be better. So hurried confidential inquiries were made to find a patriot willing to pay up to around one million pounds to keep the control of the famous paper in Scottish hands. No one would. The Canadian with Scots ancestors was the only bidder. He bought control for £393,750, a bargain price as events proved, but not perhaps a cheap one for a newspaper in dire straits. But, as Roy was well aware, the block of property containing the office of the *Scotsman* was worth one million pounds and not all of it was needed by the newspaper business. Parts of it could be sold at a profitable price. Roy soon gained five hundred thousand pounds in this way. Were the Scottish negotiators unexpectedly blind to the possibilities? Not at all. They were in a fix. They had to sell the *Scotsman* or the paper would crash when Sir Edmund Findley, chairman and chief shareholder, died. They had tried to find a Scottish buyer, but could not. Thomson was their one hope.

The bargain struck, Roy had no misgivings. Not at first, anyway. But as soon as he took over he stumbled on infuriating obstacles. He thought the *Scotsman* and *Evening Dispatch* were run in a way that in Canada would have killed them in six months. The two editors did not agree with him. They thought they knew just what their readers wanted and that the proprietor from Canada did not. In stubbornly trying to ward off too many changes all at once they were right. Murray Watson, scholarly editor of the *Scotsman*, resisted contemptuously almost every suggestion of reform. As an old friend (for I too, though English-born, had Scots ancestors, had relatives in Edinburgh, and had been deputy editor of the *Dundee Advertiser*) I told him his new chief was not one to interfere needlessly with editors, and I thought the Scotsman would be all the better for a brisker tone and broader scope to meet the increasing competition of London-controlled papers. "You don't know our type of reader," was the stereotyped reply.

Murray Watson, imbued with the spirit of the old *Scotsman*, detested the newcomer from the first. When the time came to announce in the paper the new regime, he could not bring himself to write the hated news. He got his predecessor in the chair, Sir George Waters, to do it. Sir George, a man of calm judgment who cooperated with me at the outset of World War II to improve Ministry of Information plans, had no difficulty in stating the facts without any hint of bias and without the Olympian grandeur that the *Scotsman* had sometimes displayed. Roy wanted the front page, long given over to advertisements, to be a show-place for the most important news in the paper. We of the *Yorkshire Post* had made such a change in 1939. Others had followed suit, but Murray Watson said no. The overdue change was not made in his time.

As for the *Evening Dispatch* it was full of what we used to call "British Museum matter," mainly archeological or antiquarian articles written not always by experts at firsthand but often paraphrased from old books by weary hacks. There used to be a taste for such themes, but the Northcliffe revolution has made it out-of-date in most cities by offering a livelier scope of subjects. In almost every newspaper the bygones had gone by. I learned this by painful experience in my free-lancing days. But Albert Mackie, editor of the *Evening Dispatch*, thought he understood the Edinburgh public. He believed the citizens had a character of their own, moulded by history and tradition. How often, especially at Bradford, the metropolis of wool, I have heard this theory of a community unlike any other! Roy told Mackie his paper was lousy. Mackie angrily disagreed. He was fired.

Roy chose as a successor to the conservative, antiquarian-minded Mackie an enthusiastic sensationmonger with a *Daily Mirror* training. No doubt there were many citizens who wanted something more exciting, more warm-blooded than Mackie's *Dispatch*, but Jack Miller was considered to go to an extreme, almost as if Edinburgh had the crudest appetites for reading of violence. The twofold murder by an Edinburgh man and his stabbing of a daughter gave Miller opportunity for his considerable talents. He printed photographs to tug at the heartstrings, but they aroused revulsion rather than pity among most Edinburgh citizens. Sales dropped heavily.

In fairness it must be said Roy Thomson had made some sad misjudgments and shocked Edinburgh's stiff-minded social leaders. There was instant readiness to condemn what they disliked in his papers. In the *Evening Dispatch* they disliked a great deal. It was not as bad as they thought. Anyone trained in English popular journalism would have found much dashing enterprise and emotional appeal in it, but Edinburgh was so used to sedate and senatorial journalism that to confront it with a mass of sensational innovations struck it with horror.

Nothing Thomson did—and he tried many expedients— saved him from heavy losses on the *Evening Dispatch*. He did not want to be left without an evening paper to partner the *Scotsman*. To keep the organization going night and day is standard practice in almost every British city with a morning paper. The *Manchester Guardian* has relied heavily on the profits of the *Manchester Evening News*, the *Yorkshire Post* has leaned heavily on the *Yorkshire Evening Post*, the *Liverpool Post* on the *Liverpool Echo*, and so forth. The prestige paper is rarely the breadwinner in such unions. In 1963, after losing about two million pounds on the *Evening Dispatch*, Thomson bought from Charles Harold Drayton the powerful Edinburgh *Evening News*, in return mainly for Sheffield properties, the *Telegraph* and *Star*. Now Roy Thomson merged the two Edinburgh evening papers into a lucrative monopoly.

Meanwhile the *Scotsman* had been increasing its reputation as a national institution. Murray Watson, after doing all he could to prevent drastic changes in the *Scotsman*, died in 1955. I thought his conservatism had hardened into obsessive disapproval of his chief. As an old friend I tried to show him from my own experience what could be done with gradual changes of an old-fashioned paper. I told him what had happened with the *Yorkshire Post*. Its sales went up sevenfold. It rose to the biggest sale of any provincial morning paper in England. But it was no use. Murray thought that Scotland, with her long independent history, and Edinburgh, with the status of a capital, famous culture, and proud traditions, differed fundamentally from the plainspoken industrial towns of Yorkshire and Northern England.

Roy Thomson must have found him an awkward editor, but a time came when he said, "Heck, maybe Murray Watson was right after all. I made a lot of mistakes in these first few months; I didn't realise how conservative Edinburgh was, and I tried to push it along too fast. Murray Watson may have helped me avoid other mistakes by keeping the brakes on when I wanted to go too quickly."

Roy was lucky in the new top men he chose. James Milne Coltart, an accountant managing the Glasgow *Evening Citizen*, joined him as managing director of the Scotsman Publications in 1955, showed himself as a man after Roy's own heart, with a magical grasp of figures and constant drive. He has risen to immense success in the immense Thomson organizations. Then Alastair MacTavish Dunnett, after editing the Glasgow *Daily Record*, accepted the editorship of the *Scotsman*, enlivened it richly, and made it one of the most readable papers in Britain without the slightest detraction from its dignity. Above all, he made the paper speak for Scotland more persuasively, more pungently, more successfully than it had done for many decades. The paper has received many tributes since its Thomson regime began. One, in 1963, was the Honor Medal of the University of Missouri, presented annually to a "distinguished foreign newspaper."

Coming to Scotland to run the *Scotsman* led Thomson to another triumph. He foresaw great revenues from television when some of England's press magnates still thought it best to leave the new medium alone. The Independent Television Authority gave him the Scottish contract in 1956. Many men considered astute in money matters, including Lord Rosebery and Brendan Bracken, declined to contribute to the needed capital of £400,000, but the National Commercial Bank of Scotland lent

£240,000. In its first year on the air his company made a million pounds and the delighted venturer said to a *Time* journalist it was "like having a licence to print your own money." This admission proved useful to hostile critics in later controversy. The shares became so valuable that soon the Thomson empire in Britain was worth £48 million.

There arose plenty of controversy about the man who kept on buying newspapers—after he had a hundred he went on eagerly acquiring more—and now found television a gold mine. Some of his critics, having missed a chance of easy wealth, were probably even more annoyed with themselves than with Roy Thomson. It was not easy wealth for him and for Jim Coltart, whom he had appointed managing director of Scottish Television as well as of the *Scotsman*. They had much to learn about the new medium, but, determined to grasp a wonderful opportunity, they worked with intense absorption. When STV's music and fun burst on the air on August 31, 1957, it did not please the fastidiously critical, but it fascinated the advertisers.

Soon Thomson was ready to make a take-over offer to the shareholders of the *Glasgow Herald*, the *Scotsman*'s powerful rival. The letters were ready to be posted. Then Lord Kemsley, head of the biggest and richest newspaper group in Britain, suggested that Thompson should go straightaway to London to see him. What could it be for? It must be to sell Thomson a paper or papers. Roy had been after the *Aberdeen Press and Journal* some time before. Kemsley had asked a fending-off price. Now, to Roy's well-concealed amazement, Kemsley was willing to sell control of his whole empire, including the richly prestigious *Sunday Times* and seventeen other less important but still important papers. My belief, based on talk with Kemsley, is that he had tired of the everlasting newspaper struggle. He was not a born journalist like Lord Northcliffe or a man with a passion for journalism like Lord Beaverbrook. He had financial and administrative rather than creative gifts. He had made his millions with continuous effort and become a somewhat aloof potentate. The public setbacks of some of his papers distressed him. In his seventy-sixth year he saw more setbacks ahead, more labor harassments. He was not so devoted to the exhausting claims of newspaper ownership as not to have other and more agreeable interests, such as the

creation of most beautiful homes. Why, then, not quit the struggle and enjoy all the rewards, honors and lordly grandeur he had
gained? Is it not significant that his entry in *Who's Who, 1960*,
an entry provided by himself, devoted only two out of thirty-eight
lines to his newspaper career?

Complicated secret negotiations for the sale of the Kemsley
group went on for sixteen exhausting days. The deal agreed on is
a masterpiece of its kind, if indeed there has been any gigantic
deal like it issuing from a baffling financial maze. Kemsley at
first wanted six pounds a share for himself and for any of his
minority shareholders who might want to sell—say as much as
fifteen million pounds. This seemed an impossible price for
Thomson to raise. Then an adviser, Henry Grunfeld, of S. G.
Warburgs, hit on a brilliant idea, which he called a "reverse bid."
As STV could not afford to buy the Kemsley group let the group
buy STV. It could pay Thomson with Kemsley shares. These
would give him control of the combined Kemsley and STV
forces. In the end, after various intricacies of plan had been
explicated and agreed, and later recorded lucidly by Russell
Braddon in his book, *Roy Thomson of Fleet Street and How He
Got There*, Thomson wanted three million pounds to pay to
Lord Kemsley. He borrowed the money without difficulty or
delay from the National Commercial Bank of Scotland, the bold
and lucky backer of the infant Scottish Television.

So Roy Thomson reached Fleet Street in 1959 as a national
newspaper tycoon. He had the magnificent *Sunday Times*, the
not so promising *Empire News* and *Sunday Graphic* (both have
perished), the *Western Mail*, the national paper of Wales, the
prosperous Newcastle *Journal* group, the loss-making Manchester
Evening Chronicle, the *Sheffield Telegraph* and *Star* (later to be
handed over to Charles Harold Drayton in a deal that enabled
Thomson to own the Edinburgh *Evening News* and merge with
it the *Evening Dispatch*), and smaller papers in Lancashire,
Cheshire, and Wales.

Thomson was now in what he called the Big League. Excited
with victory, he said other things that were less tactful. Visiting
Montreal he gave the impression that many British papers were
most ineptly run and that he looked forward to getting back to
London to start clearing up the mess. This angered Lord

Kemsley, a man as proud of his success as Roy Thomson was of his. Thomson apologized. A Canadian paper also apologized and said it had misreported Thomson. But was the new tycoon wrong in what he appeared to think? I should say not, if the British press were considered purely as a business enterprise. In attracting advertisements and in economical production it had much to learn from Thomson's methods. His lessons have had a marked effect in other offices as well as his own.

After acquiring the Kemsley group, Thomson went ahead at an extraordinary pace. In 1961 Illustrated Newspapers, a magazine group, was bought. In the same year the Thomson Organization, the name substituted for Thomson Newspapers the year before, took over Thomas Nelson, an Edinburgh publishing house with a distinguished history. Meanwhile the *Sunday Times* made bold improvements. It issued with the paper a costly color magazine supplement, the first in the country. Experts shook their heads over this innovation. They said it would never pay. Thomson said it would, but not at first. Thomson was right. It lost nine hundred thousand pounds in eighteen months, then turned the corner, and up rushed the profits. Beautifully printed, it soon appealed to rich advertisers who wanted to appeal to rich readers. As Thomson had said with impeccable candor, "Primarily, I'm a moneymaking man." The *Observer* and the *Daily Telegraph* paid him the compliment of following suit with color magazine supplements. In September 1964 a separate business news section increased the bulkiest of Sunday papers.

In December 1966, the organization acquired control of that most famous of British newspapers, the *Times*, which for a long time had been like the Bible in being more revered than read. Lord Northcliffe had come to its rescue in 1908 and made it flourish without losing its cherished independence. Now it was again in peril amid the furious competition from Fleet Street, especially from the *Daily Telegraph* with its far bigger circulation. This time Lord Thomson stood out as the obvious rescuer. Whatever he did to improve methods of the *Times* it was sure to lose a great deal of money before it could pay its way. Thomson did not hesitate. He calculated he could make it profitable.

His plan brought the Monopolies and Mergers legislation into action for the first time. The Monopolies Commission had to investigate a proposed merger deal between the *Sunday Times* and the *Times* and decide (a) whether or not the transfer of ownership of the *Times* might be expected to operate against the public interest having regard . . . to the need for accurate presentation of news and free expression of opinion; and (b) whether, if the merger were to proceed, any conditions should be attached to safeguard the public interest, and if so, what these might be.

The commission reported that the transfer of an important vehicle of opinion such as the *Times* to the Thomson group would represent a material increase in power for that group, but the transfer would not lead to undue concentration of newspaper power.

A feature of the scheme was the intention to appoint a single editor in chief for the two papers. Would this mean a paper coming out seven days a week like the New York *Times*? The commission, after full investigation and after assurances by the Thomson Organization and Lord Thomson, was satisfied that the two papers would keep their separate identities and the editors would be given full and independent responsibility for the opinions their papers expressed.

So the commission approved the scheme by which Lord Thomson would provide the means to carry out a program of development to lead to a *Times* circulation of four hundred thousand to four hundred fifty thousand, the minimum need for financial viability. The Times Newspapers Ltd. came into existence, with Thomson owning eighty-five percent of the equity of the company. Denis Hamilton, a brilliant executive, became editor in chief of the two papers, with William Rees-Mogg, a first-rate economist, as editor of the *Times* and Harold Evans, after a bright, innovating career at Darlington, as editor of the *Sunday Times*.

The Press Council, in an article in 1967 on the structure of the Thomson Organization said the *Times* had a circulation of more than four hundred thousand. In November, 1968, the *Times* reached 433,000. In October and November 1968, the *Sunday Times* had a sale of more than 1,475,000. Both papers were steadily gaining more readers. So the smiling, confident Roy could smile with the utmost satisfaction. He was indeed primarily a moneymaking man. After those early years of ill-rewarded struggle he was now hauling in profits faster and faster. The redoubtable Cecil Harmsworth King, with no fear of coming downfall, and Roy Thomson towered above all British competitors in the world of the printed word.

Not that everything went well for them all the time in their highly competitive field. Roy Thomson looked back in anger at certain circumstances of his purchase of the *Belfast Telegraph*, the most powerful journal in Northern Ireland. Two-thirds of the shares in the paper were held by trustees for a boy, Richard Baird. Thomson was alleged to have bought these shares secretly, and of bribing the trustees with contracts of service. In fact, Thomson had agreed to pay a very stiff price for the shares, and almost always took on executives and directors of papers he bought. At the end of long-drawn-out legal proceedings the Queen's Counsel, who had spoken sternly about the transaction with the trustees, said Thomson's integrity and honor were in no way in question and no suggestion had been made, or was ever intended, against his good name. Thomson still felt furious resentment. What man of honor, if he thought his honesty had been impugned, would not feel a burning anger?

A defeat at the hands of Cecil Harmsworth King left Thomson curiously philosophical. Fearing a take-over bid by King, Sir Christopher Chancellor, chairman of Odhams Press, publishing many magazines, the Sunday paper *People*, and the *Daily Herald*, negotiated for a merger with the fast rising Thomson group. A basis for agreement was reached. Then King made so generous an offer for Odhams that Thompson stepped out of the bargaining, apparently with no acute disappointment. King's International Publishing Corporation came into being. Thompson went on amassing more newspapers. One brilliant idea was to start what would become a ring of evening papers around London, starting with one at Reading. These would have the advantage of economical, up-to-date production in competing in their own areas with the two evening papers in London that alone remained out of the nine published there in my school days.

Though he has modestly said, "I am not a very charitable man," Roy Thomson in 1963 set up a £5 million Thomson Foundation to bring a knowledge of newspaper techniques and democratic principles to the emergent nations of Africa. His aim was to project the Western way of life. He has worked on the scheme with enthusiasm and a deeply felt belief that mass communication media have enriched our civilization, as in the main they undoubtedly have. This altruistic service, no doubt, helped to qualify him for a peerage.

Now a multimillionaire, Roy Thomson is a peer almost without a peer in his own strange way. His title, the Right Honorable Lord Thomson of Fleet (it is customary as a courtesy to term a peer Right Honorable) bears a reference to a river in Sutherland, Scotland. It happens, also, to be the brook that gave its name to Fleet Street, but that has long been converted into a sewer. Lord Thomson shines as an unparalleled phenomenon in the world of journalistic finance. Candid, honest, pleased with his abundant success, he remains a single-minded pursuer of happiness through business achievements. He has lived down a great deal of criticism. He says frankly that he buys more newspapers to make more money to buy more newspapers to make more money to buy more newspapers.

If you ask, "Why do you want so many?" he replies "They are rendering a social service. The bigger the operation grows, the greater the service rendered." If you say, "It is wrong that one man should be able to impose his ideas on millions of people," his answer is that he does not impose his ideas on millions. To begin with, he does not impose his ideas on his editors, except to tell them that he wants his papers to be successful, and he wants them to be clean. At the same time he offers them useful suggestions, based on his exceptionally wide experience.

When asked why he has killed some newspapers (for example, the *Empire News*, the *Sunday Graphic*, the Edinburgh *Evening Dispatch*) he replied bluntly, "Because not enough people wanted to read them and not enough people wanted to advertise in them. And I'm not made of money." Few people seem to remember that though he has had to kill some papers, he has saved others from death by his group economy techniques. Spreading the cost of first-rate services among many newspapers is a method the rich possibilities of which he has done more than anyone else to exploit. He is the Newspaper Group Creator Extraordinary.

Some say he is no great journalist. But he is without question a brilliant publisher in the American sense of the word publisher. He knows what kind of newspapers he wants and he gets them. I would not deny some excellent journalistic qualities to a man who has done much to improve the *Times*, the *Sunday Times*, and many others in his more than a hundred newspapers.

As a man Lord Thomson has qualities that almost everyone would admire. When negotiating to buy a newspaper he aims at a deal that will make buyer and seller equally happy. In spite of my friendly warning in Canada, he showed himself ready much later to buy the Yorkshire group of papers of which I was editor in chief. But when he found we were unwilling to sell he cheerfully accepted our decision and made no approach to the shareholders. At a Commonwealth Press Union conference at New Delhi that he attended I pointed out the dangers of one-man control of many papers. When I sat down he came over to me, shook hands and said, "That was a fine speech, Linton."

How can you not like such a man?

16

Viceroys of a Press Empire

C. Denis Hamilton *A new type of creative*
executive editor who learned leadership
on the battlefield.

You could mistake Denis Hamilton for a young general in mufti. Straight, trim, with a healthy look, a firm chin, a neat moustache, and an air of calm self-command, he has the appearance of one who has led in battle and come out of the test with the hero worship of his men. This is just what happened. Hamilton reached Fleet Street through his prowess as a young Territorial Army officer in the Second World War. He won the Distinguished Service Order at Nijmegen and was promoted to lieutenant colonel. I never knew of so young a battalion commanding officer. He was only twenty-seven when demobilized in the peaceful days of 1946, after what for Britain had been six years of war. In the year these started, in 1939, Hamilton became a Territorial officer in the Durham Light Infantry. He commanded one of its battalions and later a battalion of the Duke of Wellington's regiment.

With so brilliant a start for a very young man, he may have been tempted to make soldiering his career. Field Marshal Lord Montgomery, who admired his courage and military skill, asked

276

Courtesy of *The Times*

DENIS HAMILTON

Courtesy of H. A. Taylor

ALASTAIR DUNNETT

Courtesy of the *Belfast Telegraph*

JOHN EDWARD SAYERS

Courtesy of Thomson Newspapers, Ltd.

JOHN GIDDINGS

him to do so. A born journalist, Hamilton declined. He wanted to get back to the smell of printer's ink and the thunder of the presses. (If this seems an extravagant phrase it describes what I, too, have felt. When the First World War ended, I joined the *Daily Mail* in London, and no music ever sounded sweeter to me than the starting of the rotaries' muffled roar, down in the basement, as my first night's work at Carmelite House was ending.) Hamilton, a Yorkshireman, educated at Middlesbrough High School, determined when he was about twelve years of age to become a journalist. This ambition never left him, in spite of his rise in the army. He did not go to a university as a boy of his bright intelligence might have done, but went to the Middlesbrough *Evening Gazette* as a junior reporter.

This paper belonged to the Kemsley group, the largest group of its time. In Britain, as in the United States, newspaper groups have their critics, but they offer excellent facilities for training and promotion. There can be close contact and still closer supervisory comparison between the member papers, producing eager competition and the hybrid vigor which, as biology teaches us, often comes from cross-fertilization. Hamilton did so well as a junior reporter on the Middlesbrough *Evening Gazette* that he was moved to more important Kemsley papers at Newcastle-upon-Tyne, the *Evening Chronicle*, the *North Mail* (a morning paper), and the *Sunday Sun*, as a special writer. There, at a busy port in the midst of a great coalfield, he found scope for an agreeable descriptive style and the analysis of important regional and local problems.

He got on well with people. I have described him as soldierly. So he is after all his years in Fleet Street, but he does not resemble in the least the warrior of Shakespeare's description

> Full of strange oaths, and bearded
> like the pard,
> Jealous in honour, sudden and quick in quarrel.

He has never been in the least violent in expression or quarrelsome. Many writers cultivate a modest personality on paper, but in private life are quite different. Hamilton, in spite of his achievements, has always listened to others tactfully—an especially rewarding virtue in a journalist.

His old colleagues were warm in his praise both as soldier and journalist when Lord and Lady Kemsley visited Newcastle in 1945. This well-earned praise had an important sequel for Hamilton. In the following year he was back at Newcastle, now with ten pounds a week, not at that time a bad salary for a young provincial journalist. Lord Kemsley, like all newspaper owners, was then fiercely ambitious to improve and enlarge his newspapers and to grasp every opportunity to get ahead of rivals. Enterprise had been cruelly held in check by the war. Every newspaper owner, every newspaper editor, had office drawers full of schemes for prosperous development when newsprint rationing and all the other wartime restrictions could be stopped. The boldest of expansionists in the newspaper field, Lord Kemsley may have forgotten the young hero he had been told so much about at Newcastle. Lady Kemsley had not. She prompted her husband to inquire about him. Kemsley repentantly did so.

Everything told in Hamilton's favor. He was summoned to Kemsley House, the group's headquarters in Gray's Inn Road, London, W.C.1, and entertained at Kemsley's town home, Chandos House, Queen Anne Street, W. 1. Good-looking, eager, and modest, he made such an impression that his employer offered him almost on the spur of the moment the post of chief personal assistant in London with pay at least equal to a colonel's. Feeling that this promotion was a distinctly dreamlike transition, a heaven-sent blessing for a man with a wife (a Northumberland doctor's niece) and four young sons, Hamilton arranged to start work at the beginning of the following week, in the room next to Lord Kemsley's paneled office on the third floor of the group's massive headquarters.

The post offered remarkable scope. K, as he was known to his editors, would have scorned to break out stormily like Northcliffe or Beaverbrook. He was a resolute administrator and financier rather than a brightly innovating editor, an aloof potentate rather than an accessible leader of his numerous team. He told the first Royal Commission on the press (1947–49): "It is generally understood by those people [his provincial editors], when we have come to a decision, what our policy is, but I do not communicate myself and never have done direct with editors on policy." I have known men who worked for K for years in

London or Manchester and never had the privilege of seeing him. Once, by a misunderstanding, when I asked at the Waldorf Hotel, London, for the Guild of Editors' meeting, I was ushered into what turned out to be a gathering of Kemsley provincial editors. They had some resembalance to a group of men waiting to be taken to Wormwood-Scrubbs Prison. Though presumably wielders of power in their own communities, they gazed at me suspiciously as if I were to take over one of their editorships, but which it was to be none knew. I am sure they would be much happier when they returned to their own far-off desks. It struck me as an unfortunate atmosphere and an indication of how far they were from the chief in his gracious throne room.

Lord Kemsley certainly, as editor in chief of the *Sunday Times*, helped to make that paper extremely successful. He knew how to meet the needs of the well educated and well to do. With his papers of the popular type he achieved less success. He was out of touch with the masses, and too distant, not physically but in status, from some of his many editors. In the hierarchy at Kemsley House the new personal assistant found it possible to become an influential go-between. He knew what the great chief decided. Important men in the network of Kemsley papers looked to him to do more than communicate the decisions. They began to seek guidance from him or through him.

I have known intermediaries of the kind in lesser groups who misused their powers. Trading on the confidence placed in them by the chairman or managing director, they would issue orders of their own with a spurious air of authority from higher up. Underlings were never quite sure whether an order of the kind had the chairman's or managing director's sanction behind it or not. It is one of the sources of Denis Hamilton's strength that he never stooped to such pretensions. As Lord Kemsley's go-between he was equally respected by the giver of topmost orders and their receivers. He was discretion itself at its worthiest.

It was soon clear that he did not mean to be merely a super secretary, like Alfred Butes, who, after being with Joseph Pulitzer as confidential secretary, at length found that neurotic tycoon too cruelly exacting and worked for Lord Northcliffe, who described him as "the best secretary God ever made." Hamilton's ambitions were, above all, journalistic. Eager to know the *Sunday*

Times people, he gave the editor the benefit of his War Office contacts. First fruits were splash stories (news leading the front page) on two successive weeks about the plans for the dwindling army, now that peacetime economics took the place of striving for victory at any price. For many years he gave the paper exclusive military news and commentaries.

One article of his that aroused warm approval in Britain, whatever American readers thought of it, reviewed Eisenhower's book, *Crusade in Europe*. He respected, as all the British people did, the fine qualities of the former supreme commander of the Allied Expeditionary Force in Western Europe and future president of the United States. But Hamilton thought the book gave a somewhat distorted impression of Operation Overlord for the cross-Channel invasion of German-occupied Europe. It overestimated the American share of credit and did less than justice to the part of war-experienced, if warworn, Britain. He made a strong reasoned protest.

Among the problems in which Lord Kemsley greatly profited by the foresight of his personal assistant was the need for better training of journalists. This widespread need affected even the Kemsley newspaper empire, excellent as were the *Sunday Times* and leading regional papers of the group. The war, with its desperately necessary restrictions, had forced makeshift, temporizing arrangements on heavily reduced staffs. A strict though voluntary censorship, the rationing of newsprint, and the veto on new papers made for less competitive zeal. The standard of reporting fell. Since shortage of space cut down reports, few of the newcomers to journalism took the trouble to make themselves trustworthy shorthand writers. Hitherto shorthand had been considered indispensable to reporters. To get back to better newspapers we needed better journalists. Among veterans like myself, provincial editors who were the accepted trainers in the profession, this seemed unquestionable. We strove hard to get our professional associations and trade unions to set up a press training scheme on national lines. Lord Kemsley, exceptional among Fleet Street proprietors, took a remarkable step forward, known as the Kemsley Editorial Plan. Hamilton recruited promising young people, including university graduates, and planned a first-rate training scheme.

One outcome, full of his practical sense of newspaper needs and of his encouragement of youthful aspirants, took the form of the *Kemsley Manual of Journalism*. This was published in 1950. The Kemsley-Hamilton initiative strengthened the long-advocated but often belittled efforts of journalists, especially provincial and London suburban journalists, to set up a national scheme of press training. In 1952, after discussions in which all sections of the newspaper industry joined, the National Advisory Council for the Training and Education of Junior Journalists came into existence under a title soon changed to the National Council for the Training of Journalists. Later Hamilton greatly helped this scheme by persuading leading Fleet Street proprietors to make welcome contributions to its income.

Publication of the *Kemsley Manual of Journalism* was not the only event in 1950 that showed what a power Hamilton had become as a partner in Lord Kemsley's activities. In that year he was made a director of Kemsley Newspapers and editorial director of the group. At the same time Kemsley himself was devoting more and more attention to the *Sunday Times*. Such a situation offers a strong temptation to neglect the Cinderellas of a group and concentrate on the profitably prestigious. Hamilton tried his best, at the risk of his health, to be helpful all around. He did much for the *Sunday Times*, but some of the group's papers were already slowing down into the terminus.

His military prowess continued its useful effects. One great scoop was to buy up secretly, without telling Lord Kemsley beforehand, all rights in Lord Montgomery's memoirs. Monty, with his record of victories, had the jubilant goodwill, the acclamation, the hero worship of the British people. Whatever he said—and without question he would say it with slashing candor —was sure to be read with all-absorbed attention. The long installments (known in the office as "the big read") ran for fifteen weeks, brought ninety thousand new readers, and put the paper well ahead of its great rival for the educated and usually well-to-do reader, the *Observer*. Another serial success that Hamilton arranged was William Manchester's controversial work, *The Death of a President*.

When planning his coups, Hamilton maintained the utmost secrecy. He knew well how decisions made in a newspaper office are often the talk of the whole staff in a few hours. Office spies on some papers have been known to steam open letters from the chief. Hamilton had a healthy belief in security. But when the time came to exploit a scoop he made full and often subtle use of the promotional resources that modern mass media offer. After ten years at Kemsley House his knowledge of editorial, managerial, and promotional creativeness was probably unequaled in British journalism.

So when, in 1959, the weary Lord Kemsley, to the surprise of Fleet Street, decided to retire and gave Roy Thomson, the proud chairman of the *Scotsman* and that new gold mine, Scottish Television, the chance to take over the group, Hamilton was clearly a man with a brilliant future. The first big task the newcomer with North American ideas gave him was to launch a color magazine as part of the *Sunday Times*. Nothing of the kind had been attempted before in Britain, but Thomson determined to make it a success. Not everyone in Fleet Street imagined it would be warmly welcomed in a land which already had a wealth of competing magazines and, among people of the higher income brackets, a habit of buying the weekend reviews for leisurely weekend reading. Not everyone thought the new magazine would attract expensive advertising in a land where there seemed to be less than enough for all the existing Sunday publications. Would the newsagent tolerate the added burden of handling a magazine given free with a newspaper already bulky by British standards?

Thomson and his young henchman put immense effort into preparations for the new supplement to the *Sunday Times*. Thomson concentrated on persuading the advertising world and newspaper distributors to welcome his projected color magazine. Scepticism had to be disarmed by a long attritional campaign. Meanwhile Hamilton thought how he could make the magazine uniquely attractive. One bright idea was to persuade Lord Snowdon, formerly Antony Charles Robert Armstrong-Jones, the gifted photographer husband of Princess Margaret, sister of the Queen, to join the staff. This surprised the world, for to have somebody so close to the throne working for a newspaper showed how far Britain was moving away from its centuries-old ideas of Court exclusiveness. When news of the appointment came out, everybody talked about it, in general admiringly, and the promised magazine gained an immense amount of free publicity, and not in Britain alone. In due course readers were to see and admire the qualities that had given the young man his reputation as a photographer.

Not long before the magazine appeared, Hamilton was asked to become editor of all sections of the *Sunday Times*. He alone of those on the board was surprised. Had he not enough work to do already as editorial director of the group, with special responsibility for the color magazine scheme? Roy Thomson had other expansionist plans in mind, and Hamilton had the needed vigor and confidence to carry them through, as all his fellow directors agreed. The paper was to be bigger, a separate business magazine section must be added (Hamilton suggested this and it appealed strongly to Thomson) and a great pressroom would have to be set up in Thomson House to print the paper, hitherto produced on the machines of the *Daily Telegraph*.

It took a great deal of energy and money to build up the success of the color magazine. Critics at first shook their heads over the venture. Some thought it a wild goose chase. Lord Beaverbrook did. Cecil King is reported by Russell Braddon, Lord Thomson's biographer, to have said: "That'll cost Thomson one hell of a lot of money, and who cares? But it will also cost us a hell of a lot of money—and that hurts! Why can't he keep his bloody mouth shut?" Roy Thomson and Denis Hamilton never thought of giving in. Ultimately almost a million pounds was spent in developing this part of the *Sunday Times*. It was money well spent. The know-alls who predicted failure began to look exceedingly foolish. Advertising began to pour in and the circulation rose. Then the venture became so profitable that others rushed into the field in which the *Sunday Times* had been so enterprising a pioneer. The *Observer* and the *Daily Telegraph* decided they must have color magazines. Could rivals have shown a more eloquent recognition of a really good thing?

Amid such tough problems a new kind of editor or editor in chief was needed. Hamilton saw this more clearly than most journalists. He wrote for the *Spectator* of August 24, 1962 a remarkable statement of what the duties of the ideal editor would be under the economic conditions that were evolving.

The fact is that the finances of newspapers nowadays are very delicately attuned, and no one can tell from year to year—almost from month to month—whether financial equilibrium is to result. . . . The old type of editor, the "writing" editor, chief preoccupied with the political direction of the paper is, I think, no longer a practical proposition. We have reached a time when the understanding of newspaper economics, and the facing up to them, is just as much the responsibility of the editor as of the proprietor. The modern proprietor, in fact, should be the financier, the head of the business, one who doesn't interfere in editorial policy and is above all the chairman of the board. (This understanding is the key to Thomson's success.) And on this board the editor must have a place. If, as I believe, the object of a good editor is to achieve solvency without sacrifice of standards, it is essential for him to be what I can only call a creative executive as well as a first-class journalist.

Hamilton thought it was not good enough for the business side of a newspaper to be left exclusively in the hands of its proprietor or his nominees. "Far from being tied to his desk writing the night's leader," he went on to insist,

the modern editor should be up to his neck in the fight for solvency, having a strong say when investment in machinery is in contemplation, watching costs in every department, thinking out ways of making use of certain services, whether from his own organisation or newspaper and publishers abroad. He should know almost as much about advertising as his own advertisement manager. He should be largely in control of his own budget.

This is a good picture of what Hamilton does, but when *Punch* invited him to write about the *Sunday Times,* he disclaimed being anything like Superman. "As the week swirls past, and one problem succeeds another, I don't, I must say, feel at all like that." Nor do I think he ever will. Still, his achievements stand out with monumental prominence. He and his ambitious chief have developed the paper with ceaseless energy.

The *Sunday Times* developed on a scale Lord Kemsley had never foreseen. It was in four parts. One section consisted mainly of the latest news, editorials, and features elucidating important problems raised by events in many parts of the world. Another section, now termed The Weekly Review, appealed especially to those keen on literature and the arts, a "big read" like an astonishingly frank series on the Beatles in their scruffy early days and their later life of wealth. For women there was a good show of fashions. A business section treated the problems and the leaders of industry and finance with more insight, detail, and personality than Sunday papers had shown before. Then there was the color supplement, increasingly popular.

Hamilton must have been invited here, there, and everywhere to speak. But his public appearances are rare; he is no seeker of publicity for himself; he lives up to his vision of a creative executive, thinking always how to improve the Thomson papers, especially the *Sunday Times*. In conversation with friends it does not matter if they are only little-known country editors; he is always attentive rather than assertive. At his editorial conferences in Thomson House he encourages everyone to offer ideas. Lord Northcliffe would sometimes saw to someone who made a suggestion he did not like, "Young man, don't be silly." I cannot imagine Denis Hamilton ever playing the stern judge or sarcastic headmaster in such circumstances or being annoyed if his own ideas were not accepted as wisdom's latest triumphs.

When he was forty-six and had been editor of the *Sunday Times* for three years, he received the highest accolade in British journalism, being deemed by the judges of the Hannen Swaffer Awards the Journalist of the Year (1964). The awards are a memorial to one of the best-loved columnists in Fleet Street, who gave unstinted encouragement to youthful members of the profession. The prizes are not so numerous as those endowed by Joseph Pulitzer in a bequest to Columbia University, New York, but possess similar prestige. The Swaffer judges at the time were John Freeman, then editor of the *New Statesman*, afterwards the United Kingdom High Commissioner in India and now ambassador at Washington, James Bradley, secretary of the National Union of Journalists, and myself as chairman. When we came to name the journalist of the year we first discussed whether we should honor in this way a reporter, a political columnist, or an editor. We debated the question with judicial thoroughness. We thought the *Sunday Times* deserved an accolade. Should the

honor go to its editor? Sometimes an editor gets credit that ought
to go to a member or members of his staff or even to his employer. But we knew that Hamilton had had the utmost freedom
under the dynamic newspaperman who had become Lord Thomson of Fleet. We felt that the greater his freedom, the greater was
the editor's responsibility. As Freeman said, Hamilton exercised
the governing responsibility in the achievement of new insight,
new prestige, and now authority for the paper. Our citation of
Denis Hamilton read: "For his distinguishing work in making
the *Sunday Times* one of the great newspapers of the world."

When Hamilton received his prizes, a check for five hundred
pounds and a gold quill pen, he made a striking speech on
changes in journalism. He remembered when, among the
weightier newspapers at any rate, journalists thought it unseemly
to write all they knew. They wanted to bank down the fire of
events, to banish the glint in the eye. All this, he thought, was
perhaps a legacy before the war when newspaper proprietors
themselves were all-powerful, when public taste was at its lowest
ebb, and when Winston Churchill was a lone voice crying in the
wilderness.

This view may surprise many readers. But I know from
my own experience, when as an editor I was giving all the support I could to Churchill's warnings and urging his return to
office, how reluctant were many people to recognize the flaming
signal of events. They wanted to be reassured, not alarmed,
whatever cause there was for alarm. They spurned hearing aids
and stuffed their ears with the cottonwool of complacency. To
put it more plainly, they gave up reading such papers as the
Yorkshire Post, a stalwart supporter of Churchill and Eden on the
issue of appeasing or defying Hitler. When war came they demanded to know why editors like myself had not warned them
of its danger.

Hamilton went on to tell us it seemed to him more and more
newspapers were seeking the truth about events both great and
small. To find out the truth about great public and even international controversies needed an enormous amount of sifting and
digging, not to speak of judgment and knowledge. It cost much
money. That year's editorial budget for the Sunday Times was

nearly one million pounds. That amount was needed if you went in for a probing journalism, when a team of several men might not write a word for a month.

Then came handsome tributes. "I have a staggeringly able staff—over 100 of them, two out of three of them in their thirties. My years in the army taught me that the selection of executives is the key to everything—and able men need freedom. It has been a boost to their morale that the paper should be singled out this year, and I am personally delighted for the sake of Roy Thomson, who is the perfect proprietor. . . . He is the complete professional newspaper man and this award is a tribute to his fantastic dynamism and courage since he came to Fleet Street five years ago at the age of 65."

I have used the word "insight" several times in this chapter. It is a word now closely associated with Hamilton. He invented the expression, Insight Team, to describe a special staff for reporting in depth. It is now becoming a trade term, both in Britain and the United States. It will probably pass into common use. Perhaps people will forget who invented the technique and its name. It was undoubtedly Denis Hamilton who, more than any other editor, added this new attraction, long reports that revealed hitherto obscure truths about great events and great controversies. The Swaffer judges' award did not remain an isolated tribute. In 1966 Independent Television acclaimed the *Sunday Times* as the newspaper of the decade.

Meanwhile secret negotiations of high significance promised Lord Thomson and his faithful henchman the most spectacular achievements yet. Fleet Street knew well that the *Times* with its comparatively small circulation, though, as it claimed, a circulation among top people, must be losing a good deal of money. How long would Astor wealth keep it going against fierce competition, especially that of the *Daily Telegraph*? Who would go to the rescue?

Lord Thomson made a bid. Who else? The *Guardian* for a time shared in a not very impressive consortium to try its luck. Then it withdrew amid quaint rumours that the *Times* and the *Guardian* might merge. Another tale going around mentioned a possible take over with financial backing from the television

world. An incredible suggestion was that a public concern rather
like the British Broadcasting Corporation should run the *Times.*

Lord Thomson and Denis Hamilton remained quietly confident. The one awkward factor was the argument sure to be put
before the Monopolies Commission that while Lord Thomson
had proved himself to be a public-spirited as well as an able British
newspaper proprietor, his possessions might pass in time to persons with purely Canadian interests and without that feeling for
the British ethos, which is essential to those producing the *Times*
as a great national newspaper. But in the end a *Times-Sunday
Times* alliance, with Lord Thomson and the Honorable Gavin
Astor as partners, the Thomson interest preponderant, met with
the blessing of the Monopolies Commission. Both Lord Thomson
and his son Kenneth promised to put the whole of their fortunes
in Britain at the disposal of the *Times,* if necessary, to keep it in
being. So the famous old paper started on a terrific struggle to
restore its old standing. Denis Hamilton, the inevitable choice,
became editor in chief and chief executive of Times Newspapers,
head of all the publishing ventures and director of the editorial
strategy of the *Times,* the *Sunday Times,* the *Times Literary
Supplement,* and the *Times Educational Supplement.* He faced
calmly, like a Montgomery, a severely testing and probably long
battle to restore the primacy of the *Times.*

His masterly touch was quickly evident in a *Business News*
section and a Saturday supplement with distinguished writing
mainly on leisure pursuits. Still slim, still athletically active, fond
of sailing in Chichester Harbour, a devoted family man, a one-
man ideas department but always encouraging to others with
ideas, a careful thinker—he attributes what most of us would
call flashes of inspiration to a mysterious combination of hard
fact and imaginative interpretation—Denis Hamilton soldiers on
in the battlefields of journalism as keenly and faithfully as he
did on the battlefields of the western front.

Alastair Dunnett *Editor of the* Scotsman

We have seen how Roy Thomson, as soon as he acquired control of the *Scotsman*, faced resistance from the editor, Murray Watson, to various efforts to modernize the makeup and tone of the newspaper. (See chapter 15.)

When ill health forced Watson's retirement, Thomson's right-hand business man, James Milne Coltart, picked a successor who he believed would delight the Chairman and many more readers than the paper then had. This was Alastair MacTavish Dunnett. The choice proved first-rate for the *Scotsman* and for Dunnett. After a varied career Dunnett found full scope for his editorial quality.

A dark and dashing Highlander, fond of sailing and riding, who looks like a character out of R. L. Stevenson's *Kidnapped*, he was the son of a Caithness father and a Gaelic-speaking mother from Argyll. Born in 1908, he left Hillhead High School, Glasgow, when times in Scotland were bad. He had a piece printed in the *Glasgow Herald* when he was fourteen, but now it seemed better to place him in the security of bank employment than to risk for him the hazards of journalism. Though he served the Commercial Bank of Scotland faithfully, his heart was in writing. At the age of twenty-four he left the bank to found with a Dundee journalist, James S. Adam, the *Claymore*, a weekly paper for Scottish boys. Dunnett and Adam shared enthusiasm for Scotland the Brave. They thought the boys of their country should realize the adventurous possibilities of their own country and not be expected to concentrate their imagination on Greyfriars, the Shell and the Billy Bunters of English authors. The two young men worked with intense enthusiasm to stave off disaster, and for a time, to keep down expenses, slept without one landlord's knowledge in their one-room office. But long-established English competition proved too much for them. In 1934 they set off in single-seater canoes to explore Scotland from the Clyde to Skye. During this highly adventurous voyage, described much later in a book by Dunnett, *Quest by Canoe*, they wrote newspaper articles with a tang of salt water and a warming love of the highlands. Now there could be no doubt of the kind of future in store for Dunnett. He joined the *Weekly Herald*, then went to the *Bulletin*, and then as art editor to the Glasgow *Daily Record*. During the Second World War he was press officer to five successive Scottish Secretaries, notably that great and inspiring patriot, Tom Johnston, with whom he traveled all over Scotland and learned much of the problems of government, national and local.

After the war he became editor of the *Daily Record*. He made it a good popular paper with some graphic writing and an enthusiastic belief in Scotland. He wrote two books, *Heard Tell* and *The Highlands and Islands of Scotland*, in addition to the one on the canoe venture, and a play, *The Original John Mackay*, on why, though he may not prosper at home, the Highlander usually succeeds so well abroad.

When the *Daily Record* came under the ownership of the *Daily Mirror* group (now the International Publishing Company), Dunnett's new chiefs, Cecil King and Hugh Cudlipp, wanted changes in the paper against his wishes. He believed that with his literary qualities and his belief in the sweetness and light of culture he was not the man to make those changes. He wondered where to go. Back to commerce? To a career of authorship? In this dark perplexity the answer came like a shaft of light. A voice on the telephone—it was Coltart's—virtually offered him the editorship of the *Scotsman*. Dunnett went to see Thomson. "What is your attitude to front page news?" asked Thomson. "It is absolutely essential for the *Scotsman* to have front page news," said Dunnett.

So Thomson had no doubts, and in 1956 the spirited, adventurous Highlander, at the age of forty-eight, applied himself to the greatest task of his life. He did not attempt a violent revolution of the paper. Front page news did not begin at once. A daily conference presided over by the editor did. The *Scotsman*, though a pioneer in many ways, was probably the last important paper to adopt this method of drawing out ideas, facilitating coordination of different departments and inspiring competitive zeal.

Dunnett gave the paper a more pleasing appearance, without, of course, any corybantic headings or features. He added a Saturday magazine supplement to keep readers abreast of developments in literature, the arts, education, science, travel, and so forth, in gracefully written articles. Above all, the paper explored the problems of Scotland, gave ample space for different points of view, and wrote about the country's needs in temperate but effective terms.

Sales and advertising rose steadily. In 1959 the judges seeking the best designed newspaper in Britain for one award of a plaque chose the *Scotsman*. They said:

> *The Scotsman*, the famous Edinburgh daily, is a model of what a "quality" or "class" paper should be. The harmonious consistency of its front page, praised by the 1958 judges, extends throughout the paper; the economy of its headline typography (two styles only of Bodoni bold) is noteworthy; its halftone reproduction is first-class. It is the first daily paper—other than *The Times* itself—to win the plaque; and with the same exception, the first plaque-winner to machine-set all its news headlines from a keyboard. Broadly it may be said that we made our awards to those papers which we felt were showing the most marked individuality and enterprise in applying their typographic resources, of whatever order, to the production of a paper clearly satisfactory to their particular readers (and, we should add, to their particular advertisers). On this basis, our choice for the plaque was as instant as it was unanimous—*The Scotsman*.

The paper continued to improve. In 1960 it adopted Scotsman Royal, a typeface designed by the Intertype Company of Brooklyn with special adaptations for the *Scotsman*. This became the text type for news and features throughout the paper.

Dunnett became managing director in 1962. Friendly as always and now highly successful, he is one of the happiest and most alert editors in Britain.

John Edward Sayers *Who returned from the corridors of power to his "hometown" newspaper*

In the space of some ten years, Lord Thomson achieved the considerable feat of acquiring, among many other publications, the predominant daily newspapers of England, Scotland, Wales, and Northern Ireland, the distinctive nations which, together, are officially designated "The United Kingdom of Great Britain and Northern Ireland." (And where Northern Ireland is concerned, the word "United" is emotive and politically significant.)

Surveying today the whole range of Thomson newspapers, many of which are located overseas, the term, "empire," often applied to Lord Thomson's possessions, is not inappropriate; nor, having regard to his own definition of the authority he delegates to his editors in chief, is it incongruous to style them "Viceroys."

In this respect, however, the Thomson situation in London may appear somewhat anomalous. There, as Sir Linton Andrews has shown, Mr. Dennis Hamilton enjoys exceptional *locus standi*. Within Mr. Hamilton's territory is the headquarters of the *Times*, with its unique mystique and the rare authority with which its editor is invested by tradition and by public belief. It is a newspaper that might well share the designation which, in the ecclesiastical sphere, belongs to Westminster Abbey—a "Royal Peculiar." Whether the editor of the *Times* is accepted as being the head of his profession, as Sir William Haley claimed, is arguable, but there is no doubt that Mr. William Rees-Mogg, who succeeded Haley, is regarded as the possessor of journalistic gifts that are not surpassed, even if they are matched, by any of the exceptional editorial chiefs within the Thomson empire. But when two men ride a horse, one must ride behind, and in the light of the constitution devised when Lord Thomson acquired control of the *Times*, his viceroy in Printing House Square is Denis Hamilton.

The more typical concept of viceroyalty was evolved after

Roy Thomson (as he then was) acquired the *Scotsman*. When the lessons that followed his purchase had been learned (a process that took a little time) the new proprietor was encouraged to look for the comparable national paper in Northern Ireland. There could be no doubt of its identity—the *Belfast Telegraph*.

The *Telegraph* was not the oldest daily paper published in Ulster's captial, but it was nearly a century old; it was highly influential, and (what mattered most to its prospective buyer) it was commercially successful. For a national paper it was unusual in being an afternoon publication, though nothing in its title defined it as such. In fact, it is published in numerous editions, the final of which is prepared so late in the evening that it serves a considerable readership in the rural areas of Northern Ireland as a morning journal.

In 1961, the shrewd accumulator of newspapers whom one Canadian commentator described sourly as having "reached Fleet Street without leaving Main Street," had the *Belfast Telegraph* in the bag—or thought he had. Unfortunately, the paper could not be secured by the procedure that would have been correct and legally effective in respect of almost any other British newspaper. In this instance, however, owing to the early death of the last shareholder to have effective control, the *Belfast Telegraph* had passed to his son who had not yet reached the legal age of majority, and the right approach for purchase, in that situation, had not been adopted. Interested parties took action in the High Court of Northern Ireland to stay the completion of the sale. At that stage Lord Thomson was reported as saying that he had paid out a million pounds and all he had got for it was a lawsuit. Ultimately, under the direction of the court and with the agreement of all parties involved, it proved possible for him to get what, in good faith, Lord Thomson thought he had bought.

People who knew Ireland jested sardonically, saying that now he had bought even more than he bargained for. He had become a considerable shareholder in the country's political problems, for no one could be involved in the control of the *Belfast Telegraph* without becoming a partisan in Ireland's political—and religious—conflict. Just fifty years before Lord Thomson's appearance in Belfast, there had been a most impressive demonstration of what union with England means to the great majority of the population of the Northern Ireland. In 1911, when legislation giving Home Rule to Ireland was in process of being piloted through the House of Commons by a government with a majority sufficient to ensure its passage, men and women of Protestant Ulster were given the opportunity to express their determination never to accept government by an Irish Parliament in Roman Catholic Dublin. They were invited by local political and religious organizations to sign, individually, a covenant pledging themselves "throughout this our time of calamity" to defend their "cherished position of equal citizenship in the United Kingdom." At the city hall in Belfast, in an atmosphere of great solemnity and religious devotion, men and women signed this pledge at the rate of 540 an hour. Eventually, when the signatures given in other places had been incorporated, the total number thus pledged was 471,414. In the background, a force of volunteers and the means to buy arms were being organized.

Anyone who imagined that since the covenant demonstration ancient Irish antipathies had been banished by the partitioning of Ireland under Lloyd George's premiership in 1922 was out of touch with realities.

About the time that Northern Ireland's judges had made Lord Thomson's purchase effective, the new proprietor of the *Belfast Telegraph* accepted the BBC's invitation to allow himself to be interviewed in a television feature entitled "Face to Face," in company with one of the ablest interrogators then engaged in such duels, John Freeman, later to become British ambassador to Washington. Though the interview did not touch specifically on Thomson's plans for his latest acquisition, he made abundantly clear how the political policies of his papers were determined. Said he, "When I buy a paper I delegate complete editorial authority to the people who operate the paper in that community. They must make their own mind up, they must make their own decision; they must do those things which they believe are in the best interests of the people of that community." To Mr. Freeman's suggestion, "And they must also, if possible, make a profit for Thomson Newspapers," Lord Thomson responded, "quite so, because that's business."

In relation to the *Belfast Telegraph* the man who had been exercising the kind of authority specified by Lord Thomson was

John Edward Sayers, and he it was whom Thomson chose to continue as editor when the paper came under the new proprietor's control.

Ten years earlier, when Jack Sayers was appointed joint managing editor, those who did not know him might have viewed his promotion to editorship with some scepticism because both his father, and an uncle had edited the paper, and the emergence of a third Sayers at that level might suggest that the promotion had been determined by dynastic considerations rather than professional merit. But was there ever a young man who, having chosen to follow his father's profession, did not start with a handicap that grew as he advanced in that calling, until events had proved his merit beyond doubt?

The youthful John Sayers had given signs of a budding distinction in his own right even when he first entered the editorial department of the *Belfast Telegraph* in 1930. At the Methodist College from which he had come, he had been head boy and captain of the rugby football team, which latter position suggests possession of the kind of leadership peculiarly appropriate to the highly competitive sphere of daily journalism. For nine years he learned his job in the most practical way. Then, because he was a member of the Royal Naval Volunteer Reserve, his career was interrupted when war clouds gathered in 1939. The declaration of war on September 3 of that year found him transformed into a sublieutenant serving in the aircraft carrier *Courageous*.

Winston Churchill, in his war memoirs, relates how on the morning of September 17, shortly after he had been appointed First Lord of the Admiralty, the chief of naval staff, grave of aspect, met him and announced "The *Courageous* was sunk yesterday evening in the Bristol Channel." Later, Churchill revealed that, of the ship's company of 1,202 officers and other ranks, 687 had been rescued. The remaining 515 were the first heavy casualties of the war.

Inevitably, days elapsed before the survivors could be mustered from the destroyers and merchant ships that had rescued them, and their names ascertained. For their relatives the period of suspense was acute. For some days John Sayers, Senior, went about his duties as editor of the *Belfast Telegraph*. To those wartime problems, which all newspapers were facing, were added his responsibilities as president of the Institute of Journalists. He had been elected to that office earlier in the year and, as a special tribute to him, the Institute's annual conference was to have been held in Belfast that fall, and elaborate arrangements had to be cancelled. He was, as Ulstermen tend to be, a sturdy, unemotional man, toughened by a lifetime in journalism. He bore the suspense with great fortitude, but when news came that his son was among the survivors, he suffered a stroke, and within a few days he was dead.

After brief home leave, Jack Sayers returned to the navy, to duties which he discharged with such efficiency that he became one of the small staff serving in the Map Room of the Admiralty. Further, when Churchill left the Admiralty to become prime minister and minister of defense, this young officer also was moved to 10 Downing Street and promoted to the rank of lieutenant commander. In the course of his duties there, he attended the inter-Allied conferences at Casablanca, Washington, Cairo, and Potsdam.

In World War II military strategy was a part of high politics. Thus, it was not surprising that, on his return to Belfast, Sayers became the *Telegraph*'s political correspondent. In 1930, when he joined the paper as a youth, the paper's political importance was reflected in the identity of the then editor, Thomas Moles who for several years was simultaneously a member and Deputy Speaker of the Ulster Parliament and one of Northern Ireland's representatives in the Imperial Parliament at Westminster. Considering its long and strong tradition as a political organ, the *Belfast Telegraph* was indeed fortunate in the postwar years in having as its political commentator its former apprentice, whose last official address had been 10 Downing Street. Although, of course, service officers attached to Winston Churchill as specialist assistants did not raise their voices in Cabinet or at conferences with Allied Heads of State, such aides were privileged observers of historic events and of policy making at the highest level. A politically conscious person like Jack Sayers was certain in such an environment to undergo an expansion of outlook far transcending the boundaries of national and local government affairs.

Through his work as the political correspondent of the *Tele-*

graph, the broadcasting authorities of Northern Ireland were quick to recognize his potentialities as a broadcaster. In addition to his knowledge of his subject and his tolerant approach to it, he brought to the microphone a manner that was reasonable and carried conviction of his sincerity. He contributed regularly to a feature entitled "Ulster Commentary" and he took part with Ulster's then prime minister in the first live television broadcast made in Northern Ireland. On occasions of sufficient importance, and notably during the civil rights demonstrations and political crisis of 1968–69, he was asked by the BBC to give interpretative comment in the main news bulletins broadcast from London.

Quite early in his editorship, he attracted attention south of that border in Ireland which can be as divisive as any frontier in Europe. When news broke that Lord Thomson had designs on the *Belfast Telegraph*, Dublin's oldest and most distinguished newspaper, the *Irish Times*, had something to say. It reported a "remarkable amount of concern, evident among all creeds and classes in Belfast." The same concern "would not have been felt 15 years ago," said the paper's diarist, because then the *Telegraph* had adhered staunchly to the unionist party line and had, indeed, moved to the extreme right of that party. "However," continued the Dublin commentator, "since Jack Sayers became editor, the paper has undergone a quiet, liberalising revolution, very similar to the one brought about by [the late editor] of the *Irish Times*. . . . It has become an adult newspaper, respected and read by all classes of the Northern community. One of the most wholesome results of the new Sayers regime is that, far from losing readers under it, the *Telegraph* has gained, and keeps on doing so."

If that tribute is read side by side with what Lord Thomson requires of editors, as specified in his interview with John Freeman, it will be seen that Jack Sayers was predestined to continue in the editorship of the *Belfast Telegraph* after it had been taken over by the Thomson Organization. Indeed, the reality of his editorial control seems to have been stressed by his being given the title of editor in chief; and he has told me that he has continued to exercise, without restriction, the complete independence he enjoyed before the Thomson Organization acquired the paper.

Considerable pleasure was given to all his friends when, in

1964, the Queen's University, Belfast, conferred upon John Sayers, the honorary degree of Doctor of Literature. In the citation, delivered by the Dean of the Faculty of Arts, Professor Seth, early reference was made to one of Jack Sayers's qualities that is not evident in all men who bear the title of editor in chief—his modesty. "In spite of his many lively and vigorous—even substantial—appearances on sound radio and on the small screen," said the Dean, "the most distinguished newspaperman in the Province remains in his official capacity, a somewhat shadowy, oracular figure." The Dean regarded the subject of his eulogy as "the kind of editor that is becoming much less common today. He is not an organization man, but a political journalist in the best sense and a hardworking, well-informed *writing* editor whose dedication to the job and whose lively sense have been reflected in the paper he has edited. The *Telegraph* stands up well for the range of its interest and for its serious treatment of the news, maintaining a certain 'national' character even in its treatment of local affairs." That part of the tribute would not be regarded by Jack Sayers as the least fragrant flower in the garland bestowed on him by the university of his native city. His preoccupation with politics and the editorials would not lessen his care to ensure that the treatment of news was in harmony with the standard of journalism manifest in his own contributions to the paper.

The professor's reference to the national character imparted even to the *Telegraph*'s presentation of local news, was no doubt one of the reasons why, four years after he received the honorary degree from Queen's University, Sayers was chosen to receive the Award of the New Ireland Society (an integral part of the university), whose award is presented to the person or institution making "a significant contribution to the improvement of community relations in Northern Ireland." One of the reasons given by the panel conferring this honor upon John Sayers was that the *Belfast Telegraph*, having an extensive readership among all sections of the community, had a special relevance to that improvement of community relations with which the society was chiefly concerned. It had established itself under Sayers as a newspaper "to which all sections of the community, no matter what political opinions or religious beliefs they might hold, could look for impartial comment and accurate reporting."

Interpreting further the views of the panel, Mr. Dennis

Barritt, who was also secretary of the Belfast Council of Social Welfare, said, "Every Ulsterman must surely be aware of the changes slowly taking place in Northern Ireland. We feel that one of the chief advocates of change and improvement has been the *Belfast Telegraph* and that the community as a whole is indeed fortunate to have such a mature and responsible newspaper."

A more precise indication of the hard task to which the editor of the *Telegraph* had set his hand, came from the president of the New Ireland Society, who made the presentation. "Unless it is realised," said he, "that Protestants and Catholics must become united, we will all sink. This is our country; we love it and we want to see it made a better place." In thanking the society for the award, their guest acknowledged that the years in which the new climate of opinion was created had been exciting. The same stimulus might not remain; but "if the headlines are not so ringing in the future, do not forget that community relations will be as well served by the paper's attitude to practical matters . . . as they have been by the great debates about our divided society."

The New Ireland Society's tribute, though it lacked the academic ritual and eloquence of the conferment of the university's degree was, I know, one that came nearer to his most intimate feelings about the task to which he had set his hand. The Community Award recognized that his efforts were achieving results; and that evidence was gratifying and encouraging. He expected that future progress would be achieved in less spectacular ways, by social service given impartially to both elements; and he would prefer that the ultimate aim of eliminating enmity should be achieved by the promotion of friendliness and the force of reason.

There followed that event, however, turbulent demonstrations for and against electoral reform in the Province, marches and countermarches accompanied by rhetorical speeches which, though they did not touch the depths plumbed by some agitations of the past, did tend to confirm the paradox that hatred between peoples of differing religious beliefs has been responsible for the most ferocious wars in history. But the climate of opinion in Northern Ireland is changing, and political crises are the symptoms that a new Ireland is in process of birth.

Of Lytton's famous lines,

> Beneath the rule of men entirely great,
> The pen is mightier than the sword,

the second line is far more generally remembered than the first. The climate of opinion, which in these days determines the quality of rule, is amenable to the influence of the pen. The time is not nearly ripe for a judgment on the greatness or otherwise of his editorship, but those who constitute the increasing readership of the *Belfast Telegraph* would agree that it was indeed fortunate for the future of Ireland that Jack Sayers was rescued from the dark waters of the Bristol Channel on that September night in 1939.

Postscript. While this book was in production John Sayers died at the early age of 58, "sadly lost when most needed," as one obituary tribute said. Shortly before his fatal illness he relinquished editorial responsibility and was succeeded as editor in chief by Mr. Eugene Wason.

John Giddings *Whose world is the principality of Wales*

"The nightingale does not waste her gifts this side of the [River] Severn," said David Lloyd George, speaking to his own people of Wales about their love of song and their remarkable natural gifts as vocalists. Being a proud people, they are not averse from singing in exaltation of things Welsh. Time was when, for example, the *Western Mail*, published for a hundred years in Cardiff, advertised itself as "the only really national newspaper in the United Kingdom"—meaning of course in the whole of England, Scotland, Northern Ireland, and Wales.

With a consciousness of the need to justify so large a claim, the copywriter hastened to explain that the *Western Mail* "links itself with the lives of the people; it understands their views and their occupations. The readers know it intimately—they depend upon it. Unless this is so, no paper can call itself national."

Speculation about whether there has ever been a standard definition of what constitutes a "national" newspaper need not deter anyone from conceding that the *Western Mail* is regarded as the national paper of the principality—to which entity for the purposes of local government, the adjacent English county of Monmouthshire is added.

The *Mail's* status lays upon its editor an exceptional task in gathering news from even the most remote parts of a country, whose population of 2,700,000, and whose industries are spread most unevenly; and of ensuring, so far as editorial processes are concerned, the timely distribution of the paper throughout the land. Its area is no more than 8,500 square miles, but its natural character is unhelpful to good communications. Coal mining and the other major industries of Wales are located in the south where about 80 percent of Welsh families live. Its Northern coastline is economically important by reason of its many attractive holiday resorts. But between the extreme south (where Cardiff is situated) and those northern shores is mountainous country, of which Snowdonia is the climax. Population thereabouts is sparse; rivers and lakes assist the scenic beatuy but divert the lines of communication. Finally, to add to such territorial complexities, access to the important Isle of Anglesey is by way of the Menai Suspension Bridge.

Confronting this exceptional geographical layout, the national paper of Wales must penetrate its own territory daily in time to compete with the English national dailies, which possess some advantages. Beside having good communications between London and South Wales, those rivals can reach North Wales with editions produced on their Manchester repetition plants, with less difficulty than the *Western Mail* must encounter in traversing the principality from south to north.

It follows, then, that the editor of the national organ for Wales must be a Welshman who knows Wales and its people so intimately that he can produce a paper so strong in its national appeal and interest that his countrymen will not foresake it for those English invaders that compete with each other for a Welsh readership. Although the people of Wales are very conscious of their distinctive nationality, and have unsatisfied national aspirations, their taste in daily papers can be debased by the circumstances that, in the absence of a Welsh Sunday newspaper, they are vulnerable to the appeal of the English Sunday papers which compete for those two million potential readers beyond the River Severn.

Two highly successful newspapermen, Lords Camrose and Kemsley, knew the *Western Mail* intimately from their youth, and their acquisition of it in the 1920's gave them special satisfaction. Even after their partnership was otherwise ended, both remained on the directorate of *Western Mail* until Lord Camrose's death, when the paper became completely a member of the Kemsley group.

It was while the Berry brothers were still associated with the *Western Mail* that John Giddings, destined to become its editor, joined the staff. He had graduated in journalism on a newspaper published in his birthplace, Barry, a small seaport town close to Cardiff. Later he went to the north of the principality, serving on the North Wales Chronicle group of weeklies. He was there when, in 1939, war intervened to enlarge his world; for his army career, in which he reached the rank of captain, took him as far afield as India. With the end of that diversion, he returned to South Wales and joined the *Western Mail*. There his qualities were soon recognized by promotion to what, on any British daily newspaper, is one of the most responsible and exacting posts—that of chief subeditor. By stages, he advanced successively to the offices of news editor, night editor, and deputy editor. All this progress was achieved under Lord Kemsley's control.

Had Lord Thomson aspired to add the national paper of Wales to his ownership of the comparable papers in Scotland and Northern Ireland, it is unlikely he would have succeeded. Kemsley would have been most reluctant to detach from his group so distinguished a newspaper and one to which he, like his brother, was strongly attached by sentiment. The *Western Mail* came to Thomson in 1959 when he acquired the whole of the Kemsley organization.

At that time its editor was Mr. J. G. Davies, whose record may be judged by the fact that when, in 1965, the Thomson empire was undergoing reconstruction, Mr. Davies was invited to become editorial director of Thomson Regional Newspapers. Then, to the editorship he vacated, John Giddings was promoted.

The course by which Mr. Giddings arrived at the editorship of the national newspaper of Wales is instructive for what it reveals of the experience needed to make such journals viable, secure, and influential within the territories to whose interests they are dedicated. His appointment was completely in harmony with Lord Thomson's dictum concerning what he expects of the editors to whom he dedicates editorial independence. "They must do the things they believe in, and which they believe are in the best interests of the people of that community." Also, if Mr. Giddings's career is considered in relation to the achievements that justified the claim of the *Western Mail* to be not only the national newspaper of Wales, but the only truly national paper in the United Kingdom, the experience of its present editor harmonizes remarkably with the purposes the *Western Mail* aspires to serve.

17

Now We Look Ahead

We have looked at the lives and influence of some outstanding men who made British press history. With a host of others of varying ability and success they helped to give our newspapers the power and popularity many of these enjoy today. Now we must turn from the clear atmosphere of facts to the cloudy one of speculation. How will the press develop next in this electronic age? What kind of pioneers can we expect to be our future Northcliffes, Beaverbrooks, Kings, and Thomsons? These names suggest such different origins and such different pioneering as to make it hard to guess where the next dominating personalities in journalism will come from. Will those who wrest the mastery of Fleet Street be true journalists, learning the job as juniors, as Northcliffe did, or brilliant commercial calculators like Lord Thomson of Fleet? Will they start with very little except their brains and courage, with useful wealth, or much academic learning?

The difficulties of such prophecy might well be deterrent. Yet peering into the future is part of the occupation of the journalist. The humblest reporter on a country weekly has continually to think what may happen and how he can be on the spot to gather the details when it does happen. The news editor of a great daily gets his main scoops by imaginative anticipation. He tries to have a man wherever big news may break out.

Of this we may be sure. The mechanical resources of the press will increase rapidly. A typical headline of today is "IPC optimistic on its plans for web world beater." (IPC is the huge

International Publishing Corporation.) We shall have improved production, with more color. Hot metal setting in newspaper offices may now be in its last years. I imagine that in two or three decades our newspapers will be composed entirely by photocomposition. Britain has prophets who believe that during the twenty-first century we shall have a teleprinter in every home, no newspapers such as we have now, and far more television. That is looking very far ahead.

Let us beware of what Harry Henry, a deputy managing director of the Thomson organization, termed undisciplined speculation. Despite Orwellian-style fantasies spun out of science fiction, the general pattern of communications fifteen years from now, he said in 1968, is "unlikely to differ to any substantial degree from that prevailing today." He dismissed as a lot of balderdash predictions that each newspaper reader by then would have "his own private computer terminal." Progress seems to me assured, but not at sudden lightning speed, since vast sums have been sunk in present technical methods.

On the editorial side I feel sure that we shall have to battle still for the freedom of the press. We shall go on drawing courage and inspiration from the leaders described in these pages. Perhaps Britain will presently share the concern of American reformers —above all, that of Professor Bryce W. Rucker, of Southern Illinois University, author of that revealing work, *The First Freedom*—over the restriction of press freedom by commercial interests. A visitor to the United States, David Greenslade, when president of the Guild of British Newspapers Editors, was astonished to hear of the virtual control, by shareholdings, of newspapers, radio and television by a remarkable diversity of commercial interests, from liquor to oil, from heavy industry to chemicals. Evidence mentioned at a meeting of the International Conference of Weekly Newspapers Editors showed that such interests could and did manipulate or suppress news, without the public knowing that they had the power to do this. We in Britain believe we suffer very little in this way, but as commercial undertakings diversify more and more, a new danger may face our press.

At this point it may be well to remind ourselves that any such predictions should be offered with a modesty that is unusual

in journalism. George Eliot was right in warning that prophecy
is the most gratuitous form of error. Many journalists have badly
miscalculated future trends of the press. One example may suffice.
My old colleague, Hamilton Fyfe, who did fine work for Lord
Northcliffe, said in 1949 that though radio might become the
main source of news for the mass of people, there would still be
a large public for newspapers of widely different characters. So
far, so good. Then Fyfe let himself go.

> The number of them will increase as soon as new ones can be
> started without a million or two million pounds capital. There
> will be newspapers to suit all tastes. Everyone who wants more of
> any subject than is given by radio will find it in his own particular
> journal. . . . None of them will make much money. Nothing that
> sells purely on its merits can make much. Huge sales mean that
> huge numbers are cajoled or badgered into buying. Any article
> that relies on its intrinsic value must be content to supply a
> moderate demand. But this will be no disadvantage. Far better
> that two million should support twenty papers with circulation
> of some hundred-thousand copies apiece than pay their two
> million pennies to one.

If Fyfe thought a time was coming when national dailies
could be started cheaply he was wrong in that respect as he was in
thinking that the penny newspaper would continue to cost a
penny. His headshaking over huge sales obtained by cajolements
or badgering must have been caused by the fantastic prewar gifts
offered by so many papers, as was explained in the chapter on
Lord Beaverbrook. That form of circulation pushing was already
doomed before the starting of the Second World War killed it.
The belief, or a least hope, that each paper selling two million or
more copies a day could be replaced by twenty others with
smaller sales is far from reality and looks less reasonable today
than ever before. Hamilton Fyfe was a shrewd observer with a
remarkable journalistic record. If his predictions about the press
in which he was so successful a figure—he impressed me deeply
when we worked together on the *Daily Mail*—have gone woefully
wrong in twenty years, how can a prophet do better now, when
new printing techniques are being discussed, more or less confidently, in every newspaper office?

Sir Robert Donald, president of the Institute of Journalists

in 1913, had been a better prophet. He predicted that the movement for newspaper mergers would continue on a rising scale.
Papers which could not spend huge sums on news, features, and
circulation would be squeezed out. The paper run as a luxury
or for a mission and not as a business enterprise would become
too expensive except for millionaire idealists. He also predicted
something like radio, a prophecy which some critics ridiculed as
"news turned on like gas."

In 1928 Donald made other predictions. He expected in the
near future two more evening papers for London. Perhaps Lord
Thomson's evening papers at Reading and Hemel Hempstead,
on the perimeter of the London and southeast England conurba-
tion, may be said to fulfill that prophecy. Donald also thought
we were on the eve of radio facsimile, which would enable us to
leave a receiver on at night and find in the morning piles of pages
of news and pictures on the floor. We have been near that development, but the ordinay radio and television seem to have made
it less promising.

Journalists may be good at judging the public taste as events
develop, but they need to be first-class economists if they are to
estimate those powerful factors shaping the future of the press,
rising costs and changes in the standards of living and education.
Few journalists are first-class economists.

A recent mentor of the press, Maurice Ashley, who used to
be historical research assistant to Winston Churchill and became
afterwards editor of the *Listener*, a British Broadcasting Corporation magazine, has criticized the press for two alleged shibboleths.
One is that makeup can somehow sell a newspaper. The other
is that names make news and every story must be personalized. I
do not believe that any experienced journalist would trust
makeup alone to sell a paper. It can help if it makes the best of
the paper's contents. Northcliffe said there was splendid stuff in
the *Daily Telegraph*, but it was just shoveled into the paper
anyhow. Later the makeup was vastly improved. Up went the
sales remarkably. Makeup only did not achieve this. But it helped.

I would not say that to personalize a news story must be
deemed a distortion. No doubt as a historian, Ashley would
analyze in detail of some intricacy not only the characters of great
leaders but also the social and economic forces that sway national

destinies. But many eminent historians and biographers have looked on great leaders as personifications of the gigantic forces amid which they moved. We may well think of the American Civil War and the emancipation of the slaves largely in terms of the integrity and will power of Abraham Lincoln. Thomas Carlyle said in *Heroes and Hero-worship* that the history of the world is but the biography of great men. Why, then, if we accept his theory of heroes, must we suppose newspapers wrong to act on the principle that great names make news that people are eager to read? The principle may be worked to excess in some newspapers, but I would not term it a shibboleth or a passing craze: it responds to a widespread, long-existent human demand. I see no reason to believe that personalization of news stories will go out of fashion, no matter how many of our people go to universities and no matter how many have bigger incomes.

In spite of the critics and censors, some statements can be made with fair confidence. The *techniques* of news communication will continue to change and may be revolutionary, but the *principles* of news communication will remain. Suppose wise men of the Middle Ages, instead of developing the art of printing, with its enormous effect on civilization, had invented radio: would it have become the chief instrument of communication, the chief means of education? Would books and newspapers never have gained the hold they have on so many millions of people today? I cannot think it. The printed word has a power which in some respects the spoken word cannot rival. Pictures, especially moving pictures, have a unique appeal. Television has a unique grip on the minds of many. But in some respects it cannot rival, still less outrival, the printed word. How could radio and television furnish their listeners and viewers with the mass of financial details and small advertisements to be found in so many papers? Fancy having to listen to a complete stock list to know the latest prices of the five, ten, or twenty equities in which you, if a small investor, have invested! Fancy having to listen to many columns of small advertisements if, say, you want to buy a second-hand baby carriage! Pictures can be most attractive, most enlightening, but there are many important subjects calling for the formulation of ideas that pictures could not convey. It needs no plunge into the philosophic doctrine of conceptualism to prove that assertion. Many of our own experiences in ordinary debate make it a common-sense statement.

So, although some newspaper managers fear increasing competition from the present commercial (or, as we say in Britain, independent) television and the possible introduction of commercial radio, a wide area of the advertising field is reserved and must be reserved for newspapers only. It is an area which I believe will increase. The United States and Canada have set an example of what can be done to encourage newspaper advertising. The Canadian-born Lord Thomson of Fleet has taught us valuable lessons on this subject. Some managements have learned them well, but others, both advertisers and newspaper managements, have a long way to go before they will fully respect and profit by American experience, as Northcliffe did. We are too ready in Britain to believe ours is a special case, that our newspaper readers would always resent change—they would if it were made too suddenly, too disturbingly—and that what made ours the leading press and ours the leading Empire in the past will keep us to the forefront in the future, if only (as John Citizen often adds) we curb the trade unions, or keep out more foreigners, or improve the laws of cricket.

Some newspaper businesses are run by men who hate competition and dread inevitable changes. If the reader suspects that I have an imperfect sympathy with British newspaper managements, I must disclaim this. As a newspaper director for years, I know the painful problems of having millions of sterling invested in printing processes under threat of rapid obsolescence, the danger of spending several millions more on machines that before long may be competing with still better ones, and the fears of being no longer needed that haunt trade unionists when new machines call for new manning agreements. It is often said that we are in a contracting industry, and that soon other once successful papers will fade away like the *News Chronicle*, the *Star*, the *Daily Dispatch* (Manchester), and the *Leeds Mercury*. These fears impose caution. Control of newspapers is only for the stouthearted, ready to fight competitors, ready to experiment, ready to keep up with the tide of social change. But for them the outlook is not too dark.

They can give a service which nothing yet invented can

wholly replace. What they need, especially in London, is to provide newspapers that the reader will not toss aside with the impatient exclamation, "Oh, we heard all this on the telly last night"
or "It's not as up to date as the radio was at breakfast." Newspapers must seek out news on which radio and television are
silent, and provide features of the utmost readability. In many
respects the great rivals of our London newspapers are not the
papers on the other side or at the other end of Fleet Street but
the radio and television enterprises. I expect that before long we
shall have breakfast television, as Americans have, enabling us
to watch the news as we eat our bacon and eggs instead of having
to read a paper propped against the coffee pot. When that habit
is established we may find commercial television scooping up
more advertising of motorcars, foods, cosmetics, and detergents.

Then life will be harder still for those newspaper companies
that have stayed out of a share of television profits on the specious
ground that they know all about newspapers but nothing about
these newfangled contraptions that would cost so much to develop. They underestimated the damage that a new kind of journalism—for such it is—and a new kind of advertising could do to
their kinds of journalism and advertisement media. They will
learn in time, perhaps soon. Then they may find radio and television give indirect help to newspapers by creating deeper interest
in events and their causes.

Among other problems that first-class managements will have
to tackle is that of distribution. As Hugh Cudlipp, chairman of
the International Publishing Corporation has pointed out in the
Times, our excellent newsagents are likely to be forced out of the
High Streets by supermarkets and chain stores. They have done
first-rate service. At one time we had perhaps too many of these
agents. What was termed the distance-limit tended to thin them
out. A man would be given a district free from any danger from
a new rival. Even so, the little man who sold cigarettes, sweets,
magazines, and papers had his troubles. Authority often looked
askance at the employment of schoolboys to deliver morning
papers. Some harassed agents gave up this method of delivery.
The customer had to call at the shop for his paper. Now that so
many people do not work on a Saturday, that is a day when some
shops find fewer papers are being picked up. With papers and

magazines much dearer, the newsagent is less inclined to take risks in ordering papers which may or may not be sold. It may be more profitable to concentrate on cigarettes and sweets. New ways of getting papers into the hands of the customers may have to be tried before long. My fear is that if newsagents generally gave up delivering morning papers it would mean a grim time for those papers.

Turning to predict what may happen on the editorial side, we find ourselves hampered as in mechanical production matters by a foggy future. Will the freedom of the press, as now understood in the United Kingdom, less happy in this respect than the United States, continue? It comes under frequent attack on one ground or another, sometimes with few cries of protest. Still, we have worthy champions of press freedom in such editors as Alastair Hetherington (*Guardian*), Derek Marks (*Daily Express*), David Hopkinson (*Birmingham Post*), Clement Jones (Wolverhampton *Express and Star*), Peter Harland (Bradford *Telegraph and Argus*), and David Greenslade (*Mansfield and North Nottinghamshire Chronicle-Advertiser*) and in such enlightened public men as Lord Francis-Williams, Lord Devlin, and Lord Shawcross.

Parts of our freedom, notably in the process of law, have been recently whittled away, no doubt with an honest desire to produce fairer trials, though this desirable aim seems to me unlikely to be realized. Journalism can be a noble profession. It can also be a dangerous one. Libel, contempt of court, disclosure of official secrets—these words are charged with a sinister significance for newspapermen. They betoken threats always hanging over newspaper editors and reporters. Champions of press freedom have to cope with much distrust of newspapers. Some journalists share that distrust. As long ago as April 1963 the *Spectator* bluntly declared that the "real restrictions of the freedom of the popular Press consist not in those which are so modestly imposed by the State but in those imposed by a few monopolists who, controlling the vast mechanism of allied papers and chains of papers, seek to force their own wills on the community, using the journalists, in so many cases, as their instruments and chattels." This argument has often been heard in Parliament and elsewhere. It persists to this day. It is used against Lord Thomson of Fleet. Yet the truth is that the men directing great newspaper groups are no more eager to force their wills on the community than the directors of single papers. They are usually less so, since, like Lord Thomson, they realize the value of local editors who understand and share local community feeling, which on many issues may be out of sympathy with Fleet Street outlooks and those of other towns. For example, Norwich, with its interest in agriculture, is unlikely to feel as strong as Newcastle the closing down of coal mines.

We hear less of the arguments against press monopolists than we did when Parliament voiced the grievances that led to the Royal Commission on the Press in 1947. The assertion that the growth of newspaper groups had created a monopoly and that the groups were deliberately driving independent newspapers out of existence was disproved by the commission's findings. It was generally agreed, the commission said, that the British press was inferior to none in the world, but all the popular papers and certain of the quality papers fell short of the standard achieved by the best, either through excessive partisanship or through distortion for the sake of news value.

In agreement with this verdict much propaganda has been directed against the press for alleged unfairness, undue exploitation of crime and sex, and intrusion into private life. A Press Council was set up to defend the press where it deserved to be defended and to curb misuse of press freedom. My experience as a member and for some years as chairman of the Press Council convinced me that many of the critics who attacked us, perhaps with a sincere sense of wrong, could not prove their allegations, brought no evidence to support them, but went on with vague and general complaints as if they would rather have their grievances than have them remedied. The investigations and verdicts by the Press Council have been fearless, thorough and just, wherever specific grievances have been brought before Lord Pearce and his colleagues or, for that matter, their predecessors. Nevertheless, there remains much of the old distrust of the press. It is not confined to one political party.

Politicians generally are ready to blame the press for unfair use of excessive powers. We can well understand why. A politician may spend many hours in preparing a speech. He may believe it to be a momentous pronouncement. The press may disagree and print only a small paragraph of the laboriously prepared utterance. Or perhaps an editorial writer, making a cursory comment which has not been fortified by more than ten minutes' thought, if that, may demolish the speaker's long-mediated arguments. No wonder the hapless politician wants to damn the press. When he blunders he is likely to use the readiest of all excuses and blame the reporter for misrepresenting him. There certainly is excessive partisanship, but more, I think, among the Whip-coerced politicians than among freedom-cherishing journalists.

I do not say the feeling against the press is purely political. Many people think well of their own favorite papers, but have been led to believe that others which they scorn to read are more sensational and less trustworthy. Efforts to curb and censor the press, in the name of freedom, can be highly dangerous, as we know from experience in Russia and her satellites and in Nazi Germany. Such efforts are characteristic of would-be dictatorships. But Britain believes so strongly in popular freedom that few of us imagine it to be possible that we could fall victims to a Russian-type dictatorship. No leading journalist, so far as I remember, warned us it might happen in Britain when in 1968 we watched in horror the television pictures of the rape of Czechoslovakia. But the thought must have troubled some citizens if they looked far ahead to changes that might happen some day if American isolationism, increasing, led to the sharpening of the struggle for power in much-divided Europe. We certainly cannot afford to be complacent. If ever by lack of adequate preparation we let ourselves be crushed by an enemy we may be sure that the destruction of our press freedom would be one of the first penalties exacted from us. The proposition that the pen is mightier than the nuclear bomb or the intercontinental ballistic missile is not one in which I should have any confidence if it came to the test.

Thomas Jefferson said no government ought to be without censors, and where the press was free none ever would. If we had to choose between a government without newspapers and newspapers without a government he said he would dispose unhesitatingly with the instrument of government. Choice between these alternatives is not likely to be demanded of us. The British government will be subjected to many critics, as it is now, and so will newspapers, quite rightly.

As we peer into the future we should never forget to envisage as clearly as we can the changing social background. More people are now well educated than in my younger days. Far fewer people are illiterate. When I was a young reporter it was not unusual for witnesses to make their mark on depositions because they could not sign their names. As educational standards rise and educational opportunities improve we shall have to satisfy a more critical public. That means the press will need to draw its beginners from a higher level and make its national training scheme for junior journalists more exacting. In the course of this process we must convert many teachers to a better appreciation of the improving newspaper press. At present some British universities and public schools, when helping to get their students into careers, are inclined to warn them off journalism.

Why? Partly because it still has a somewhat Bohemian reputation, without the prestige of more ancient professions. My form-master at school deplored what he thought my folly in choosing to join the press instead of training to become a clergyman. "You'll die in the gutter," he said. "Journalists are smart and unscrupulous. You haven't the brains for that life. Far better take Holy Orders. Yes, you young fool, you'll die in the gutter." Today many journalists are well paid, and we do not hear of even the less able or the less fortunate ones dying of starvation in the gutter. A more even distribution of wealth, such as most political sections aim at, will encourage more lavish productions, as is already happening in the magazine world and with the publication of expensive, well-illustrated books of knowledge in serial parts.

One of the fashionable predictions in Fleet Street today is that before long there will be fewer national papers (that is, London papers sold in almost every town of our smallish island). Some prophets imagine we shall be reduced to three such papers —one great paper of record on the pattern of the *Times, Daily Telegraph*, and *Guardian*, one popular paper for quick reading such as the *Daily Mirror, Sun*, and the *Daily Sketch*, and one middle-of-the-road paper like the *Daily Express* and *Daily Mail*. Lord

Thomson of Fleet is probably right in saying there is not advertising at present for all the national papers. But individual taste will assert itself. How could an amalgam of three such different papers as the *Times, Telegraph,* and *Guardian* please all their readers? The recent progress of the *Times* and the *Financial Times* shows what can be achieved by a determined, strongly financed appeal to a special class of reader.

London is more likely than the provinces to have a shake-out of weak papers. A well-established provincial paper has less competition to fear. It can be *the* chief channel of communication by news and advertisement within its community. If well edited it will have a most loyal readership.

Finally, amid all the criticisms directed against the press and all the loyalty many papers inspire, how will these elements coalesce? They won't. There will always be angry critics and grateful readers. If journalism continues to watch the public interest, as it should, continues to strive for social reform, as it should, and continues to defend the weak victims of bungling bureaucratic tyranny, as it should, it will continue to rouse antagonists. It has always done so. I have no doubt that twenty years from now we shall have censorious people, many of them honest but misled, blaming the press for its attacks on constituted authority, blaming the Press Council for not achieving more reforms, blaming our press training scheme for not producing better journalists. But I also believe that newspapers, under the spur of fiercer competition from other news communicators, will remain an indispensable and most welcome part of our lives, the watchdog of the citizens' rights.

Bibliography

SPECIAL MENTION should be made about the manuscript sources used in the compilation of this work.

A comprehensive history of the *Manchester Guardian*, now the *Guardian*, based on primary material in the newspaper's archives, has been begun by David Ayerst, a former editorial writer on the paper. It is hoped the book will be published in 1971.

An entire library of books and a vast number of newspaper and magazine articles have been written about Lord Northcliffe. He figures in many First World War memoirs. *Opportunity Knocks Once* by Sir Campbell Stuart tells much about Northcliffe's American Mission.

Three volumes of J. L. Garvin's *The Life of Joseph Chamberlain* were completed in 1932–34, taking Chamberlain's life to 1900. A fourth volume. "At the Height of His Power, 1901–1903," was added by Julian Amery. A. M. Gollin's book, *The Observer and J. L. Garvin, 1908–1914*, is a first-rate piece of research about Garvin's career up to the outbreak of war in 1914. Dr. Gollin, an American, has had access to a vast number of papers and letters belonging to the late J. L. Garvin. Miss Viola Garvin made them available under the terms of an agreement with the *Observer*. The *Dictionary of National Biography* contains a notice of Garvin by M. Barrington-Ward, who wrote with personal knowledge of his subject.

The following materials were also extremely important and helpful —annual reports of the International Publishing Corporation, interviews with Mr. A. P. Ryan and Mr. John Maywood of the London *Times*, documents from the Thomson Organization, and Sir Robert Donald's private papers.

Of particular significance were the valedictory articles on William Haley by Irverach McDonald, associate editor of the London *Times*, and Mr. Donald McLachlan of the *Spectator*. Scores of articles and editorials in the *Belfast Telegraph, World's Press News, Sunday Times, Daily Press,* and *Westminster Gazette* were also used as references, including a biographical sketch on J. A. Spender that appeared in the *Western Mail*.

Also, much of what has been written is based on Sir Linton's and

Mr. Taylor's personal knowledge through their business and social relationships with the men discussed in this book.

Andrews, Sir Linton. *The Autobiography of a Journalist*. London, 1964.
Baistow, Tom. "When Editors Edited." *New Statesman*, Nov. 29, 1968, 736–37.
Baxter, Beverly. *Strange Street*. London, 1935.
Beaverbrook, Lord. *Canada in Flanders*. 2 vols. London, 1916–17.
———. *Success*. London, 1921.
———. *Politicians and the Press*. London, 1925.
———. *Politicians and the War*. 2 vols. London, 1928–32.
———. *The Resources of the British Empire*. London, 1934.
———. *Men and Power, 1917–1918*. London, 1957.
———. *Friends*. London, 1959.
———. *Courage: The Story of Sir James Dunn*. London, 1962.
———. *The Divine Propagandist*. London, 1962.
———. *Decline and Fall of Lloyd George*. London, 1966.
———. Introduction to *The Abdication of Kind Edward VIII*, by A. J. P. Taylor. London, 1966.
Blumenfeld, R. D. *R. D. B.'s Diary*. London, 1930.
———. *All in a Lifetime*. London, 1931.
———. *The Press in My Time*. London, 1933.
Braddon, Russell. *Roy Thomson of Fleet Street*. London, 1965.
Brittain, W. J. *This Man Beaverbrook*. London, 1941.
Brodzky, Vivian, ed., et. al. *Fleet Street: The Inside Story of Journalism*. London, 1967.
Burnham, Edward Fredrick Lawson, 4th baron. *Peterborough Court*. London, 1955.
Byng, Lady Alice Strafford. *Up the Stream of Time*. London, 1903.
Camrose, William Ewert Berry. *Newspapers and Their Controllers*. London, 1947.
Christiansen, Arthur. *Headlines All My Life*. London, 1961.
Clarke, Tom. *My Northcliffe Diary*. London, 1931.
———. *Northcliffe in History: An Intimate Study of Press Power*, London, 1950.
Coote, Sir Colin. *Editorial*. London, 1965.
Cudlipp, Hugh. *Published and Be Damned*. London, 1953.
———. *At Your Peril*. London, 1962.
Cummings, A. J. *The Moscow Trial*. London, 1933.
———. *The Press and a Changing Civilisation*. London, 1936.
———. *This England*. London, 1944.
Dark, Sidney. *Mainly about Other People*. London, 1926.
Documentary Evidence. Vol. 1. Her Majesty's Stationery Office, 1962. (Report of the Royal Commission on the Press.)
Driberg, Tom. *Beaverbrook: A Study in Power and Frustration*. London, 1956.
Fyfe, Hamilton. *Northcliffe: An Intimate Biography*. London and New York, 1930.

Gardiner, A. G. *Many Furrows*. London, 1925.

Garvin, J. L. *The Life of Joseph Chamberlain*. London, 1934.

Garvin, Katherine. *J. L. Garvin: A Memoir*. London, 1948.

Gibb, Mildred, and Frank Beckwith. *The Yorkshire Post: Two Centuries*. Leeds, 1954.

Gollin, A. M. *The Observer and J. L. Garvin, 1908-1914: A Study in a Great Editorship*. London, 1960.

Haley, Sir William, A. P. Wadsworth, et. al. *C.P. Scott, 1846-1932:The Making of the Manchester Guardian*. London, 1946.

Haley, Sir William. "Lord Beaverbrook." *11th Annual Report of the Press Council*. 1964.

Hammerton, J. A. *With Northcliffe In Fleet Street: A Personal Record*. London, 1930.

Hammond, J. L. *C. P. Scott of the Manchester Guardian*. London, 1934.

Harris, Wilson. *J. A. Spender*. London, 1946.

History of the London Times, 1785–1948. 4 vols., London and New York, 1935–1948. (Vol. IV, pt. 2 1921–1948.)

Mackenzie, F. A. *Beaverbrook: An Authentic Biography*. London, 1931.

Magnusson, Magnus, et. al. Introduction to *The Glorious Privilege: The History of the Scotsman*, by Lord Thomson of Fleet. Edinburgh, 1967.

Middleton, Edgar. *Beaverbrook, the Statesman and the Man*. London, 1934.

Mills, W. Haslam. *The Manchester Guardian: A Century of History*. London, 1921.

Mosley, Leonard. *Castlerosse*. London, 1956.

Oral Evidence. Vol 1. Her Majesty's Stationery Office, 1962. (Report of the Royal Commission on the Press.)

Political and Economic Planning. *P.E.P. Report on the British Press*. P.E.P. Organization.

Pound, Reginald, and Geoffrey Harmsworth. *Northcliffe*. London, 1959.

Ryan, A. P. *Lord Northcliffe*. London, 1958.

Spender, J. A. *Comments of Bagshot*. London, 1907.

———. *Campbell-Bannerman*. 2 vols. London, 1923.

———. *The Public Life*. 2 vols. London, 1925.

———. *The Changing East*. London, 1926.

———. *Life, Journalism, and Politics*. 2 vols. London, 1927.

———. *The America of Today*. London, 1928.

———. *Sir Robert Hudson: A Memoir*. London, 1930.

Spender, J. A., and Cyril Asquith. *Asquith*. 2 vols. London, 1932.

Spender, J. A. *Fifty Years of Europe: A Study of Pre-War Documents*. London, 1933.

———. *Short History of Our Times*. London, 1934.

———. *Weetman Pearson* (Lord Cowdray). London, 1939.

———. *Last Essays*. London, 1944.

Stead, Estelle. *My Father*. London, 1913.

Stead, W. T. "The Maiden Tribute of Modern Babylon." *Pall Mall Gazette* extra. 1885.

———. *The Truth About Russia*. London, 1888.

———. *The Pope and the New Era*. London, 1890.

———. *If Christ Came to Chicago*. London, 1894.

———. *Mrs. Booth*. London, 1900.

Stuart, Sir Campbell. *Opportunity Knocks Once*. London, 1952.

Taylor, H. A. *Robert Donald: The Authorized Biography of Sir Robert Donald, G.B.E., LL.D*. London, 1934.

———. *The British Press: A Critical Survey*. London, 1961.

"The Head of His Profession." *New Statesman*, Feb. 6, 1954, 156–58.

Vines, C. N. *Little Nut-brown Man*. London, 1968.

Waterhouse, Nourah. *Private and Official*. London, 1942.

Whyte, Frederic. *W. T. Stead*. London, 1925.

Wrench, John Evelyn. *Geoffrey Dawson and Our Times*. London, 1955.

Index